David Kerrigan was born in Melbourne, Australia, in 1974. As a first generation Australian, he's the son of an Irish father and a Maltese mother. He's travelled to over 45 countries: having often earned his way by playing live music. By definition of taxpayer, he's officially lived in the UK and the USA.

MAN, DOG, BIKE

A Ride Between Head and Heart, via India

CONTENTS

This memoir is a true story, but was manufactured in a mind that may contain traces of fiction.

AUTHOR'S NOTES

Some trees grow without knowledge of a seed being planted. The materialisation of this book was much along these lines. As its author, it was never my intention to hit the travelling road to come out with a book on the other side. But when a friend set the ultimatum that he *expected email*, I took to the road with perhaps a hungrier eye.

The challenge was set by one of my greatest of mates, whom I give the alias *Manuel*, and thanks to the canvas of his heartfelt attendance, a string of emails began to unfold.

Despite his comments to 'keep the tales coming,' and 'this captain's log is turning into a book,' I, at first, found it implausible to consider myself a bona fide writer or appreciate that I was producing just that.

Months on the road passed, and with the wealth of written work only growing—and including, over time, some profounder tales from certain historic events—I ultimately subscribed that I was writing what was the fair portion of a book, hence, *Man, Dog, Bike* was realised.

But it's not myself I wish to commend, for if not for the original ultimatum from my friend the seed of this book might have never sprung. And for that I, as its author, am to him ever grateful.

TEXTUAL AID

Australians speak their own unique version of English—
a colourful derivative of British English where the object is to
express oneself with as much novelty as possible.

In habit, Australian English tends to shorten long words
and lengthen short words, converting terms into affectionate
diminutives wherever possible.

In terms of its evolution, it's felt that Australian English
derives from Cockney English, but in regards to grammatical
rules, the only tangible rule is that Australians treat English as a
game to be played.

In attempt to maximise fluency, I've devised an *Australian
Glossary of Slang, Terms, and Things*. For non-Australian readers
it could prove to be a useful means of guidance. For readers
bearing an Australian passport it could prove a relative means of
entertainment. Nonetheless, please visit, for without the scan of
your eyes it will grow to feel inferior to the narrative.

For Brady Thomas, and all those that lost their lives in the
Boxing Day Tsunami 2004 and the London Bombings July 7th, 2005.

1. Breathe

The most profound experience that ever happened to me was in a dorm room of a hostel in Dublin, December 1999. But to explain its significance, I need first to go back.

All my life I'd been diagnosed as asthmatic, and from the dawn of my existence had been in and out of hospital with bouts varying from mild to life threatening. Apparently I flatlined when I was three years old.

But I was never saddened by my condition, as I'd never known life without it. As a kid, I'd run around playing cricket, footy, climbing trees, get subsequently wheezy, have a puff of my inhaler and get straight back out there amongst all the sights, sounds, and smells that constituted boyhood.

It was a similar story throughout my teen years. But around the age of eighteen, just as I finished high school, and, ironically enough, when young people are thrust into the pressures of adult life, the asthma medications that had served me until this point appeared to no longer work.

Standing in front of the mirror, I'd look myself square in the eye and puff and puff with all my might. But no relief would come. I assumed I'd become immune to the old medications, and I sought the advice of countless doctors and specialists who, for the most part, would scratch their heads and prescribe the same old stuff over and over.

Five or more very difficult years passed during which I continued to feel, quite literally, permanently unable to breathe, or at least unable to catch my breath fully as I could when I was younger.

In June 1999, I decided I was going overseas, independently, for the first time. Seven years earlier I'd visited Irish relatives in America with Dad and my older brother Stephen, but this trip was to have no guardian or restrictions.

My main objective was to reach the motherland of Malta and the fatherland of Ireland, where I had numerous relatives whose names were like folklore to us first-generation Australians down in Oz. The trip also included a chocolate-box tour of mainland Europe. But with the unwanted extra of permanent breathlessness, I less so relished sites such as the Eiffel Tower, St Mark's Square in Venice, and the Alps of Switzerland, as I gazed at them with strained eyes and accelerated heartbeat.

I reached Ireland by December that year, and having caught an asthmatic's nightmare—the flu—my breathing was at such a record low that I considered cancelling the rest of my trip and flying back to Australia. But barely having the strength to make the phone call, as opposed to that to endure the long haul flight, I settled into a dorm room in a hostel in Dublin.

With countless anonymous backpackers checking in and out, my makeshift ward was far from private, and taking my inhaler up to 30 times a day—which, although it would "work" by way of making my hands go shaky, but never would it relieve my breathing—I spent most of the daylight hours in bed.

This was the first time in my adult life when I actually fretted for my parents. But as much as I was here, they were in Melbourne.

I'd been there for almost a week, successfully avoiding social contact, when an unsought voice made its way into my ear. 'What's wrong with you? You look terrible.'

'Nothing. I'm fine.' I said, wishing this man would catch the soonest bus to the universe's outermost corner.

'You're not fine. I would know.'

'How would you know?'

To this day his name eludes me. He was Indian, about middle-aged, and he was proud to tell me that he was a general practitioner in London.

'Do you have asthma?' he asked.

'I do, but—'

'—And have you taken your Ventolin today?'

'Yes, but it doesn't seem to—'

'—Son, if we meet in 50 years, I want to hear you tell me that you take your inhaler two puffs in the morning and two puffs in the evening.'

'I do, I've probably taken it over twenty times today, but it doesn't—'

'—Son, you have oversensitive airways. The inhalers relax them so as to facilitate natural breathing. This is why it's so important you take two puffs in the morning and two puffs in the evening.'

'I've been taking them all my life! But for the last five years I seem to have become immune to—'

'—Son, another remedy is to wear an undershirt at all times, to avoid sudden changes of temperature getting into your chest.'

'I sometimes do, but—'

'—But more important is that you take two puffs in the morning and two puffs in the evening. In fact, it's getting dark, you should take it right now!' he said, gesturing towards the dorm bathroom.

I felt the 'v' of my forehead increase from lowercase to capital. 'I'm not taking those stupid inhalers, mate! All they do is make my hands shake—'

'—Son, come on! Take it right now. No more backchat!'

Feeling like a child being sent to his room, I snatched my inhaler from my backpack and stomped into the bathroom. I flicked on the light, belligerently; the only trace of compensation being that the door was heavy enough that I could grumble without him being able to hear me.

'Stupid inhaler.'

I turned towards the mirror and looked myself square in the eye.

'I should just change my flight and go home.'

I exhaled until my lungs were almost empty.

'One more taste of this evil shit and I'll vomit.'

I put the inhaler to my mouth, pressed and inhaled mightily.

What happened next was the closest thing to a miracle I'd ever experienced.

As though an invisible corset had been unfastened, or a padlock on my ribcage suddenly unlocked, I felt a massive pressure fall away from my chest where from one neighbouring second to the next, I could breathe! I could breathe! My god, I could breathe!

Propelled into a state of natural ecstasy, it was as though I'd swapped bodies, or had reverted to the blissful state of childhood. I stood there for some seconds, gazing with disbelief into the mirror, breathing deeply, freely, and relishing each full inhalation like a smoker does with a cigarette.

In disbelief, I walked back into the dorm room where my Indian friend was waiting.

'Well?' he asked.

'It worked!'

'Of course it bloody worked!'

'Yeah, but… it hasn't worked for like five years, and, like, I mean, it *really* worked!'

'Son, if we meet in 50 years, I want to hear you tell me that you take your inhaler two puffs in the morning and two puffs in the evening.'

'I'll do that. I really will!'

I went to bed soon after, and as though an unconscious curse had been miraculously lifted, I remember waking through the night—in my squeaky top bunk bed—in such a state of bliss that it brought tears to my eyes. I woke the next morning feeling more rested and energised than I could remember ever, and just as the doctor ordered, I took my morning puffs.

I walked all around Dublin that day in what was, I guess, the closest state of enlightenment I'd ever known.

As though a veil, or constriction, had been removed from my senses, I could see, hear, taste, smell, and most of all *feel* with a heightened awareness that, for the first time in my life, made me realise I wasn't a separate entity floating aimlessly in a callous universe, but an intrinsic part of some sort of singular collective consciousness that forms the universe and all life in it. Be it the collective squawking of the seagulls reeling above, sounding, to me, as pure as dripping glass, or the icy sea breeze blowing off the Irish Sea feeling like a life-giving coverlet brushing against my face, or the white rays of the winter sun feeling as though they were stirring me on a cellular level, every sensory experience seemed so amplified that it rendered me in awe of all life and the very concept of it.

Where there was once great heaviness, there was now tingling lightness, and as though doing away with an age of pain and blockage, I wandered until dusk through the streets of Dublin, and up and down the length of the River Liffey, coughing up an indescribable amount of rubbish from my lungs. Each fragment discarded making way for even more glorious capacity to breathe.

It was no mystery that my new condition was bequeathed via the portal of good breathing, but *how* the breathing had unlocked was an utter mystery. I mean, all I'd done, as I'd been doing hourly for however many years previously, was take a whack from my inhaler, and—*bang!*—I was fast-tracked to comparative enlightenment. The spiritually inclined would later suggest that through some sort of trick of the mind occurring inadvertently by the doctor having taken control, I'd had a massive release from my heart chakra. Whatever that meant.

I left Dublin the next day on the ferry, and as the only soul standing on its stern side; I watched the small windblown city, with its famous Poolbeg chimneys, diminishing in the distance. It had truly been the scene of a miracle.

I arrived in London the next day, to be told vivaciously by my friends how well they thought I looked. I told them the story, sparing the details, to which with faces that suggested they had no personal experience with such matters, they made a sincere effort to show interest. My victory was a personal one, though cherished nonetheless.

I lived in London for the next twelve months, existing day and night in a continual state of bliss.

Saturday mornings were a particular treasure—where I'd lie on my bed in Tooting, relishing the ability to breathe as though with every breath I was having a sort of healing-conditioner massaged through my soul.

With my head, my body, and most importantly, my heart, now completely clear, it was as though I'd become who I *really* was: my true untainted self according to spiritual hypothesis, which at the time I knew little about.

Around 7.30 a.m., I'd open my bedroom door, which opened onto the backyard, and wait, ritually, for the sun's rays to creep around the brick wall corner. While listening to the sounds of Hindu music wafting from the shops of Upper Tooting Road, I'd sit on my floor and be filled with ecstasy by seemingly nothing— or equally—by something as inconsequential as watching an ant crawl up a wall. Along with meeting my doctor-friend in Dublin, it was perhaps here that my interest in going to India began.

There was no amount of money on Earth I could be offered to revert back to my pre-Dublin condition, which I referred to as the "cursed me". As now, able to feel it in the very air around me, I resided in a permanent state of love; love for all life, love for all matter, and most importantly, love for myself. I would smirk at the thought of the old me as I would at the thought of a bumbling child, who, lost in the perpetual state of fear and tension that I was, would battle my emotions via my head as successfully as one dodges machinegun fire. I was hereby at the summit of health and happiness; for by whatever means people were trying to acquire it, I now had it. But all of this was about to be lost. I went back to Australia.

2. Downfall

For the next four years back in Melbourne, I was haunted by a recurrent question: 'Stick a stick in the ground, or set sail?'

My return from London had, for the first few months, felt like a triumphant one. Feeling an inch or two taller, I was now a *traveller*, worldly, experienced, a young man who'd had the chivalry to trace his family roots and so on; all such titles more than welcome on my imaginary business card.

Adding to my height, having written my first ever songs when I was overseas, I also formed a new band called *Audioride*.

As its singer/guitarist/songwriter, I was also its manager—booking all gigs, handling promotions, recordings, and everything else that contributed to the endless stream of emails and phone calls that came with the job. But where other bands, with no especial desire to make it, might have been content to tinker on the scene, I, wishing to create a validating footprint, suffered the burning ambition to turn my dream of making it in music into the reality of it.

Playing all over Melbourne as much as possible—and all the while writing and improving the set—blood, sweat and tears we slogged it out. But like trying to paint a wall red with the colour pink, I found the process of getting a break largely frustrating; that no matter how much I applied, I couldn't quite reach what I wished.

With permission to use the cliché, the highs were high and the lows were low. We played to some amazingly receptive crowds, and I even had the honour of meeting some self-professed fans. I was once even asked to sign an autograph. But contrary to this, we often played to crowds whose numbers were fewer than in the band, and we once had a bloke heckle after the first song, 'Jeez, youse need a new singer!' Although I brought to his attention that the venue's door was wide enough to accommodate a tool as big as he, his words cut me quite deep and made me truly question whether I was kidding myself in thinking I was a contender for stardom.

But more than just the doubts of one's abilities that typically arise when pursuing a creative endeavour, what wore me down the most was that little voice in my head incessantly fretting over conventional concerns—house, job, future stability, was I wasting my time and dreaming too far from the mark of what I was capable of? Perhaps if I'd had less aspiration invested in the band I'd have been less anxious, but along with this pressure, when our bass player left to take on a job interstate, I lost the last of my energy to continue and Audioride folded.

Over the next two years I became a very jaded version of myself. Back doing my old trade of graphic design, jeans were replaced with trousers, crinkled t-shirts with ironed business shirts, and a nocturnal life of gigging in pubs and clubs with the routine grind of nine to five.

But comparable to how Mr Bucket from *Charlie and the Chocolate Factory* found his job of screwing the caps onto toothpaste tubes, I found the office job so spectacularly monotonous that it made the word monotony seem comparatively enthralling. I'd become Jack on the corporate beanstalk, with over 3,000 other lemmings all herded into one monstrosity of an office building. I was surrounded by David Brent equivalents by the dozen. Each sad, water cooler-bound lemming—the sort that says *Happy New Year* up until January 10th—starting their day by marching up the long grey stairs from the car park to their desk, to sit behind a window that doesn't open, at a grey computer with a picture of a tree as a screen saver. Although I was earning the most money I'd earned in my life, it compensated little the sense of tragedy I'd become a part of. How, in the name of advancement, society degenerated so far away from nature's will, is, remains to be, and always will be, utterly beyond me.

Above our desks was a large customer counter, a sickening electrical sign that ticked over the number of customers we'd successfully imposed our products on, the only supposed motivation to work harder being to push the grand number higher and higher. One needed little morality to discern its evil, and its lustful objective to sell and sell was indeed a stark contrast to the statement of one of my all-time heroes—an old hippy I'd seen in Byron Bay, fantastically weathered from having spent his life walking around with a sign that read: *Nothing for Sale*.

I gathered I wasn't the only one in this corporate hell dreaming wider than the width of its walls; still, this didn't lessen the ritual irritation by many around me. Everyone would complain about having headaches, sore backs, or bad skin. 'No wonder!' I wished to scream. 'When you're in an environment devoid of inspiration, pumped with recycled air, and cornered in the toilets by the world's unfunniest blokes boring you with their heyday fishing stories, how could you *not* have a headache let alone refrain from jumping off something high!' Perhaps this was why the windows didn't open.

In what were, I guess, imperceptible increments, somewhere along the way my old state of breathlessness mysteriously returned. I considered, vaguely, that it may have been due to the range of things I loathed about life—my horrible job, the folding of the band, the humdrum, the routine, the monotony, the soul-destroying busyness and familiarity, the monthly payments, the traffic jams, the shopping centres, the idiotic crap on the telly, and—to the extent this chapter would need to be printed on an everlasting roll of toilet paper—so much more. But due to my inability to understand the cart before the horse in question, I was convinced my breathing relapse was less a byproduct of my dread list than it was a mysterious physical problem. And knowing what it felt like to breathe well, it this time felt even worse than my pre-Dublin condition.

Desperate to reclaim my lost fortune, I'd eyeball myself in the mirror and attempt—daily—to recreate the Dublin miracle. But with the mouse on the wheel in my head well and truly resumed, desperation proved no porthole to relief, and falling only further down its rabbit hole, my decline was as continuous as it was steep.

As the weeks turned into months, and months into years, my attempts to seek help were exhaustive—general practitioners, asthma specialists, every allergy and blood test known to medicine, anti-anxiety meds, hypnotherapy, counselling and more. I even had a bronchoscopy, where doctors put a camera into my lungs. The verdict? 'All good in here'—words of the like translating into 'we can't help you', filling me, in turn, with even more desperation.

A textbook case of the chicken before the egg—'Am I anxious because I can't breathe? Or can I not breathe because I'm anxious?' Although over time I considered that my downfall was perhaps an emotionally based one, it was impossible for me to discern either way.

With the breathlessness came a suite of crossover symptoms:

a continuous sinking feeling in the stomach, permanent fluttering in the chest, the inability—particularly in the mornings—to stop my hands and feet from shaking, weight loss so dramatic that my cheekbones began to look like handlebars, my skin turning grey, my hair starting to thin, and incapacitating insomnia.

As for the emotional beach upon which I felt washed up, where on the good side of the breathing fence I'd felt utterly connected to all life, I now felt precisely disconnected and adrift in a sea of anxiety where there felt an almost blur between myself and the muddled cosmos that surrounded me.

This experience, be it real or unreal, physical or emotional, constituted the densest feeling of loss I'd ever experienced. However unwanted the sticker, I had well and truly reverted back to the cursed me. As much as friends and family would encourage me to just *relax past it all*, it was difficult for them, or anyone, to understand that what I was going through was far more life threatening than something that could be remedied by a night in with a DVD.

I'd heard it said that the longest journey someone can set out on is the one between head and heart. The solitary gain, so far, of my personal crisis—or as the spiritually predisposed would later advocate, 'my personal painbody granted to help me on my path to self-realisation'—was that I'd come to better understand that I was constituted of two parts: Me *the doer*, the guy who eats, brushes his teeth, and gets in his car and buzzes all around; and me *the watcher* or voice that, welcome or not, constantly narrates my experience.

The doer felt, for the most part, like a slave at the end of some whip of obligation, constantly expected to be here and there, doing this and that. And the watcher, although guilty of being an incurable dreamer, was like the wiser half, always reminding me that I am worth more and that no matter what circumstance I find myself in, I always have a choice.

But with these two parties came party members, backers of the doer, saying, 'Ah well, this is how it is in the adult world! Head down, arse up! You got to do the right thing! Everyone hates their job so get used to it!' And the quieter and wiser voices of the watcher: the spokespeople of the heart, always fighting for what was, and, remains to be my truth. Like Democrats and Republicans, it was hard to know if the two parties disagreed for the sake of it. But I couldn't deny that if the fight turned to one of ten paces, I hoped the watcher would turn about-face and blow the other idiot away.

So there it was, the same old question, sitting heavily on my chest four years later: 'Stick a stick in the ground, or set sail?'

Stick a stick in the ground: suck and see, buy a house, get an Ikea membership card, find a girl, settle down, and all such things from a Cat Stevens lyrics jacket. Or *set sail:* shoot for the horizon, cast for that beyond my eyes and keep scratching the travel and curiosity itch—the societal c-word I'd always felt a certain pressure to forbear. For the fact I could breathe when overseas—and that there was nothing that meant more to me than to reclaim my ability to do so—was there any question at all?

As I pondered day in and day out, the clock on the wall at work refused to change its pace. The same went for the one on my bedside table, and the dozen or so at Flinders Street Station. Their permanency was just too symbolic; I was going back overseas.

AUSTRALIA

3. The Last Supper

Twasn't the night before Christmas, nor was it bin night, but it was Thursday, April 8th, 2004.

As far as my friends were concerned, my leaving was worthy of a roundtable conference, so we gathered at Nick's Greek Tavern.

With blue shuttered windows, whitewashed walls, and the smell of olive oil wafting throughout, the restaurant was decked out in Greek authentic. Our crew arrived one-by-one, and we were seated at a long candlelit table in the back corner. The room hummed with conversation, and as we pored forth over matters like 'if not mint-like, then just what flavour is regular-flavoured toothpaste?' conversation at our table flowed as it should.

We were mostly settled in, with eleven mates present, yet one key figurehead was still missing.

'Hey Dave, where's Jude?' asked Matty, as he lowered himself into his seat.

'Dunno, but he's pretty allergic to punctuality.'

'Should we wait for him before we order?'

'Nah, it could be to the detriment of the lamb.'

With all at our table turned to each other, a waiter approached. But with a wig of such poor quality strapped to his head that it looked little dissimilar to a dead dingo sticky-taped to his scone; this was no ordinary waiter. 'Excuse me, sir, do you have any questions?' he asked.

'Yes. Does that thing stuck to your nut double as a watchdog? Do you believe you've got the rest of us tricked into thinking it's real? And do children, running into the arms of their parents, explode into tears at the sight?' My face, in its strain and confusion, surely said.

'Excuse me, sir, do you have any questions?' he repeated.

'No, no questions. Actually... do you serve hare?'

'Hair?'

'As in rabbit?'

'As in hare?'

'Yes!'

'No, we do not!'

'I'm sorry. Can we have some menus, please?'

'No!' he replied, holding his hands behind his back and pursing his lips.

* *A note to all men wearing wigs:* as the spiritually inclined believe that 'destruction can only lead to destruction', a wig can only lead to awkwardness and humiliation. So for humanity's greater good, have it euthanised by a vet, bury it in the backyard, and let us get back to singing Kumbaya.

In a tone of overt defiance, he addressed our table. 'At Nick's Greek Tavern we don't have any menus! The customers get what they're given!'

'I can't believe how rude this waiter-bloke is,' I said, turning to my mate Mick, 'I hope his ears turn into arseholes and shit on his shoulders.'

'I think the forced-menu is a novelty service. Besides, if he's getting tetchy, it's because you've cornered him.'

'What?'

'Haven't you heard why Greeks aren't any good at soccer?'

'Why?'

'Coz every time they get into a corner they put a milk bar on it.'

Scribbling on his pad—and if happening to have overheard us hopefully not including cyanide fried cheese—the waiter announced a list of dishes we should *expect* to receive. He was an unpleasant piece of work, but hearing words like *saganaki* and *tzatziki* somehow compensated his crabbiness. Having cleared the irritation from his throat, he whipped his pad into his pocket, turned and departed.

Observing them snowball into conversation, I fell into a moment of pride while looking around the table. There were more good people present than in some nations combined. Sitting beside me was one of my best mates: one of the forefrontal soldiers on the battlefield of life, who more times than we could account for, we'd sat beside each other dissecting the good, bad, and any area of life that urged use of the word ugly. He was tall, dark blonde-haired, and so good-looking he made James Bond look like a ham-slapped version of his own reflection. His name was Manuel.

'So,' he said, 'you've been threatening to go back overseas for years. I can't believe you're really going.'

'I can't breathe knowing the flavour of every tomorrow.'

'Anything particularly wrong with Melbourne?'

'Other than the six o'clock news?'

'That bored here?'

'The grind just isn't life; just a contrived nightmare that gets in the way of it.'

'Do you reckon you're still hung up on what happened with that doctor-bloke in Dublin?'

'Completely.'

'So where are you off to?'

'I'm flying to Kathmandu, having a squiz through Nepal, and working my way through India before settling in London. I'm keen to ride a motorbike across India, but I'm still just thinking about it.'

'Half your luck though.'

'Luck? If I ride over a cliff and land on a pillow factory, more than half.'

He cracked open a long neck of Melbourne Bitter. 'So can I ask why a neat freak would want to take on such a jaunt?'

'A good man once told me, "don't aim to be material-rich, aim to be story-rich."'

'Who told you that?'

'You.'

The waiter returned with our food, and his wig—having slid leftward in the course of his busyness—now looked little better than an upturned bird's nest. He laid the plates on the table. 'Happy with the lamb, sir?' he asked in a tone of residual displeasure.

'Ahhhr… yes,' I said, turning to my mate Donnie, 'I'm just glad I didn't order the quail, or anything reminiscent of egg.'

'So where's Jude?' asked Donnie, 'Hasn't he fronted?'

'Nup, he seems to live via an imaginary daylight-savings change.'

'He must be out the back winding his clock.'

Conversation lessened as everyone began tucking into the food. Manuel emptied the long neck into two glasses and placed one before me. 'You playing any gigs while you're away?' he asked, a writer by trade, who himself was adept in sowing story and song.

'I've had a major songwriting block for the last eighteen

months. I doubt I've got it in me anymore.'

'Music or not, when you're trekking through Nepal, or barrelling across India on your bike, spare a thought for me sitting back at my desk in Melbourne.'

'What?'

'Don't *what* me; you're the only bloke I know that can take something that happened to you in a supermarket aisle and turn it into *Bridget Barry Jones*.'

'I'm sure there'll be tales to tell.'

'So cash in on your Irish storytelling genes. I expect email: glorious, elaborate, and bar the garlic bread, home-delivered.'

'Thanks.' I said, feeling a certain pressure to perform.

The night grew later than before, and it was then that I overheard Vic speaking quietly to Rach. 'Everyone's talking about Dave as if he's dead.' Although unaware I'd heard, she was right, and I sat there listening to the group talk about me as though reminiscing at a funeral. The regard warmed me more than any might have known, and brought home more than ever that as per the old cliché, friends—born with no predetermined connection, yet with something innate drawing us together—really are the family you choose.

Keasy raised his glass. 'To Dave Kerrigan and the obnoxious bastard he is!'

I sat there with a dumb smirk, daring to consider the journey ahead. Although it was a loose sketch of glistening uncertainty, I knew there'd be many a grim moment on the road where I'd wish I were back at this table.

'Do you realise what day it is?' Keasy asked.

'Thursday?'

'Yeah, but *what* Thursday?'

'Thursday the 8th?'

'Think about it: you're the man of the match, there are eleven of your mates gathered for your parting dinner—and there'd be twelve if the one whose name starts with "J" hadn't betrayed the arrangement—it's Easter on Sunday—'

'—Holy Thursday?'

'J.C. Kerrigan Foot Washing Services.'

It was a fantastic coincidence, for although I was no aspiring messiah, this really had been the Last Supper. 'And to think I didn't get a kiss when he betrayed me.'

And as on the third day, when Jesus ran out of tomb beer and ascended into a 24-hour bottle shop in heaven, by the Sunday, I was gone.

IN THE AIR

4. Melbourne to Kathmandu

Another world I barrel towards,
no one to have to bow.
A clean slate, an open floor,
no when, or where, or how.

We were high in the air when a flight attendant came walking up the aisle. 'Excuse me, sir, tea or coffee?'

'No thanks, I'll just have a tomato juice.'

I leant back in my seat, pondering the joyous combination of tomato juice and altitude.

Australia was somewhere beneath, and although the odd bit of turbulence inspired the odd bit of white knuckles, I was happy to be there. In fact, I'd never understood the aversion of flying. Fair enough if someone was terrified of any highly unlikely events, but I'd never understood how back-to-back movies with back-to-back martinis could be considered a sufferance.

Turning right to economy never left to first class, when

boarding planes I'd always taken the aisle of the commoner. And sitting, on this flight, in the Anti-VIP section of the back row, it growingly intrigued me as to why anyone would care to be in first class anyway. Sure, you get more legroom and an umbrella in your cocktail. But unless those in economy had to flap their arms to power the plane, I failed to see the value.

Australia was long gone, and although it had been night for most of the flight, the deepened sky didn't dissuade me from gazing out the window. We were somewhere above land, and like a pointillist pattern drawing up a foreign picture, down below was the twinkling of a thousand lights.

Some hours later the Asian sun snuck over the horizon. Breathing by its own lung, Kathmandu—in a vast stretch of winding streets, narrow laneways, temples and shanty shacks— was revealed through the breathless pollution. 'This is really it!' I thought, as the plane descended. All that I'd prepared for was about to happen. But armed with little more than a toothbrush and a credit card, was I prepared at all?

THE KINGDOM OF NEPAL

5. The Prison Soul

With a course of freshly-squeezed naivety running through my veins, I walked through the airport corridors and approached the customs counter.

'Good morning, sir,' said the officer, as he flicked through the pages of my unused passport, 'where is your visa?'

'Ahhhr... I didn't know—'

'—Don't worry,' he said, sensing I couldn't differentiate travel-arse from travel-elbow, 'you can pay upon entry. Twenty-five American dollars.'

'Sweet,' I thought, getting my credit card out of my daypack, 'do you take visa?'

'No, sir, I give visa.'

'No, as in do you take visa credit card?'

'No, sir, cash only.'

'But I don't have any cash on me.'

'Then you cannot enter the Kingdom of Nepal. Step aside.'

It was as simple as that. I couldn't enter, and feeling myself turn burgundy as the wave of stupidity ran through me, I stepped aside as ordered. 'How had I failed to know this?' I thought, wondering if when my travel agent had likely told me, that, much like the frame of mind I'd endured school, I simply wasn't listening.

Like a Bloodhound sniffing nearby, a security guard armed with a machinegun approached. 'Come with me, sir,' he said in tone grave enough to make me nervous. Adding to my unease, as we walked away, he and the customs officer spoke in their own language.

We continued down a long grey corridor. Until finding it sufficiently secluded, the security guard stopped me at its dead end. 'Are you American?'

'No!' I said, quickly displaying my passport.

'I can help you.'

'How?'

'I can escort you to a cash machine outside, you withdraw your money, I'll bring you back, you pay up and you'll be allowed entry. But—' he paused, taking the time to pick at some dead skin on his hand, 'afterwards you must do something for me.'

'What?' I asked, nervous to hear the terms of his conditions.

'The Maoists have upset the economy very much, and tourism in the city is very bad.'

'And?'

'And so you must—' he broke, looking over his shoulder.

'Yes?'

'You must…'

'Yes?'

'Stay at my cousin's hotel.'

The drumroll in my head ended. 'All right,' I said, having thought I'd be required to pay an amount of money breaking records in extortion, 'I'll stay in the hotel.'

He clapped, quite girlishly at that, which rather contradicted the man-with-machinegun image. He next escorted me into the mayhem outside the airport.

With a flock of taxi drivers circling tourists like vultures on dying prey, the madness beyond the doors was enough to justify an Aspirin addiction. Myself being ritually pecked, my bodyguard was quick to allow their eyes the sight of his gun. 'Come!' he said, anxious to get back inside who was presently an illegal immigrant. I withdrew the money, went back to customs, and was lastly stamped through.

Next came his end of the bargain. 'My cousin is a very nice man, with a very nice hotel, in a very nice part of Kathmandu,' he said, seeming to acquire perverse pleasure from use of the word *nice*. He took me back outside, and having previously played the role of bodyguard, he was now that of bellboy, hailing me a taxi and throwing my bags and guitar in its boot.

In a tone so firm it sounded little less than shouting, he gave the adolescent driver specific instructions as to where I was to be taken. As for the noted violation of my free will—settling on the idea that the task of finding a hotel was now taken care of, I opted to look on the bright side of my potential abduction.

As the taxi drove away from the airport, within minutes the horizon presented the snowcapped mountains of the Kathmandu Valley. Taking it in for the first time, I struggled to believe that here in my own skin I was in Nepal.

We bounced along the pot-holed road, when an older man, frantically waving his arms, came running towards us from an adjacent field. The young driver stopped our car in a skid, leant across my lap and wound down my window, whereupon the older man grabbed me by the arm. The young driver exploded into a rage, and I ripped my arm back into the car as he hit the accelerator.

'What was that about?' I asked.

'Oh nothing, sir, he's just another driver looking for business.'

Having made it into the guts of the city, we bumped along the dirt streets. Laid before my eyes was a world they'd never conceived; streets strewn with litter, people spitting without reserve, others shouting across the market stalls, trails of goat's blood running from the open-fronted butcher shops, and as many stray dogs as oxen and carts. I sat bolt upright, conceding that if my eyes were any more open my brain might have rolled out.

'Look out!' I yelled, pointing to a cow lying on the road, to which all too immune to such sights, the driver wobbled his head and smiled.

And so it is, that despite the disruption to the narrative, here is the necessary introduction of the Nepali/Indian head wobble.

In India, the famous head wobble actions from left to right, in a symmetrical motion. But in Nepal it's more of a singular flick to the left only, its shortcomings making the Kingdom a chiropractor's heaven. Technicalities aside, they served the same communicative purpose—to accentuate the expression on the face at any given time, whether happy, sad, angry, in agreement or disagreement. Applied well, it was limitless in creating a range of communications, from yes, no, maybe, get fucked, to 'excuse me sir, I was in your shop half an hour ago, did I happen to leave my tweed cap here?'

The taxi pulled into the proposed hotel, and I approached reception with my bags over my shoulder.

'Good day, Mr David,' said the man behind the counter. 'I am being the manager.'

'Ahhhr... g'day. How did you know my name?'

'My cousin called from the airport. You know, the nice man

with the gun?'

'Yes.'

'And where is your wife?'

'I don't have a wife.'

'Well, I have booked the honeymoon suite for you and your wife anyway.'

'But I don't have a wife.'

'Why no wife?'

'Because there *isn't* one.'

'What is the problem?'

'There is no problem.'

'Are you gay?'

'No, I'm not gay.'

'Then why, Mr David, are you having no wife?'

'I just don't have—'

'—Well, I have booked the honeymoon suite for you and your wife anyway,' he said, and with a casual flick of the wrist concurrently ringing a bell—*ding!*—'Please, Mr David, it would be my honour to offer you some complimentary chai.'

A nearby door squeaked open, and a diminutive man appeared carrying a tray with a tea set. 'Please,' he said, pouring a cup, 'drink.'

Upon following his instruction, it was nothing less than love at first sip. It was hot and sweet; with more sugar than I dared to know. But figuring someone else had put it in there I considered it my responsibility not. Knocking back cup after cup, my head filled with a sugary music, and my mind couldn't but go for a little imaginary wander into *Sugar Land*—a faraway place where children made of sugar all hold hands and skip through sugary fields. And little marshmallow lambs with sugar-coated tails jump through sugar-coated hoops, and everyone is sugary and gay—

'—Gay? Why like that?' asked the manager.

With my bags slung over his shoulder, although I'd respectfully declined his services, another man escorted me to my room upstairs. He dropped my bags by the door and smiled widely. I gave him some local tender, and closed the door on him at a speed slow enough to be polite, during which he kept looking back and forth from his hands to me. The door clicked shut, and the discontinuation of its squeak added to the room's stale aura.

I sat on the bed and attempted to spend some quality time with the closest thing to my wife—my guitar, but feeling as blocked for anything useful as the last eighteen months, I laid it down. I noticed the clock on the wall, which seemed to tick at the exact pace as the one on my bedside table in Melbourne.

*****

Dear Manuel,

I'm in Nepal. Hot, humid, and as non-alphabetical as two scrabble trucks in a smash, it's like someone has taken what I know as a normal world, shaken it like a snow globe and called it Kathmandu. I guess I'm still looking at things through my first-world glasses, but seeing a third-world country for the first time makes me wonder how a place becomes and remains this chaotic.

Firstly, it seems that dogs and cows have swapped places on the social spectrum. Cows, regarded as sacred, lounge around on the roads playing the part of unwanted roundabouts, while dogs, viewed as vermin, are left looking for love in all the wrong places. Try to pat one and it'll run from your hand like you're the hangman putting a rope to its neck.

I might do some volunteering while here. I initially thought it was a fabulously original idea, until I caught on that two in three westerners are here for this reason. We'll see.

*****

It was 9 p.m., and like a city with a sore gut, pouring in through my hotel window was the noise of beeping horns and wailing locals. As I sat on my bed, looking down at the flashing of neon streetlights, and the occasional smoke-blowing motorbike passing by—a world that although foreign, seemed to come with such parallel commonalities to my own—something unwelcome rose within me. It was a feeling as unsettling as uncontainable that I only then realised came with the endeavour of solo travelling: the feeling of loneliness. Perhaps I'd expected that having put myself on a big plane, much within would be left behind. But realising, now, that my soul was equally the prisoner of my body, no matter where I put myself, the bubble of this expectation was popped.

Sitting in the darkness of my room, with no one but myself as my mate, I felt it came down to a simple choice—*apply* or *don't apply*. Strapping on my shoes and standing up, I headed into the hustling inner-city area of Thamel.

Thamel. Once upon a time some traveller discovered it before us all. Standing there among the glittering mishmash of Internet cafés, restaurants, and Everest trekking agencies, I was by no means that pioneer. White eyed, I'd wandered through the tangled streets until my legs grew fed up.

I sat out the front of the Kathmandu Guest House gates, happening for no reason to be gazing up at the Irish pub opposite, when a voice spoke, 'you should go in there.' I turned to make its acquaintance; sighting a petite-sized local man sitting on the doorstep of his jewellery shop next door. 'It's very good, that Irish place.'

I smiled faintly.

'My name is Bali. It means, Monkey King. What is your name?'

I looked away.

'I'm not wishing to hassle you, my friend.'

I turned back to him. He was slightly older than me—more than a kid, but less than what I regarded a man.

'So where are you from?' he asked.

'Australia.'

'Oh! My best friend lives in Darwin, and my favourite album is INXS *Kick*!' he said, breaking into a spontaneous version of *Devil Inside*, although with a touch less finesse than Michael Hutchence. 'I know you think I'm playing the tourist game, but I never do business with friends, and any Australian is a friend of mine!'

'Thanks,' I said, standing up to leave.

'What are you doing tonight?'

'I'm not sure, mate.'

'I am going to the casino. I know the boss, so everything is free. You should come!'

'Ahhhr... I don't think I—'

'—Really! It will be fun!'

Although the only thing I'd place a bet on was the fact I was no gambler, I figured I had nothing to lose.

Casino-bound, by the time we reached Freak Street at the opposite edge of Thamel, the night sky had collapsed with rain. We sought shelter under the corrugated roof of a shop front. He began telling me he was originally from Kashmir in North India, and had come to Nepal ten years earlier to seek refuge from its political troubles. I listened with a heart halved in compassion and wariness, still wondering if his sorrow-laced story was designed to soften me before asking for measures of charity.

Having worked our way through the puddle-strewn streets, we arrived at the Kathmandu Casino Royale. We were met by a guard at its main entrance, who performed a military salute with such passion I could discern a dent on his forehead from long years of duty. The casino's outside was built of red brick, and it had richly carved windows and eves. Inside—with its lazy ceiling fans, gold banisters and plush red carpets—felt like a hybrid of James Bond-meets-Indiana Jones.

'It was built by the Rana Kings of old,' said Bali as we entered. 'Magnificent, isn't it!'

'It is.' I said, feeling that save for the absence of seasickness, I was boarding a cruise ship.

As the sole westerner in his sights, the proprietor, wearing a black suit and tie, was quick to approach.

'This is David from Australia,' said Bali. 'He is my best friend!'

'Best friend?' I thought, feeling it was a fraction premature for such regard.

'Good evening, David, you are my most welcomed guest.'

I smiled politely, concealing I had zero intention of throwing my life's savings at his tables.

To the snap of his finger, a young waiter rushed over with a couple of drinks. I reached into my pocket, to which Bali was quick to remind me that everything was on the house.

We lowered ourselves into facing armchairs.

'So—' Bali began, 'I want you to meet my friend Nisha.'

'Who's that?'

'She is very beautiful,' he said, stirring the ice in his drink.

'I'm not really one for setups, mate.'

'No need to worry.'

'Worry might not be the word, but…'

'But, what?'

'It doesn't matter.'

'No, speak freely.'

'But wary could be..'

'Meaning what?'

'Meaning that at least some of the moisture behind my ears dried up years ago.'

'I don't understand, but really, I think you should meet her, then you'll see there's neither cause for worry, nor dampness behind your ears.'

'I think I should get going, mate.' I said, standing up.

'No, please sit!'

'Look, I appreciate that you brought me here, but—'

'—You westerners worry too bloody much!'

'I'm happy to hang out with you, but I'm not interested in anything for sale.'

'Of course, of course,' he said, gesturing for me to sit back down.

The night rolled on, and regardless of the flow of free drinks, my suspicion withstood. We positioned ourselves at the main roulette table, and as Bali threw down the dice, a small crowd gathered. To my surprise, he was proving to be pilot of the hour, and I, by default, was his wingman.

Over the noise of the crowd, he fired off some instruction to a waiter; the waiter soon returned with two celebrative cigars. 'Nisha is here somewhere,' he said, and although I responded with a faint smile, I decided it best I part ways with him.

He turned back to the table, and I headed for the main door, but while so, I couldn't but become entranced by the voice of the local woman fronting the in-house band. She was singing in an eastern style. Until hearing it live, I'd struggled to believe someone could sing as high and transcendentally. She manoeuvred her hands in a wave-like motion, as her voice emanated off stage like a column of smoke.

I walked away soon after, but as I headed for the door, I felt a hand on my shoulder. It was Bali. 'Where were you?' he asked. I didn't respond. He was visibly drunk, and oblivious of my plan to cut and run, he attempted to give me half of his winnings. 'Come on, man! I am the king! I am the king! I am the Monkey King!'

'I can't take your money, mate.'

'But we are brothers, right?'

'Brothers?' I recoiled, the sentiment making me even uneasier than *best friends*.

We reeled through the main door a lot less sober than when we'd entered, and the same guard mechanically smacked himself in the head with a military salute. Bali tipped him kindly, to which the guard broke into a fit of salutes so vigorous I feared he might clout himself into the 31st century.

A taxi pulled into the turnout. We got in, and as I slid around on the backseat as we tore through the rainy streets, I felt my adventure had officially begun.

The next morning, when I walked out the hotel door, a young local lad jumped into my arms. 'Vun chotlat! Vun chotlat!'

'What?'

'Vun chotlat! Vun chotlat!'

'Chocolate?'

'Yaaay! One chocolate! One chocolate!'

I considered refuting his request, but knowing I'd be no match against his will, we walked to Durbar Square, I bought him a chocolate, then—*plop!*—I was thanked by the universe by being shat on by a pigeon.

'Ha ha, mister!' he laughed, running out of the square having gotten double for his money. Despite being left with a bruised ego—and having to spend the day reminding myself that being shat on was a heavenly-sent virtue—the joy in his eyes rekindled my interest in volunteering.

It was my intention to teach English or music, but learning that many organisations required first-time volunteers to pay joining fees of up to $1,000—I soon realised the world of volunteering had in no way escaped the corruption brush.

My interest was starting to wane, until some days later I met a volunteer in a bookshop in Thamel. We initially stood alongside each other in perfect anonymity, thumbing through our books of interest, until he made a large whiney yawn. 'You an Aussie, mate?'

'Yeah, Hervey Bay Queensland. You?'

We stood there making our introduction, during which he told me he was volunteering at an orphanage outside Kathmandu. His homegrown colloquialisms couldn't go unnoticed, but they were not without an effortless theatrical charm that made me proud to be a member of his clan. His name was Lars.

'There's a group of us volunteers meeting for dinner tonight, mostly girls. You should come, mate,' he said, writing the details on a piece of paper.

I said I'd be there, although I wasn't sure I'd front.

7 p.m. had been the proposed meeting time. Lying on my bed at 6:30 p.m., milling on my theory that the only way to offset travel loneliness was to *apply* or *don't apply*, I figured I should sign on. While tying my shoelaces, I grew nervous, remembering his words, *mostly girls*.

Prepping for social battle, I shaped my hair into what I believed to be its most attractive mould, put on my cleanest dirty t-shirt and applied some pretend aftershave. But when I arrived at the designated place there was not a soul about.

I pulled up a seat at the empty bar, and as though sensing I'd been stood up by not one, but many, the barman offered a sad smile. I ordered a No Mates martini, and grumbled to it like Humphrey Bogart in *Casablanca*.

I stood up to leave when Lars ran in. 'Sorry, mate!' he said, catching his breath, 'we had a last-minute change of heart. We're at the rooftop restaurant up the road.'

Having reached the restaurant's door, we scaled the stairs up to the rooftop. In its centre was a long table with some twenty western girls, their voices morphing to perplexing effect from the distance we stood.

Lars and I approached, and I pushed out my chest in the hope of making my pectorals look less insufficient. 'Everyone—' he said, their voices stopping as they turned around, 'this is Dave the Aussie.'

'Ahhhr… g'day.' I said in a fractured voice.

Cutting across me like knives across a carcass, eye contact shot between them. Knowing that I was being pored over, scrutinised, studied, dissected and analysed in that heavy-browed manner that the female of the species habitually employs, all I could really do was pretend to be exotic.

Associating me as just another male, some—like a bad dream—were probably rerunning past unsuccessful relationships, others—looking slightly dreamier—perhaps wondered of the sort of husband I'd make, while others again—looking concerned— possibly speculated the fruits of my endowment or lack thereof.

But as I stood there I felt I understood, for although I was born on the male side of the fence, I felt I had some understanding of a woman's mind and heart.

Doing a systematic scan, when a woman meets a man for the first time, she accesses him closely—the appeal of his looks, the sharpness of his wit, his intuition and so on. If he's funny, it displays intellect and that he'd likely have the ability to provide. If he's serious, that he has the emotional IQ to more fully understand her. With all these factors determining if she'll entrust her heart and body to him, it's in the blinking of an eye— the speed of a woman's mind being that in the time a man may spend readjusting his armchair she can devise a dozen plans of how to dispose of any no-longer-wanted-parties—that from out her mind is produced a result receipt.

The table held their attention on me, and knowing my voice had to be strong for the coming torrent of questions, I cleared my throat as discreetly as possible. All the girls present were very attractive, perhaps with the exception of one. I took a seat next to someone in particular, but I was instructed, emphatically, by the one of exception to sit next to her. I obliged.

'So what's your story?' she asked.

'Excuse me?'

'What's your story?'

'Ahhhr… I'm from Australia.'

'Another disgruntled westerner with something to prove?'

'What?'

'You're all the same, you boys; here to prance and impress the girls.'

'Are you always this shy at first?' I asked; having deduced in under three seconds that this corpulent little woman made dragons seem like bunny rabbits that poo-pooed marshmallows and wee-weed lemonade. She was Norwegian. Her name was Ingrid.

Everyone at the table were volunteers, folk with good hearts and good intentions. I'd primarily fronted to get information, and I foolishly gave Ingrid seniority by asking her a question on the subject. 'Ok—' she said, 'this is how it is…' launching into a protracted spiel about how men—being without the sensitivities of women—shouldn't bother with volunteering. There wasn't a chance my face was hiding my offense, and as though familiar with her lack of diplomacy, some of the others looked over with faces of unease. The shine of this volunteering idea was starting to dull, and I changed seats soon after.

'Sorry about that,' said my new neighbour.

'I feel like I'm on trial here.'

'She detests men.'

'And I get the feeling *carpet* is what comes to mind when she hears the word shag.'

She smiled and looked downward. 'So what's your name again?'

I told her. She explained that she was volunteering at an orphanage outside the city, giving me information without me even needing to ask. She had dark almond-shaped eyes framed by her long dark hair. She was English. Her name was Jane.

Over much group conversation, a rather tall girl addressed me from across the table. 'So tell us about yourself!'

Everyone went quiet.

'Ahhhr... well, I just flew in from Egypt where I was teaching yoga on the banks of the Nile.'

'Really?'

'No... but I've heard of the Nile, and of Egypt.'

Some smiled, others slouched, and Jane turned to me. 'I'm taking the kids to the zoo tomorrow. You should come.'

It was a volunteering date.

Tomorrow became today, and this volunteering idea as yet untested, I grew nervous as Jane and I took a taxi to her orphanage.

As soon as we arrived, Jane was swarmed by the resident kids, yelling 'Sister! Sister!' while tugging at her dress and quarrelling for rights to hold her hands. Noticing me standing back—yelling 'Brother! Brother!' and clutching at my hands also—they soon turned their attention to me. These kids were raised entirely by women, and remembering then the words of Ingrid, who'd passionately rejected the need for men in orphanages, my aversion for her increased.

We walked into the orphanage, where for the first time the stark reality of poverty truly hit me. Ranging from ages one to fourteen, some 25 children lived in a concrete-floored room about the size of an average bedroom. Like a prison yard, it seemed to be divided into social sectors—boys along one wall, girls along another, each child seemed to be wishing for a slither of breathing space. Some were quick to come over and hold our hands, while others cowered in the corner in a ball of tears.

'Namaste!' greeted Jane in a qualified tone, to which all replied in choral union while palming their hands together.

All orphans, she explained how many had come to be here, most of their parents killed by the Maoists. I'd heard of the Maoists, but as yet knew little about them.

(Starting out as a group of gun-wielding insurgents fed up with the political squabbling, the Maoist Rebel Army began in 1996. Originally disregarded by government, having risen—by 2004—to a force between 10,000 to 15,000 fighters, the Maoists were a well-organised, heavily-armed force who had many parts in the country's west entirely under their control. They'd demoralised the Nepalese Police Force, and many speculated the Royal Nepalese Army—directly under the king's control—was frightened to confront them. Their blatant objective was to lead the country to a Marxist republic, and so powerful they'd become it was felt few would defy them when they inevitably struck Kathmandu.)

Although the Maoists may have had tangible justifications, it was standing back at the orphanage that the reality of violence as a means to change anything painted a less noble picture.

'Who wants to go to the zoo?' Jane sang, causing the room to explode into a choir of endorsement.

With ice-cream devoured, elephants and tigers waved at, and tears cried and dried, the day at the zoo came and went. Perhaps having been her biggest kid for the day, Jane guided me with a knowing smile.

It was dusk by the time I made it back to my hotel.

'Good evening, Mr David,' said the manager behind the counter, 'and where is your wife?'

'I told you, mate, I don't have a wife.'

'Why no wife? Are you—'

'—No, I'm not gay!'

'Come come,' he said, ringing his bell—*ding!*—'You will now be having your complimentary chai.'

Again carrying a tray with a tea set, the same diminutive man appeared. 'Please,' said he, pouring a cup, 'drink.'

As I poured the hot sugary tea down my fat neck my head once again filled with a sugary music, and my mind drifted back into *Sugar Land*—that faraway place where children made of sugar all hold hands and skip through sugary fields. And little marshmallow lambs with sugar-coated tails jump through—

'—Mr David,' said the manager, 'there's someone here to see you.' I turned around, and standing there was Bali. 'Come with me. Nisha is ready to meet you.'

My wariness rose like a rash as we barrelled through the streets of Thamel, not at all soothed by him singing INXS' *New Sensation*.

We arrived at the door of a small bar. 'Look, mate,' I said, over the noise of the eastern music coming from behind it, 'I told you I'm not interested in anything for sale!'

'Stop bloody worrying,' he said, and when he pushed open the door, standing on stage was the lady I'd seen singing at the casino. 'There is Nisha.'

'Her?'

'Yes.'

'Her up there?'

'Yes! She is my friend!'

'Then why didn't you tell me that was her at the casino?'

'Because, man, I was too busy winning! I told you she was around though.'

With both of us nursing a glass of local rum, we sat at a nearby table, and manoeuvring her hands in the wave-like motion she did, her voice seemed to fill the room without effort. She had exceptionally long hair and deep brown eyes. As soon as she got off stage, Bali seized the moment. 'This is David. He is my best friend!'

'Nice to meet you,' she said in a voice so quiet it was hard to believe it was the same one she sang with.

'Ahhhr... likewise. I really like your voice.'

'Thank you,' she said, sitting opposite.

'Is it falsetto or full voice?'

'It's a blend. I hear you're a singer also?'

'Half,' I said, wondering in what context Bali had referred to me.

'You should do some singing in Kathmandu. They will love you here.'

I certainly hadn't exercised the idea, but after a ten-minute pep talk figured the only thing I had to lose was the non-existent reputation I had in these parts.

Like a manager satisfied with his efforts, Bali leant back with a contented smile as Nisha returned to the stage. I was starting to see him in a new light, convinced the only thing he was guilty of, so far, was having brought together two musicians. He pulled out a packet of thin cigars. 'She's like a princess,' he said, exhaling his debut puff, 'not that anyone would want to be royalty in this country.'

'You're referring to the shooting?'

'Yes, and wasn't that an international embarrassment.'

'I saw something about it on the news at the time.'

'It was three years back; the entire royal family was massacred by the son of the king, Prince Dipendra. He killed his father, mother, sister, brother, aunts and then himself. The old king, Birendra, was a wonderful man, and everybody believes his brother, the new king, Gyanendra, had hand in it to claim the throne. Now Gyanendra rules a country that hates him!'

He offered me one of his cigars.

'I tell you, this country is a mess, and nobody wants to clean it up. Men are wretched and lazy, and pride themselves in it, especially in government; those bastards sit around never doing a thing. And all this bullshit with Iraq.'

'What shit?'

'Come on, man!' he said, giving me a light. 'Do you live under a bloody rock? Right now there are twelve Nepali hostages being held in Iraq—cooks and cleaners. But the Iraqis haven't made any demands for their release, giving the Nepali government even more excuse to do nothing. But that's the way of things in this country; you watch, the government will sit on its hands, and those hostages will be killed.' He sank into his chair, seeming to take a moment before again leaning forward. 'I am just a simple businessman, and all this nonsense is frightening away the tourists! Between the uselessness of the government, the tension of the Maoists, and the corruption of the royal family, the people of this country are going to explode! It will happen soon! You will see it!'

As per Nisha's advice, the next day I went rallying to get a gig in Thamel. Typically, upon approaching several pub owners I was met with the who-*the-farck*-are-you-and-why-should-I-give-you-a-gig attitude. It was less than uplifting, but after explaining to one owner that I'd play his venue for free, he gave me the green light. The catch was that the gig was to be that very night— a Saturday night. I'd rather have had a couple of days to rehearse, but I led my new friend to believe I'd be hunky-dory by nightfall.

It was midday, and when I walked into one of Thamel's most popular eateries—famous for serving only chai, chocolate donuts and fried eggs on toast—I bumped into Lars and, sadly, Ingrid.

'G'day,' he said, as Ingrid failed to pay me more than burning eyes. 'What's going on?'

'I just organised a gig for tonight.'

'Where?'

'At the Buddha Bar.'

'Cool. I'll round up as many of the crew as I can. So what are you doing for the day?'

'Not sure.'

'We're going up to our orphanage. You should come, mate,' he said, and although I wondered if along the way Ingrid might push me out of a moving vehicle, I accepted.

Having soon arrived, their orphanage proved to be a very different place to Jane's. More like a monastery, it was a huge cobblestone building whose weatherworn exterior was covered in thick dark moss.

We barrelled along a lengthy internal corridor, aligned with door after door of rooms concealing secrets I'd never know. Ingrid appeared to have not a bee but a terradactyl in her bonnet.

'What's going on with her? I asked Lars, the two of us lagging a safe distance behind.

'Just stand back, mate,' he said, as we turned left into an office full of men caught sitting idle. *Three Men Fill Three Diapers* should have been the headline, as one of them switched off the telly at a speed as though it were an Olympic event.

'Please, miss,' said another, sitting bolt upright, 'we were just—'

'—Enough!' she snapped, before doing her nut in a froth-based language.

Lars looked at me knowingly. 'Word is these blokes were using donation money to buy alcohol. The blokes in this country are useless, mate, the women do everything, even laying the roads.'

With Ingrid's heart rate having returned to her version of normal, the three of us made our way to the baby room.

The room was lined with some twenty cots, some with up to five babies in each. All of them were Nepali, and all were orphans. The nursing of these babies was carried out solely by volunteers. Lars went from one cot to the next, as natural as though he had a few of his own back home. 'Each baby deserves one volunteer,' he said jovially. (So fine a bloke was he that he later went on to start his own orphanage: *www.forgetmenot.org.au*)

This dome-roofed room, filled with infantile hollering, was in essence an inadvertent concert hall. Lars handed me one of the star vocalists, a baby boy, and he lessened his song to a murmur after a few minutes in my arms.

'Dave, look at this,' said Ingrid, calling me over to the other side of the room where lying in a cot was a Caucasian baby. 'This little girl was left on the doorstep through the night—just three nights ago. No one saw who put her there. We have no name and no way of even knowing the nationality.'

'So what happens now?' asked Lars.

'The only thing that can. I'm going to adopt her.'

It was then that I better understood, that although hell hath no fury like the brimstone in her heart, it definitely beat for the greater good of the kids.

When I made it back to Thamel later that afternoon I ducked back into the famous eatery for round two of fried eggs and donuts.

I sat quietly to myself, a thing at which I was becoming quite adept. I noticed a western girl sitting at the neighbouring table. She had large blue eyes, and medium-length blonde hair. Perhaps

I had x-ray hearing, but when she sneezed—*och-choo!*—I was sure I detected a hint of tartan.

'You Scottish?'

'Aye? How can ye tell?'

'No reason. D'you want some of my donut?'

'Whot?'

'D'you want some of my—'

'—Noo thanks. Soo furryboots are ye fae?' she asked in an accent as Scottish as a bagpiper choking on a shortbread.

'Pardon?'

'Och, I jist flew in fae Glasgow there, so ah'm stell oan home patter. I meant, *where aboots are ya from*?'

'Melbourne.'

We spoke for some time, and although we'd been perfect strangers a short time earlier, there was a forthright honesty about her that seemed above the need for the usual pleasantries. She seemed to have an ability to look through you, not in an invasive way as one might read the secrets in your face, but as though able to see *you* better than you yourself, she spoke straight to the bone of what mattered. Her name was Ange.

'Soo whot brings ye here?' she asked.

'To this donut shop?'

'Tae Nepal, ya dafty.'

'What's a dafty?'

'Someone who's an inch thicker than their national average.'

'I see, so what brings me here? In a word, dunno, but I'm pretty keen on the chai.'

'Deep.'

'And you? The prospects of enlightenment?'

'Include the prospects of a tan and ye might be gettin' close. I guess ah'm takin' a leap of faith. After Nepal ah'm away tae India.'

'So am I! Perhaps I'll see you over the border?'

'Perhaps, but it's a big old place this.'

'What? Kathmandu?'

'Noo. Asia.'

With her body language looking like a snake getting out of its old skin, I figured I best not push the partners in crime thing. 'Well, I'll see ya around then,' I said, standing up. 'It's been nice talking to you.'

'D'ye knoo whot?'

'What?'

'It has.'

I walked onto the street before turning around and walking straight back inside. She looked bemused as I reappeared and cleared my throat. 'If you're at a loose end, there's a few of us getting together at the Buddha Bar tonight. Should you fancy it.'

'Och, we'll see.'

It had been a long enough day, but I was yet to get through the gig for the night—which was going to be little more than a slapdash case of swinging by the hotel, grabbing my guitar and crossing my fingers.

Barrelling along the streets at a large pace, running over in my head what I was going to play—a mix of older originals and covers I felt I could do justice in a solo acoustic format—I was running far later than I wished.

I arrived and ran up the entrance stairs—past a handwritten sign: *Saturday Night... One Night Only... David Kerrigan from Australia.* It was frighteningly official.

The venue was small: with plush red carpet, dusty chandeliers and crushed-velvet cushions strewn across the floor. I felt instantly partial to its dynamic, especially thanks to the ceiling-to-floor window next to the stage that opened to the street below.

There were some anonymous souls sitting nearby, probably

oblivious there was going to be live music at all. I proceeded to set up, and the manager eyeballed me from the bar. I felt bad enough for being late, but remembering I was playing his gig for free, my guilt stood little chance of survival.

I plugged in, got comfortable on the rickety stool, and the first song—an older original—began.

KICK THE MOON

(♪ featured on the *Audioride* album *Join Like Water] Move Like Tides*)

And so you're lost
In the four-walled house of glass
You float across
Wading through the smoke
And I know

Take my hand
I almost know where I am
Let's spin and dance
And watch this world dissolve

Climb on up the fairy tale vine
Watch your feet now you're getting high
Kick the moon, steal the light, up you come
Forget your feet, forget your mind
The world will be there next time
Climb on up the fairy tale vine

It's night, I'm tired
Let's drag ourselves outside
Like rope entwined
So slowly we unwind

Climb on up the fairy tale vine
Watch your feet now you're getting high
Kick the moon, steal the light, up you come
Forget your feet, forget your mind
The world will be there next time
Climb on up the fairy tale vine

As did I feel on this night, something always happens when onstage. Where although my mind is occupied by the situation itself—remembering the lyrics and chords, being mindful of my voice, and, projecting the masquerade that being onstage requires—I'm equally consumed by a recurring reflection where I wonder how the little kid I was—one whose life was occupied by talking to ants in the backyard, mowing the lawns, and toking hourly on a Ventolin puffer—ever came to be here.

I sat by the open window as I played, and with the comings and goings of hundreds beneath—some stopping to listen, and some waving up—I had a clear view of the bustling laneways of central Thamel. The night was hot and airless, until, with a boisterous crack of thunder it began to rain. I finished the first song somewhere around then, and the room filled with gentle applause.

Now starting to relax, I kept on, and due to the music pouring onto the street below; the venue began to fill with unknown faces. Lars was the first comrade to front, and as per his proposal, he'd managed to scout several of the volunteers. Ange the Scot soon followed, and soon after came Bali and Nisha. I was particularly self-conscious to have Nisha present, herself being a singer far superior to me. She offered an encouraging smile as she stood by the bar, next to the manager, who, happy with gamble, gave me a thumbs-up any time we made eye contact.

With one song blurring into the next, and all going to plan, the room, to the surprise of all, fell to darkness. I stopped midsong and tapped on the dead mic. The bar staff surrounded me at the feet with candles, so I continued without the mic.

Having already experienced that citywide blackouts were just a part of life in Kathmandu, I was less than surprised to be singing in the dark. But coming to the conclusion then that somewhere underground, in a damp room, was an exhausted turtle peddling a unicycle hooked up to a generator that powered the city, and, too rooted to continue, had to on occasions burn down a cigarette, neck a cup of earl grey, and punch down a prawn by way of self-elected smoko, never before had I stopped to wonder why.

With the intimacy of the blackout having proven to be the highlight of the night, when the power resumed—and the lights filled the room—so too did an air of disappointment. But the show went on nonetheless, and just when I thought I was far enough away from Oz to never hear the words again, some squawky Aussie yelled from the back, 'd'ya know any Chisel?' I sunk, filled with disbelief that the same words that had haunted me at numerous gigs in Melbourne had found me in Nepal. All in all it made for a well-received laugh, and I scratched out a two-bob version of *Flame Trees*.

With drinks having been drank, hands having been clapped, and my voice getting a fraction too close to cactus for my own liking, I signalled the gig's end by laying down the guitar. And with Nisha quick to approach and explain she felt my voice was good, but better in its projection when singing without the mic, and the Chisel-requesting-bloke explaining that my version of *Flame Trees* made him so homesick he was flying back to Sydney the following day, and the owner of the Israeli bar across the street offering me to play his venue at my soonest convenience, although I wished to pick my performance into a platter of critical pieces, I was left no choice but to be happy.

*****

It was some time later that the Maoists gave official warning they'd be striking Kathmandu in the next few days. There was no telling if their act to block the capital was merely symbolic, or, like in Cambodia in 1975—when the Khmer Rouge marched into Phnom Penh, took control, and eventually wiped out two million of its own people—if it was the start of something more sinister. Bearing in mind the Maoists were responsible for the deaths of 11,000 Nepalese—and their plan to topple the monarchy was widely-known—no one could know the lengths they'd go to for political validation.

With speculation rife, and tourists being warned to clear out while they could, a cloud of unease descended on the city. Although I'd had in mind to spend more time involving myself in volunteering, I wasn't prepared to risk staying.

I packed my bags the next morning, but I was going to leave, by no means, without first saying goodbye to Bali.

'You know the Maoists are coming?' I said, having found him, to style, sitting on the doorstep of his jewellery shop.

'I had wanted to take you to that Irish pub,' he said, gazing up.

'Aren't you going to get out?'

'They serve big glasses of dark beer.'

'I know, it's called Guinness. So aren't you—'

'—Maybe we should have one now?'

'I would, but I'm about to leave, mate.'

'Where are you going?'

'To Pokhara and then south into India. What about you?'

'I'm not moving from this step.'

'Why?'

'Because fuck the Maoists, that's why,' he said, using my hand as a jimmy to stand up. He brushed off his jeans as he faced me.

'You know, I'll miss you, you bastard.'

'Thanks, mate, you're one of the good ones.'

I proceeded to walk away, but was summonsed just a few steps later, 'David?' I turned around. 'If I was a girl I'd marry you!' It was a comment to which my brain failed to find a reply, but breaking the silence for us, he broke into street-wide swan song—'don't ask me… what you know is true… don't have to tell you… I love your precious heart…' it was INXS' *Never Tear Us Apart*.

I swung back to the hotel to get my bags and guitar, to find the manager, to style, standing behind the counter.

'Goodbye, I'm getting the bus to Pokhara.'

'Ah, very good, Mr David. Are you taking your wife?'

6. The Spark

I hopped on the bus an hour later, and it pulled out of Kathmandu just in time to see a string of armed Maoist trucks entering the city. The outgoing traffic was painfully slow; with a multitude of locals with the same escape plan in mind.

Once out of the red zone, the journey to Pokhara was constituted of two hundred kilometres of slow-winding roads back-dropped with snowcapped Himalayan Mountains. And no complaints from me.

The fresh mountain air struck me as we disembarked at Pokhara bus station. I grabbed by bags and wandered the high street, mesmerised by the reflection of the panoramic mountains in the giant Phewa Lake.

I settled into a hotel, and I sat on the bed and tweaked a few chords on the guitar. I laid it down soon after and walked over to the mirror. Suddenly, I suffered the grave realisation that my hair was so big it looked as much like a dead bandicoot as a woollen helmet. I found a nearby barbershop and entered.

'How would you like it cut, sir?'

*****

Dear Manuel,

Things are pretty tense in Nepal, the Maoists are moving into Kathmandu, and right now twelve Nepali hostages are being held in Iraq. The Iraqis haven't made any demands, only encouraging the Nepalese government to be "doing all they can" by sitting around watching WrestleMania.

In other news, I've shaved my head. I'm told it's mandatory for those entering India. The fact I look like a fat version of E.T. is nobody's business but mine.

*****

The next day I walked into a chai shop on the Pokhara high street when—*och-choo!*—I heard a familiar sneeze come from a table at the back. It was Ange.

'G'day!' I said, genuinely delighted to see her.

'I didnae recognise ye, look at yer shiny bawheid!'

'What d'you reckon?'

'Yoo look like an erse with eyes, or an egg without the other eleven. But it's soo much better. Before ye looked like a prize yopper.'

'What's a yopper?'

'Someone employed under Thatcher's *Youth Opportunity Program*.'

'Thanks.' I said, sitting at her table. 'So when did you get here?'

'Jist last night.'

'And where are you off to after Pokhara?'

'I cannae wait, finally ah'm heidin' tae India.'

'Same, I'm catching the bus from here at the end of the week. You?'

'Ah'm gonnae get the bus back tae Kathmandu tomorrow,

then fly tae Delhi fae there.'

'Fair enough.' I thought, happy with the budget option.

Perhaps being sentimental toward our initial meeting, I ordered some chai and chocolate donuts. We moved to an outside table, and as she gazed at the lake her eyes grew wistful.

'Decent view?'

'It's gorgeous,' she said. 'The mountains look so much like the highlands it's makin' me homesick.'

Our food arrived, and the waiter slapped a newspaper on the table. I was more interested in the food, but when my eyes scanned the front-page of the paper, my guts sank: *Nepali Hostages killed in Iraq.*

'We've gotta get outta Nepal!'

'What? Why?'

'They've killed the hostages!'

'Whot are ye talkin' aboot?'

'Beheaded one and shot the other eleven. We should catch the bus to India right now!'

'But I wis gonnae fly oot fae Kathmandu!'

'This place is going to go arse up!' I said, sliding her the newspaper.

Bali was right, upon news of the executions the patience of the Nepalese was utterly broken, and from one neighbouring hour to the next Kathmandu went into severe rioting. Thousands of infuriated locals took to the streets, and set ablaze the city's largest mosque and the offices of Qatar Airways and Pakistan Airlines. The king immediately called for a dawn-to-dusk curfew and troops took to rioting crowds with batons and tear gas.

Ange put the newspaper down. 'D'ye knoo whot?'

'What?'

'I better get the bus with ye.'

We made our way to the bus station within half an hour, braced for what was going to be a twelve-hour journey to the Indian border. As the ramshackle bus filled with worried-looking locals, Ange and I were relieved to be in the company of each other.

All seats were soon filled, except for the one behind the wheel. And when a hefty man wearing a yellow turban—less a contender for the cover of Men's Health than a poster child for a hotdog-eating contest—climbed in, turned around, and grinned openly at Ange, I instantly disliked him.

He turned the key, and the trip began.

The journey was to be a straight line from Pokhara to the border town of Mahendranagar, which, relying on the sole and pot-holed highway of the steep terrain of western Nepal would cut like a blade through Maoist country. The bus screeched along the jerky road, grinding its gears as though it'd never so much as heard of the joys of oil.

Ange turned to me after a couple of deafening hours. 'D'ye knoo whot?'

'What?'

'When I first met ye I thought yoo were a big dumb bastart.'

'Do you like darts?'

'Whot?'

'Do you like—'

'—Whot's that got tae do with the price of shite?'

'I was just getting that dartboard-vibe for a minute there. So, dumb bastard ya reckon?'

'Aye!'

'And why's that?'

'Coz of yer fanny-erse hair, yer guitar, and that crap ye put oan.'

'Well, my hair is gone, and what ever I had on must have worn off by now.'

'Ah'm no' talkin' aboot aftershave, ya bamstick!'

'What's a bamstick?'

'Someone who's a danger tae themselves.'

'If you dislike musos it's perhaps coz you've sat around one too many bonfire ruined by one too many out-of-time bongo player.'

'Ah'm guessin' *muso* means musician?'

'Aye.' I said, making my debut attempt at Scottish.

We were now deep into the west of Nepal. The bus had been moving at a reasonable pace, so it came as cause for concern when with a sudden jolt the driver pulled over.

'Whot's gaun oan here?' said Ange, the two of us gazing out the window.

The locals became straight in their seats, and the driver looked equally tense, with sweat teaming down his forehead as his eyes fixated on the door. Sitting directly behind him, Ange and I were at the very front.

The door opened, and on walked what looked like a snotty-nosed teen; dressed in blue army pants, an old grey t-shirt, and heavy boots. He stood at the front of the bus with intense eyes, and in his arms was a machinegun so comparatively big that all you could do was hope if he tripped arse over it that it didn't go off. He began to slowly walk the aisle, eyeballing each passenger, and when he passed by Ange mouthed the word *Maoist.*

Turning away from the sound of his boots, the passengers avoided eye contact at all costs. All were granted pardon so far, but for reasons unknown he stopped at one man at the back. The two conversed in their own language, and the sweaty suspect quickly handed over some paperwork. The Maoist broke into a performance of harsh words, and he grabbed the man by the arm and escorted him outside.

Witnessing him being marshalled to the roadside, it was

impossible to know what to expect, and shooting through my mind images of the man being gunned down, I dared to imagine tomorrow's headlines.

The driver started the engine and pulled out, but was instructed to stop after just 100 metres. The door was opened with force, and the same Maoist boarded, holding the same man by a fistful of his shirt.

The Maoist marched the man down the aisle, and giving him a subsequent dose of stern words he pushed him into his seat. He turned around abruptly, as though angered by the thought of watching eyes. He scanned all passengers as he walked back towards the door, casually tapping the trigger of his gun. With a commanding nod, he instructed the driver to open the door before he disembarked.

It was now night, and with not an artificial light for miles, wrapped around us was a darkness I'd never known. It was breathlessly hot, and like points of light to a neighbouring realm, the stars flickered above the snowcapped mountains.

For all the natural beauty on hand, though, our disposition felt otherwise, and wondering why we were long past the ETA, I leaned forward to the driver. 'Excuse me, how much longer to India?'

'Oh, very far just yet,' he shouted over the roar of the engine.

I sank back into my seat, and Ange and I fell asleep somewhere around then.

I was awoken, an indefinable amount of time later, by the bus coming to another halt. We were caught in a long line of traffic, and Ange was asleep on my shoulder. 'Ange, Ange, Ange…'

'Whot's gaun oan now?' she said, her voice cracked with well-earned fatigue.

I stepped outside, to find standing on the road a crowd of hundreds who'd abandoned their vehicles. At the far end of our sea of traffic was a wall of fire as tall as a double storey house.

'What's this about?' I asked the local man standing beside me.

'Those bastards killed those hostages! This is the protest of the rural people. They're as sick of the government as the monarchy and the Maoists!'

I wondered why I was here, and wondered if Australia even existed anymore.

The blaze relented after an hour, which we'd spent protecting our noses from the smell of burning tyres. The first of the daredevil drivers drove towards the hotspot, and inspired, or, equally unwise, our driver started the bus. I sat back onboard, watching us inch closer to the flame.

'This is bullshit…' said Ange under her breath.

'Not safe!' I yelled to the driver.

'No no, the bus is diesel!' he said, causing me in my lack of scientific knowledge to wonder if diesel was inflammable. Gambling our lives for peanuts nonetheless, he drove through.

It was now so late that if the time existed I wouldn't have been able to guess it at all. Having driven further dark and countless miles, we pulled into an abandoned petrol station.

Gazing around at the other passengers, who, in their fatigue and boredom seemed to be filling their time by cleaning their fingernails, blowing their noses, or watching those around them cleaning their fingernails or blowing their noses, I felt it safe to assume we were stopping for a short break.

'Excuse me, why are we here?' I asked the driver.

'The people are angry and there are too many fire blockades on the highway.'

'And?'

'And so we must stop here for the night.'

'Whot now?' asked Ange, yawning.

'They're splitting the journey in two.'

She put her head in her hands.

'Well, it's all because of that shite that went down in Iraq, so once again you can blame George W. Brainwave.'

But with all the locals disembarking, and stretching out on concrete floors, in doorways, next to petrol bowsers, and some even laying on the roof of the bus, Ange and I—still in our seats— were the only ones complaining.

A few uncomfortable hours passed, and when Ange stirred in her sleep, the driver—slouched in his chair—turned around. 'Hello, mam,' he said with an oily grin, bypassing me as though I had powers of invisibility, 'are you married?'

My blood pressure rose. 'Yes, *we* are married!' I said, taking her hand into mine, 'and we have two kids—a son called Haggis and a daughter called Tartan.'

His face performed an awkward smile.

'Fair dinkum,' I said, turning back to her, 'there are quicker ways to kill me.'

'Och, don't yoo fret darlen.'

The sun climbed over the mountain peaks, and we'd soon been driving towards the border on the same rutted road for a string of blurry hours. The road was dotted with the smouldering remains of the many fire blockades that had burnt out through the night, and we were regularly pulled over for Maoist checks.

I could deal with the heat, the hard seat, and the cacophonous whine of the engine, but dealing with the ongoing checks was, for those as impatient as Australian and Scottish nationals, as fraction too rich for Christmas.

The bus stopped yet again, and when another Maoist-kid

fulfilled his duty of modelling his dumbest face expression by way of authoritative scan and not two minutes later another pimply-faced halfwit paraded on with his machinegun to do the same, I'd officially reached breaking point.

Refusing to believe that a face of such naivety could understand or even care about the Maoist objective—but to him this whole Maoist-thing was a game that gave him a gun and a sense of worth—I wanted to kill him, and after killing him, I wanted to kill him again. Down to my last bead of patience, I reached for my water bottle, filled my mouth, and spat into Ange's face. She retaliated with the same, continuously, until the driver—caught in the cross spray—swung some behind-the-back haymakers.

With visuals of blazing street riots, Maoist revolts, and the beheadings of hostages in Iraq, after spending what was supposed to have been a twelve-hour bus journey speculating the state in which Kathmandu had fallen, it was 32 hours later that we reached the Indian border. We disembarked, got stamped, and with the orange dusk crawling out of the sky, we crossed over the border bridge by foot.

INDIA

7. The Holy Town

We stood on the dusty red road as the darkness deepened.

'How do you like India, sir?' asked a local man.

'I only just got here.'

'And?'

'And, so far it seems pretty good.'

He smiled, wobbled his head, and wandered into the darkness from whence he came.

'Jeez,' said Ange.

'What?'

'Try not tae overwhelm him with detail next time.'

'Well, I've only been in his country for 45 seconds.'

'I cannae believe we're here.'

'I've been fixated since the Tooting days.'

'Rooting days?'

'That too. Where are we anyway?'

'Banbasa, Uttaranchal.'

'There's not exactly a lot going on.'

'No' exactly.'

'I hadn't thought beyond getting out of Nepal. So where now?'

'Ah'm up fur gonnae Rishikesh.'

'Never heard of it.'

'It's a pilgrim town with loads of ashrams, it's the yoga capital of the world.'

'That's nice.'

'Och, don't be like that! D'ye no' wannae come?'

'Nah, I'm not into daily stretches. *Plan A* is to buy a motorbike.'

'Fur what?'

'To ride to the south.'

'Got somethin' tae prove?'

'Why?'

'Coz whot sort of numb-nut would wannae take on these roads?'

'I'll be fine.'

'You'll be dead.'

'Better to croak on wheels than sitting at a computer.'

'Spoken like a true wanker.'

'Anyway, I'll come to Rishikesh. I've gotta look for a bike somewhere.'

The heat of Nepal was behind us, as politically India was far safer, but we were yet to endure another ten-hour bus ride to Rishikesh. Burdened with much reluctance, we boarded another of the subcontinent's tin gems, and as it trundled through the night, we strayed in a kaleidoscope of low-grade slumber.

An indefinable amount of time passed.

'Dave, Dave, Dave…'

'What? Where? Wh—'

'—Shut up! We're here.'

We disembarked, and having saved my drool for a drool-less day, we walked along the banks of some river; its framing mountains, like shy faces, being slowly revealed in the pink veil of dawn.

'Is that the Ganges?'

'Aye, I think.'

'It's quite murky, isn't it?'

'Well, it doesnae exactly get a lot chlorine, does it?'

'Look!'

'Whot?'

'There's a cow licking its bum.'

We found a small hotel, at which time the final tally of hours since leaving Pokhara bus station was a mere *42*. I sat on the bed, reminisced about the long lost laughter of kookaburras, and untied my shoelaces with the last fumes of energy.

I was awoken a few hours later by eastern music blaring across the Ganges. I stood on my balcony, and perched in the sky as always was the most well-travelled voyager of us all—visa-less, passport-less, and crossing each and every border each and every day—the sun. Perhaps I was riddled with romance, but it looked the reddest version of itself I'd ever seen.

It was high noon when I knocked on her door. 'Ange?'

'Whot?'

'Have you ever been to India?'

'Whot?'

'Well, get this—*In-di-ya*—you're in India!'

She opened her door, revealing that her eyes had glazed over like a donut. 'Ye're a dough-heid yoo are.'

'What's a dough-heid?'

'A person of known idiocy.'

I coughed. 'Anyway, rise and shine. It's gunna be next week before it's tomorrow.'

We took to the river town soon after. The day was glisteningly clear, and we walked slowly along the riverbank, as though simulating the ease of its sluggish flow. It was perhaps in contrast to the shadiness of Nepal, but with the locals on hand offering welcoming smiles, and the pace of the things seeming to dally as opposed to bustle, this small pilgrim town offered a sincere feeling of safety.

'Are we really in India?' I asked.

'Och I knoo, it's soo quiet, and spotless,' she said, her blue eyes looking even brighter than usual.

We walked further up the river, and found a man serving chai from a pushcart. We ordered a hit and took up a seat under a nearby palm.

Bathing in the tranquillity, we sat quietly for some time. 'Mad isnae it? I never expected it tae be soo calm.'

'Me either, I think people have one of two reactions when they arrive—freak out and leave, or realise it's a place they'll come back to.'

'Whot's yers?'

'I'm still deciding.'

Our chai arrived, and we paid the man the princely sum of one rupee per cup—about two cents Australian.

We sipped quietly away, when another local man approached. He was wearing tattered orange attire, his arms were smeared with mud, and his forehead was covered with white paint. He stared at us intently, leaning on a cane and rattling a begging tin. Ange deposited a few rupees, causing him to put a hand to his chest and duly depart.

'He's a sadhu,' she said quietly. 'They renounce all material possessions and survive oan donations alone.'

'I see.'

'Whot?'

'It's just...'

'Just whot?'

'Just… he looks more like a bludger chucking a long-term sicky.'

'Och, speak English, no' that Aussie pish!'

'Ya know, when you skive off work so you can go down the beach with your mates. And a bludger is a bloke who tends to do it on a Friday.'

'Well, he's no' a bludger, ya bampot!'

'What's a bampot?'

'Someone who's clearly unhinged. Sadhus are highly regarded in India, wanderin' fae place tae place and livin' in caves and forests.'

Although I wished to hold onto my scepticism, I was impressed upon later learning the lengths some went to for spiritual purification—some acts even making it into the *Guinness Book of Records*, like sitting in the same place for twenty years, standing in one spot for seventeen years, and one sadhu who crawled for 1,400 kilometres.

We finished our chai, and along with the growing assemblage of cows and people, we continued along the river.

'I can't get over all the cows. My Irish granddad was a butcher, if he'd had his way he'd have taken to 'em with a boning knife.'

'Which in India would equal jail. They're considered holy coz they symbolise the mother—the source of milk and all.'

'Moo juice, as my people call it.'

'Whot?'

'Nothing. That's fair enough, that holy stuff, but to him they were subject to the Irish belief that if you can't drink it, eat it.'

She rolled her eyes and walked ahead. 'Tomorrow ah'm gonnae check into the ashram over the other side of the river—d'ye wannae come?'

8. Plan B

Although I'd come to India with one eye on freedom, and the other on seeking answers that could shake me off emotionally, I'd become deeply adverse to the leagues of try-hard western spiritualists I'd observed along the way. They were a dime a dozen, yoga pant-wearing enthusiasts donning beads and wristbands as though the official decoration of the spiritual soldier. Most seemed unable to tell you quick enough just how "into it" they were. I'd been privy to conversations so toxically pretentious, I sometimes wondered if I should check myself into an infirmary.

Many such exchanges took place, but none stood out as much as with one American bloke, who overflowed with pride as he told a room of some thirty people—mostly girls—that he'd found his way back to god by drinking his own piss; his self-serving homily closing with a look as if expecting a round of applause.

These types, I felt, constituted the perfect circle of contradiction, in that they failed with flying colours to understand that genuine spirituality is defined by the degree the ego is dissolved, not fed.

That if their transformation from jeans and t-shirts—to loose pants and sandals—was done in the name of impressing others, they were walking through the backdoor of the very house they'd tried to vacate.

Ange was by no means one of these, but was a dignified student in the Earth School. The others seemed to multiply when they got wet, and I knew any ashram would be rife with their kind, hence I wanted no part.

The next morning, nevertheless, Ange convinced me to go for an inspective wander at the ashram over the river.

Leading us away from the racket of the street, we walked up the long entrance ramp, where its vast flowery grounds unveiled themselves like a grand opening. The gardens were dotted with shady palms and tranquil seating areas, and the sound of nearby monkeys carried on the breeze.

Set high above the street, we gorged on the panoramic view of the Ganges. Ange turned to me with a broad smile. 'Why don't ye toss the bike idea and stay here fur a wee while.'

'I'm tempted, it's just… I'm not currently asylum seeking.'

'Och, don't be such a Jessie.'

'Me? What about this lot of whitewashers? They look as if they'd be hard pressed to make a cup of tea between 'em.'

'Don't be such an erse.'

'I'm just not such a fan of these spiritual types, folk into their star signs and chakras, and those who claim to be so *connected* they can't sleep during a full moon.'

'Ah'm like that.'

'Three words: al-co-hol.'

'Look, why don't we go doon the office and ask a few questions?'

'I'll come for a walk with ya, but that'll be me.'

We entered the rudimentary office. The fly screen door slowly closed behind us, screeching a melody so unpleasant it could make a dead man frown.

'Good morning, sir,' said the man, rising from his desk.

'Good morning, what's the minimum stay, please?'

'Fourteen days, sir.'

I turned to Ange. 'Nah, that's a bit rich, I'm going to head into town and start looking for bikes.'

She shrugged her shoulders.

I headed for the door, but it was perhaps from not wishing to hear it a second time that I turned back around. 'Excuse me, are there any peanuts in the cooking?' I asked, myself being deadly allergic.

'Actually, in fact, probably definitely yes or no,' said the man, in an accent so thick that without a personal linguist on hand I'd have done better with Pythagoras' theorem.

'Sorry?'

'Let me explain more clearly, sir,' he said, inhaling as though about to launch into a more thorough explanation.

But performing a head wobble composed of neither a nod meaning *yes*, nor a shake meaning *no*, he fell to complete silence.

I stood before him, conflicted with feelings of irritation and awe, for this head wobble was so symmetrical, so utterly buoyant, and such the heir to the perfect circle's throne, that it could surely bring a tear of appreciation to mathematicians and scientists alike.

The silence drew on, and I frowned and puckered, and puckered and frowned, until some years later he spoke. 'Have I made myself clear, sir?'

'Crystal,' I said, turning back to Ange, 'd'you know what?'

'Whot?'

*****

Dear Manuel,

I'm in Rishikesh, and much to my surprise I'm staying at an ashram. I didn't really know what they were previously, other than some sort of hippy refuge sought by westerners seeking budget enlightenment.

The word *ashram* means *place of aspiring*, so if a crack o' dawn rise, two times yoga classes, two times meditation sessions, and three times eating the same food each day, defines aspiration, then an aspirant I am.

There are about a hundred inmates in stir. Each gets a small room, a bed with no mattress, and a pillow less comfortable than a chip of Ayers Rock. It's a bit of a contrast to the motorbike plan, but here goes I s'pose.

*****

We were still standing in the office, when—*ding!*—the man rang a bell, prompting two other men to enter. Both were armed with keys and blankets, and they eyeballed us with a fraction too much intensity to call friendly.

'Follow me,' said one, as the other said the same to Ange.

'Hang on,' I said, 'can't we get a room together?'

'Men and woman are separate in the ashram.'

He led me onto a balcony with a generous view of the river. 'This isn't so bad,' I thought, taking it in as he fished the keys out of his pocket. He unlocked the door and we entered.

The room, however, if such cells were worthy of the title, was little more than a white concrete box with a hard wooden bed, a hole-in-the-floor dunny, and metal bars on the windows.

'Any chance of an upgrade?'

'Lunch is at twelve o'clock,' he said in answer, handing me a blanket and rulebook. 'Don't be late.'

It was 11:50 a.m., and feeling like a prisoner unsure of his crime, I sat on the hard bed. 'Because this is *far more* fun than a motorbiking tour of duty?'

I changed into loose white attire and made my way to the eating hall.

The hall was long and yellow; it had a grey tiled floor, and on the wall was a small music box playing a crackly Hindu mantra. There were as many westerners present as Indians, and all sat cross-legged on the floor, eating by hand from their metal trays.

I spotted Ange in the far corner. I walked over and sat next to her, as happy to see her as though we'd spent a lifetime apart.

'Good'arvo, my name's Dave. What are you in for?'

'Illegal importation of Aussie zoomers.'

'What's a zoomer?'

'Someone of an unstable disposition.'

Sitting opposite was an older western man. He was both handsome and ugly all in one, leading me to think he was French. 'G'day, Pierre.' I gestured by a raise of the eyebrows, to which he broke eye contact at record speed.

'Wanker..'

'He's in silence, ya eeejit.'

'Why? Frog got his tongue?'

'Cat ya uncultured galoot! Anyway, shut it with yer Aussie piss-fartin' aroond. We're supposed tae be quiet and reflective.'

'On what?'

'Oan things.'

'What things?'

'Any and all things. Now shut it!'

'D'you know what?'

'Whot?'

'You'd think they could have thought of a better name for it than sticky date pudding?'

'Everybody silent!' said one of the chefs, standing in the centre of the hall. All closed their eyes and fell pin-drop quiet.

As though psyching himself for the gig of his life, he closed his eyes and palmed his hands into prayer position. I kept one eye open, and several long seconds passed before he began singing some mantra. His voice, however, perhaps the very thing used to convert the ashram's milk into curd, was about as in-tune as a cat being castrated with a can opener.

Trying not to think of Ange, I sat on the cusp of a total laughter breakdown, and I ran a scan of other-things-to-think-about-in-case-of-an-emergency. It would have been to my advantage to think about global warming, or the escalating concern of housing affordability for young Australians. But with the sound of Ange struggling to my left—and the chef wailing upwards as gracefully as a chicken, with a cape, trying to take flight—an avalanche gave way and I spurted aloud.

He stopped abruptly and made firm eye contact.

I tried to disguise my laugh as a cough, by intentionally continuing it and beating myself on the chest. Unconvinced, he held the stare, until after a few long seconds he turned away and recommenced.

'I'm sorry,' I said to her when he finished, 'but it's like needing a wee during hide-and-seek.'

'Dear me...' she sighed, 'I think I ought tae be reprimanded fur bringin' a fannyboz.'

'What's a fannyboz?'

'A bloke with jacobs that look like a fanny.'

Everybody started tucking into their food—a hotchpotch mix of clotted rice, lentils, and stuff that looked like a hybrid of the two.

'This is pure mingin', she said.

'Is that Scottish for shithouse?'

'Aye.'

'Not a trace of Viagra in it.'

'Maybe it's the very thing that groond the French bloke tae silence?'

'Maybe.'

The French bloke sneezed aloud, making me wonder if he'd just broken his vow.

Later that day was our first yoga class. The large breezy hall was already full of students sitting cross-legged, so I was mindful to stop the rickety aluminium door from slamming behind me. I chose a mat at the back and sat down.

The yoga teacher entered. Standing over two metres in height, he was the tallest Indian I'd seen. He stepped onto a raised platform at the front of the room, and lowered himself down like a resting insect. He scanned the room intently, before he closed his eyes and proceeded to meditate. The class followed his lead.

The hall fell quiet, and despite the monkeys screeching outside, it entered a tranquil state. I sat with eyes closed and legs crossed, and reflecting on the trip so far, I waded into nostalgic waters—to my mates at the Last Supper in Melbourne, to the power-generating turtle peddling his unicycle in Kathmandu, to the wall of fire on the highway while fleeing Nepal, when—*bang!*—the hall door slammed shut. I opened my eyes, and standing in the doorway, fidgeting with his gonads and wearing a blank face as though surprised it'd happened, was an Italian.

Bang! the next day came and he let it slam. *Bang!* and the next. *Bang!* and the next again, and each day he would stand in the doorway, interfering with himself and looking equally surprised.

Time passed slowly at the ashram, and little by little I settled into the disciplined life of yoga and meditation. Due to the gender segregation, I spoke to Ange during meal times only, so I'd spend a lot of the day to myself wandering the florid grounds. The grounds were usually dotted with others, almost always keeping to themselves, but one day I struck up an unlikely conversation with an old local lady that lived at the ashram fulltime.

'I have seen you here for some time,' she said, stopping on the cobblestone path.

'Hello, I've been here for almost two weeks.'

'Then it's time we were introduced. My name is Mamma Sharvari…' she had long white hair, large Bambi-like brown eyes, and despite being what I guessed to be about 80, her face radiated a certain light and youthfulness '…and this is Mr Teen Tang.'

Mr Teen Tang was a frail old dog. His ginger coat barely masked his emaciated frame, and clearly a soldier with a story he was missing a leg. I knelt down to pat him, and when his tail responded with a generous wag, the old lady broke into a gentle laugh. 'Oh! He doesn't normally like people patting him, but he seems to like you.'

'Dogs are the best people.'

'And I trust his screening. You must come to my house for chai.'

We walked at a pace gentle enough to accommodate her age, until we reached her residence in the ashram's farthest corner.

Her place, like my own, had a balcony with a view of the Ganges. Unlike the starkness of mine, hers was garlanded with ferns, and even had a large bird aviary with a few screeching contenders. One of the birds—a large red parrot—was in a separate cage. It banged its head as though recalling an Iron Maiden concert, and it greeted me with what I could discern were the words 'Hari Om.'

'What's his name?' I asked.

'Harry the Parrot.'

'And what's *Hari Om*?'

'Harry is a practicing Hindu, and *Hari* means god while *Om* is the vibration that emanates through all creation. Including Harry!'

She invited me inside, which not dissimilar to my own room, was little more than a white concrete box. In heed to one's home being the externalisation of their internality, hers had an old woman's touch of floral curtains, hanging plants, and colour-coordinated spice tins perched on 360° of shelves. Its walls were the perimeters of such sincerity and welcome; I couldn't but feel as though I'd entered the house of long-known family.

'Please, David, sit. One or two sugars for your chai?'

'Just one, thanks.' I said, knowing the obnoxious sweetness of the subcontinent's chai.

She dug elbow deep into a sugar bowl, as though rummaging for the Crown Jewels of Ireland.

'And how long have you lived here?' I asked, grappling with her definition of *one* sugar being a tablespoon.

'We moved here from Goa in 1988, and my husband died in this very room in 1992. He died at the ashram and I will die here too. But for now, while I'm alive, he's with me anyway.' I leaned forward and she slowly stood up. 'It's a sin to sit inside, young man, when the sun wants to say hello.'

We walked onto the balcony and took a seat.

'The day after my husband died, Mr Teen Tang appeared on the balcony. He was just a puppy at the time—'

'—Hari Om! Squaaaaaawk!'

'Ssshhh, Harry!' she said, 'I like to think of him as the reincarnation of my husband.'

Her belief was indeed alien to western rationale, but coming from such a veteran soul I wished to honour it.

As though aware of being the topic of conversation, Mr Teen Tang hobbled over with his three legs. Where he might have been a puppy when he first arrived on the scene, he was these days old enough to be his own father. He sat by my feet, and he gazed up, leisurely wagging his tail.

'So how did he get the name?' I asked.

'In Hindi, *Teen Tang* means *three legs*.'

'How did he lose it?'

'When he was young he used to chase the Bandar monkeys, but one day he was attacked by a large group. They mauled his leg and it had to be amputated.'

'So what was his name beforehand?'

'Mr Chaār Tang.'

'Meaning *four legs*?'

'Yes!' she said, laughing, and although I wondered if when the monkeys happened to reef off his head, she'd switch his name to *Mr Three-Legged Headless Mongrel of Rishikesh*, I smiled in response.

'So are the monkeys a danger to people?'

'Oh very much!' she said. 'The grey Langurs are fine, but the red Bandars are aggressive. They attack in packs. Be very careful of the red monkeys, David, never ever look them in the eye.'

Home time came, and when I stood up to leave, she slowly rose to her feet and handed me a tin. 'Take this with you. It's a coconut chili chutney; you will like it very much. And remember what I said about the monkeys.'

One-by-one the stars punctured the sky, and with the rising moon just shy of full, I sat on my balcony taking it all in.

My room was neighboured by another room next door, both fronting onto the same shared balcony. The other room was untenanted, or so I thought, until its door unlocked from the inside and out walked a local man.

'Good evening,' he said, pulling up a seat beside me.

'Hello,' I replied tentatively, secretly agitated that I had to share my beloved balcony.

He was quite short, solidly built for an Indian, and resting rather regally on the tip of his nose were thick-lensed glasses. I guessed him to be about 50.

'So why are you here?' he asked, with a fraction less reservation than made me comfortable.

'I'm not so sure.'

'Come on! All you westerners are here for some reason or another.'

'It's all a bit new to me, this ashram stuff,' I said, starting to wriggle in my seat.

'Meaning?'

'Meaning it's all a bit of a mystery, really.'

He sat forward, as though expecting more, while I had an internal debate as to whether impertinence was a viable option.

'I guess I'm here because my head is like a speeding train, and I want to slow it to the point it's safe to jump off.'

'Good answer! That's why I'm here also.'

I was disappointed he'd so easily made sense of my analogy, but I was yet to learn his intelligence was far superior to mine.

'Would I be right in saying I detect a lack of faith?'

'Mate, when we live in a world where a hundred people can be gathered at a pedestrian crossing, waiting as one for the green man, and some chump comes along, parts the crowd, and pushes the button as though none present had thought to do so, it's pretty hard to have faith.'

'Very true,' he said, sinking back into his seat. 'My name is Professor Pramesh; I'm a history professor from Delhi. But don't fear.'

'Fear what?'

'I look far smarter than I actually am.'

'I doubt it.'

'And you are?'

'Dave.'

'And?'

'And, what?'

'Your profession?'

'Ahhhr... a yahoo.'

'Which is?'

'A philistine whose ignorance outweighs their intellect.'

'But your wit so far suggests you enjoy more intelligence than ignorance, so to the contrary you're in fact *not* a yahoo.'

We shook hands.

The night stretched forth, and the stars settled into a glittering lightshow.

'I've been coming to this ashram every year for ten years,' he said, 'I need it to get away from Delhi. That city has no breath.'

'As in the pollution?'

'And the rest.'

'Being?'

'Being the contradictions between day-to-day reality and religious philanthropy.'

I sat forward in my seat.

'I'm not just talking about Delhi, my friend,' he said, pushing his glasses north up the ridge of his nose. 'This country is sick with hypocrisy. It bathes in double standard.'

'How?'

'Look around! India likes to consider itself the world's spiritual homeland, but it turns a blind eye on a lot that needs seeing— overpopulation, environmental neglect, discrimination through the caste system...'

'I've heard of the caste system, but I don't know much about it.'

'It's a five-tiered Freemasons club, designed to keep order from the top down. No matter what caste you're born into, you must live, marry, and die within it.'

He then gave a more comprehensive breakdown.

(Brahman—the highest caste, including priests, politicians and other educated members of society. Their qualities are peacefulness, self-control, strictness, tolerance, wisdom and religiousness. Any Indian rich enough to travel outside of India is typically Brahman.

Kshatriya—known as the *Warrior* or *Ruler* caste. Its members are landowners. Their qualities are heroism, power, determination, resourcefulness, generosity, leadership and courage in battle.

Vaishya—merchants and farmers. They're considered important for providing food to the community, and sacred for being land and cow protectors.

Shudra—the broadest caste. Its members are the general working class, who provide a particular service or work in non-polluting jobs like artisans, labourers and agriculturalists.

Harijans—formerly known as *Untouchables*. They are the lowest caste, and work in degrading jobs such as cleaning, sewage and anything considered unsanitary. They acquired the name because people of higher castes believe they're too contaminated to be touched—and that even to come into contact with their shadow as polluting. They're forbidden to enter temples, and the houses of higher castes. In ancient India, Untouchables who made physical contact with higher castes were often beaten to death. They were given the name *Harijans,* meaning *Children of God,* by Mahatma Gandhi who sought for society to accept them as equal. Musicians are considered part of this caste, as the act of blowing saliva into wind instruments is considered unhygienic.)

Mr Teen Tang, the three-legged dog appeared on our balcony and sat by my feet. When I reached down to pat him Pramesh jumped like Jack out of his box.

'What's wrong, mate?'

'He'll bite!'

'Why?'

'Because he has teeth!'

'So do children.'

'But they only have two legs.'

'Just shoot the love through your arm and spread it over his head.'

'No thanks.'

'No thanks?'

'Yep.'

'Why the defiance?'

'I've never patted a dog in my life.'

'Of course you have, so as I was saying—'

'—No, I haven't.'

'As in *never*?'

'That's right. Never.'

'That's a fair old clutch of your stalk, mate.'

'Is that a euphemism suggesting the grasp on one's penis measures the authenticity of his claims?'

'Exactly!'

'Good. I'm fascinated by degenerative dialects.'

'So you've never patted a dog?'

'Nope, I'm more of a cat person.'

'It figures.'

'It figures?'

'It does.'

'And what's that supposed to mean?'

'Me, I'm a man of the dog, first and foremost.'

'And what's wrong with being into cats?'

'Nothing, if that's your thing?'

'My thing?'

'It's just…'

'Just what?'

'Just… it's a bit dainty, isn't it?'

'Dainty?'

'With their nutritional requirements of caviar and salmon?'

'What?'

'And the fact that no cat in the world every knew its own name..'

'How dare—'

'—And that no cat in the *universe* ever ran into a lake to retrieve a duck..'

'I tell you, young man, you have a nerve I'm glad I don't have in my tooth! Is this deliberate?'

'What?'

'The incivility?'

'Mate, I swear on the life of every cat—that ever sat on command—that I'd never be so underhanded.'

'Maybe you are a yahoo?'

I fought back a smile. 'Cats have their place. I just prefer an animal I can walk down the shops.'

As though on cue, Mr Teen Tang limped over to Pramesh and sat by his feet. The cat man gazed down, and his eyes grew decidedly pointed.

Bang! the next day came, and the Italian bloke slammed the door of the yoga hall. It left me wondering that if lab rats could be trained, by repetition, to not touch an electrified object, why—*the farck*—he couldn't. Standing in the doorway, fidgeting with his olives, still he looked surprised it'd happened.

After yoga I made my way over to the eating hall. The room seemed busier than usual, and the air was crammed with the music box's crackly mantra. I spotted Ange halfway along. I sat next to her. I was just about to speak when the prayer-singing-chef proceeded into the centre of the hall.

I turned to Ange regardless. 'D'you know what?'

'Whot?'

'Have you ever wondered why they don't call the littler ones Shetland potatoes?'

'Shut it,' she said, as the chef palmed his hands into prayer position.

'D'you know what else?'

'Whot?'

'It's my birthday.'

'Everybody silent!' said the singing-chef. All closed their eyes and fell pin-drop quiet.

His singing was as woeful as always, and sounding, on this day, as majestic as a squirrel choking on his nuts, it seemed to be getting worse.

Having resisted the need to laugh, Ange turned to me when he finished. 'Is it really yer birthday, or are ye talkin' Turkish Delight?'

'What's Turkish Delight?'

'Shite.'

'Yeah, it's my birthday. It's pretty cool to be in India for it too. I'll always remember this one.'

'We best commemorate then, whot d'ye wannae do?'

'Let's go down to the river.'

It was September 28th, and the day was as hot and colourful as you'd expect from India. We walked along the bustling roadside, during which a young local boy ran up to us with a cricket bat in hand. 'Hello, mister! Your country?'

I told him.

'Australia is number one! Shane Warne! Glenn McGrath!' he shouted, giving us his best air-bat before running around a corner.

We reached the river soon after, and with kids swimming and locals whack-washing their clothes, its banks were as lively as the images that had lured me here. The riverbank sand had a glittery metallic quality, and I walked ankle-deep into the water. 'Shit! It's freeeeezing!'

'Aye, whot were ye expectin'?'

'This is India, everything's supposed to be balmy!'

'Aye, but we're near the Gangotri Glacier.'

Anytime I'd imagined the Ganges I'd envisioned an unsavoury picture of decomposing bodies and contaminated water, but with Rishikesh nestled in the Himalayan foothills, this section was as unspoiled as you could wish for.

'I think I'll go for a swim,' I said, 'but I dunno if I should take my pants off here?'

'Why no', huv ye got varicose veins?'

'No, coz I've only got these translucent undies on.'

'Och, ye're in India the now, nobody cares!'

'You coming in then?'

'Noo, ah'm no' strippin' aff in front of these blokes over here.'

She was right, for the notion of privacy being utterly alien in India, as always we'd attracted a crowd. It was even common for western girls, daring to swim or suntan, to catch local lads wanking themselves in the reeds of the riverbanks.

I swam around until the holy water washed away enough old sins to make room for new ones. When I got out and dried off, the growing crowd circled in. 'Hello, sir, will you be my friend?'

'No.'

I sat on the bank, and Ange turned to me, her eyes seeming expressly occupied. 'Can I ask ye something?'

'I guess you just did.'

'Don't be daft. Why exactly did ye set oot oan this trip?'

I felt a familiar tension come over me as the inner *breathing article* loaded onto the front page of my head.

'I'm not sure I want to bore you with it.'

'Thanks,' she said, 'anyway, ah've been sittin' here watchin' the river, and thinkin' aboot yer birthday, and I dreamt up a wee verse I wannae sing tae ye.'

She inhaled.

'Ange?'

'Aye?'

'I'd prefer birthday bashes with a loaf of salami.'

'Och, ah'm only jokin', ya numpty! I knew it would get up yer kilt.'

'Aye.' I said.

'Well, happy birthday and all. Ah'm gonnae heid up the hill fur arvo yoga, ya comin'?'

'Nah, I'm going to hang down here. But I'm dead proud to hear you using the word *arvo*. I mean, why go to all the trouble to saying three syllables when you can achieve the same desired effect in two?'

'Dave?'

'Yeah?'

'Ssshhh..'

She walked off, and as I strolled along the same cricket-kid from earlier ran up to me. 'Steve Waugh!' he shouted, giving me his best air-bat again before running around a corner. Curious, I followed, to find a group of some twelve kids playing street cricket.

With an old crate for a wicket, and a plank for a bat, their equipment was as elementary as you could imagine. Standing at the crease—having marked it in the dirt with his bare foot—was my little mate.

'Sachin Tendulkar!' I said, to which when the ball met with his bat it shot down the street and smacked into a cow.

It was still my birthday, so I figured I'd indulge in a self-bought present. I walked into a nearby clothes shop. The merchant smiled widely, and followed me around at a proximity close enough to be grating.

I browsed for a matter of time, until I spotted an item of interest. 'How much for this orange shirt, please?'

'One hundred rupees, sir.'

'I'll give you fifty.'

'No, sir, one hundred.'

'I'll give you sixty.'

'No, sir, one hundred rupees, last price.'

But the notion of fixed-prices being blatantly un-Indian, I was offended by his obstinacy.

Trounced, I resolved to leave, but it was then that one small question passing his lips would change our dynamic forever. 'Your profession, sir?'

A little-imaginary-devil-with-little-fluttering-wings appeared at my left shoulder. 'I'm a professional cricketer, recently drafted.'

It was hard to know if it was from excitement or nerves, but a muscle began to twitch in his temple. His brow grew damp, and having shot some command at his wife, she brought out a tray of chai in under a minute.

'So tell me, sir,' he said, dusting off a stool, 'do you know Ricky Ponting?'

'Yes. He is my cousin.'

'Really?'

'And I was best man at his wedding.'

He broke into girlish laughter, clapping his flippers like a delighted seal. 'And tell me, sir, are you in India for the Test Series?'

'Yes,' I said, having precisely zero idea that the Australian team was currently in India.

He gathered his children for a group photo, and knowing that somewhere in hell Satan was dusting off another stool in preparation of my coming, I smiled for the camera.

Conversation turned back to business.

'Please, sir, have this orange shirt, no money for you!'

'Now now, I don't want to be unfair, or least of all dishonest. I'll give you fifty.'

'Ok! Ok!' he said, inserting the word between his shortening inhalations.

I was in his shop for half an hour, and I acquired a bundle of clothes at a heart-warming price. I could have let myself feel guilty, but figuring it was my birthday I was quick to grant myself pardon.

We parted with a reverent handshake, and as I exited his shop I noticed, a couple of doors along, the same group of kids still playing cricket. The little Tendulkar-batsman was again at the crease, and I acknowledged him with a faint nod.

My intention was to keep walking, but the merchant, moseying out of his shop, announced to the kids I was an Australian cricketer. My heart stopped as their faces lit. 'Shane Warne! Jason Gillespie!' they yelled as they exploded into mergers of child and pogo stick. I smiled dumbly, and although I'd hoped the moment would pass without consequence, one of the youngsters threw me the ball.

I stood with the ball in hand, but for the one, single, and inarguable fact that I bowl with the finesse of an orangutan, I was quick to chuck it back. 'No, mate. I'll bat.'

I stood at the crease with the bat in hand. Dozens of folk had gathered, and none were watching closer than the merchant, leaning against a wall with his arms folded.

I swallowed hard as the bowler took his run up. 'Steve Waugh! Ricky Ponting!' his teammates yelled as he unleashed like a muscle arm shotgun. My hit had to be a belter, for to be discovered as a fake could result in the burning of my effigy. The ball hurtled towards. My whole reputation was on the line, my whole career—perhaps my fear of clowns had returned, when—*whack!*—I belted it high.

Relieved, I stood back, and watching the ball soar through the air, it—*plop!*—landed in the Ganges.

'Yyyaaayyy!' the pogo-kids burst into a choir of approval, and guilty only of being in character, I lay the bat down and pointed their way.

'Good luck at the game, sir!' said the merchant, the twitch in his temple having resumed.

'Thanks,' I said, re-entering his shop for some subsequent bargains.

It was night by the time I made it back to the ashram, and the yellow moon hung low in the north Indian sky.

I sat on the balcony, eating Mamma Sharvari's chutney, just breathing the silence and savouring the serenity... so much serenity... not a sound...

*****

Dear Manuel,

I've discovered a new mortal enemy—crickets! If they'd heard of the concept of a moment's peace, I'm sure they'd use it as rehearsal time for the gig they play in my room every night.

I'm still at the ashram. With each day bleeding into the next, there's no point of reference, like the garbo on a Monday, to know what day of the week it is. I still have mixed feelings: not only that you have to wear abrasive gloves in case of any moments of weakness, but that I'm privy to conversations none should endure outside a padded cell.

It has its pluses, I guess, it's quiet and there are no distractions. I sometimes even enjoy the complimentary discomforts, my personal favourite being the bucket and cold-water tap in place of a shower.

*****

Splash! the next morning came. As naked as the day I was born, I crouched down on the bathroom floor and poured a bucket of cold water over myself. 'Jesus, Mary and her mates!' I jumped up and shook off, feeling as miserable as drenched.

I walked over to Mamma Sharvari's residence. As I walked up the balcony steps—'Hari Om! Squaaaaaaawk!'—Harry the Parrot greeted me. Mr Teen Tang was present, and his tail offered the wag I knew it would. He looked sadder than our original meeting, and it occurred to me that—waiting to be fed, patted, for you to get home from work, off your phone, to be let in from the rain, or let out to have a wee—dogs spend the majority of their lives in a perpetual state of waiting.

I was just about to knock when the old lady spoke through the fly screen door, 'Oh! He likes you very much, that dog.'

'Hello, I'm here to return your baking tin.'

'And how was the chutney? Not too spicy?'

'No, it was lovely, thanks.'

'Please, David, come in and sit. I've just made some chai.'

I went inside and she handed me a cup.

'I hope it's not too sweet? I've already put two or three sugars in it.'

I took a sip, to which sweeter than all the Wonka Bars in Willy's factory, my tongue filed for same-day divorce.

'How is it?'

'Just right, thanks.'

She took a seat next to me.

'I feel quite good today, young and light,' she said, and her face, framed by her long white hair, still radiated its light and youthfulness.

The door was ajar, and the frail dog limped inside and sat by our feet.

'The nights are getting colder,' she said. 'I'm not sure he'll survive the cold season this year.'

'Maybe we should ship him to Goa?'

'Maybe, failing that, I should make him a dog jacket. He's more arthritis than muscle. Curse those monkeys for ruining his leg. Remember what I said, never look the red ones in the eye.'

Later that afternoon, after yoga, I made my way to the eating hall. I spotted Ange by the door, and when I plonked myself next to her she took a clumsy sip of her chai. 'Och, av missed ma mooth and splootered all doon ma shirt!'

I handed her a small piece of paper.

'Whot's this?'

'An invitation to speak English.'

'Och, yoo can talk!'

The singing-chef palmed his hands into prayer position, and proceeded into the centre of the hall.

'D'ye knoo whot?'

'What?'

'Don't make us laugh with yer crap today.'

'I won't, but did you hear the one about the bloke with the five dicks?'

'Whot?'

'Condoms fit him like a glove.'

'D'ye knoo whot else?'

'What?'

'Tomorrow's ma last day at the ashram.'

'Everybody silent!' said the singing-chef. All closed their eyes and fell pin-drop quiet.

Pavarotti still he wasn't, and as we sat there enduring the torturous sounds in which he specialised, I leant over to Ange. 'D'you know what?'

'Whot?'

'Have ya ever thought this chef-bloke sounds as melodic as a walrus getting its knackers waxed with gaffa tape?'

'Ssshhh!'

'It's just… perhaps the imagination boggles, but it's like all but two of the Three Tenors.'

'Shut it!'

'Or being witness to a botched circumcis—'

'—Excuse me, sir!' bawled the chef, 'is there a problem with my singing?'

Ange exhaled deeply.

'Ahhhr… no.' I said, battling with his eye contact, which he held for a few long seconds before he recommenced.

I turned to Ange when he finished. 'So are you really leaving tomorrow or are you talking Turkish?'

'Aye, ah'm gettin' the train south tae Pondicherry tomorrow mornin'. Whot d'ye wannae do darlen?'

That night I sat on the balcony, gazing at the Ganges. 'Freedom at the flick of a wrist…' I thought, dreaming about the motorbike plan. 'Or perhaps I should embark on the unknown with Ange? Or stay here until I can do the splits?'

'—Stay here!' said a voice—it was Pramesh, appearing from out of his room.

'How did you know what I was thinking?'

'You were talking to yourself.'

'For how long?'

'About the last two days,' he said, pulling up his seat beside me.

'I'm at a t-intersection: *Plan A* to the left and *Plan B* to the right.'

'What happens if you go straight?'

'The ditch.'

'I've towed myself out of that many times.'

'To be honest, mate, I never really meant to stay here.'

'So what's keeping you here?'

'Not sure. Can I ask why you come here?'

'Because, Mr Kerrigan, my head is like a speeding train, and I want to slow it to the point—'

'—Is that you thieving my analogies, Professor?'

'It is. I come here to be revived by the simplicity, so when someone asks, "How are you?" I can feel comfortable answering.'

'It's a trite question.'

'And you westerners ask it as a pleasantry, but it lacks sincerity. It seems what you're interested in is *"who* are you?" I find the competitiveness repugnant, and the lust for validation pitiable.'

'And Indians are above this?'

'Somewhat. We care less for appearances and possessions, but how someone is *really*. So if it helps you decide which way to turn at your intersection, let me ask plainly: how are you?'

Asked so directly, I found the question, his tone, and the strength of his eye contact positively confronting.

So how was I? I was tired, full of doubt, wondering why I was here at all, what to do next, and why. I missed my mates. I missed

Vegemite. I felt the same, down to the last cell, as did I look it in the mirror, or a puddle at that. This jaunt to India had less than lived up to the brochure, and every clock in the country ticked at the same pace as those at Flinders Street Station. I had no idea what the smartest next move was, but I couldn't, for the life of me, find a coin to aid the decision.

The sun had barely rubbed the sleep out of its eyes when I knocked quietly on Ange's door.

'G'morn,' I whispered, mindful of any nearby horizontal aspirants.

'Soo whot are ye gonnae do darlen?'

'I'm going to stay.'

'Really?'

'Ironic, isn't it? The endorser is off and the sceptic is staying.'

'I'm dead surprised tae be honest.'

She closed the door gently behind her and we started walking through the leafy gardens with her backpack in hand.

'So where will you go after Pondicherry?' I asked.

'Ah've no' got a Scooby Doo.'

'I'm guessing that means a clue?'

'Aye.'

We walked for a while longer, ruminating our story since Thamel, but when we stopped at the ashram's front gate, we fell to a definite silence.

'D'you know what?'

'Whot?'

'You know how you asked me why I set out on this trip?'

'Aye?'

I looked downward.

'Whot?'

'It doesn't matter.'

'Soo whot aboot the motorbike plan?'

'It's on ice.'

'Personally, I think it should be put oan fire.'

'Now now, I subscribed to your world of daily stretches.'

'And fur how much longer ye reckon?'

'Not sure really, it'd be nice to see you in the south though.'

There was something palpably sad in her blue eyes, causing me to battle the same in mine. 'It's jist, like we said in Nepal, it's a big old place this, and the plans of backpackers aren't the most dependable things.'

'I know,' I said, looking downward again, 'so this really is goodbye?'

'Aye,' she said, and she walked down the long exit ramp and was gone.

9. Journeyism

I sat on the balcony with Pramesh, gazing mindlessly at the river while he flicked through his newspaper. 'Bloody silly bastard!'

'What's that?'

'You wouldn't read about such stupidity!'

'Sounds like you are.'

He performed a long sequence of tutting.

'What happened?'

He closed the paper. 'Just yesterday a fireworks factory was burnt to the ground. A group of workers were taking a cigarette break and one sod flicked his butt and sent the whole bloody place into the sky! It was a fireworks show to mark a millennium new year! Everyone was bloody killed!'

Although empathy would have been an appropriate response, I struggled to overlook the comedy.

'Anyway,' he said, 'the good news is that tomorrow morning we have karma yoga.'

'Karma what?'

'It's doing house-cleaning and menial choirs for others.'

'I see.'

'It's considered good for your karma and greatly therapeutic.'

'Like getting a foot massage?'

'Yes.'

'Or doing an impressionistic painting of water lilies?'

'Exactly! In fact the person you're serving considers himself to be doing you a service by allowing you to do his dirty work.'

'Hang on, so you want to tell me that getting up before the sun and vacuuming some other bloke's house makes him the hero?'

'My friend, things work differently in India than in Australia.'

'You got two hopes—no hope, and Bob Hope. I mean, call me ignorant, but my idea of therapy is having an hour-long sauna while watching a documentary about blue whales.'

'Mr Kerrigan, things work in karma—an act of doing good equals good fortune for yourself, as an act of doing bad equals the equivalent negative; whether granted in this life or the next.'

'That's all very nice, Professor. But the laws of karma aren't confined to India; they're universal. It's exactly why I save dogs and help little old ladies cross the road. As for some bastard humbling himself as the man-of-the-match for letting me clean his shed, well… do you remember that comment about the grasp of a man's stalk?'

'You have an awfully strenuous outlook on things. Never have I known someone to probe life's complexities with such forcefulness.'

'Thank you.'

The sun never slept in the next morning, and before I knew it my concrete cell was filled with the tingle of a new day's light.

The day was hot, hotter than most. 6 a.m. karma yoga proved to be the thankless monotony I suspected. I was so glad it was over I promised I'd celebrate its end, annually, for the rest of my days.

Afterwards, I went for a wander through the leafy gardens. I sat on a garden bench under a large palm. Aside from the nearby monkeys doing their monkeying-thing, there was not soul about, until an old local man, one of the ashram's permanent residents, shuffled over and sat beside me.

He was old, in the vicinity of 90. If I was an aspirant, then I guessed him to be a graduate.

'Namaste,' I edged.

He turned and gave me a polite smile that suggested he was more interested in the silence of the setting.

I sincerely understood.

He was dressed in white, and he was frightfully skinny. 'My name is Swami Deepak,' he said finally. He had a long white beard, which made his croaky voice sound like he was talking through a sock. I'd seen a few such elders around the grounds, but I'd never spoken with one.

I cleared my throat awkwardly. 'I know a sadhu is someone who renounces all material possessions, but I'm unclear on the definition of a swami.'

A dense silence ensued, as though he was choosing his words, that, or further debating his interest in conversation. 'A swami is a Hindu elder who devotes himself to spiritual practice, and complete mastery over all primal urges.'

I nodded civilly, masking my inexperience with such thinking.

'The word translates to *Master of Oneself*.'

We sat quietly for some time, surveying the immense river. 'So how is your practice going?' he asked.

'Ok, I think, though I have some breathing difficulties. It's just a physical thing.'

'You'll find it's a heart thing.'

'A heart thing?'

'That your heart chakra is in need of release. Then you will breathe.'

I wasn't so sure. 'I'm quite new to yoga and meditation, if that's what you're referring to as practice. I guess I'm feeling pretty run-down.'

'I'm not surprised; you westerners eat too much and rest too little. Nature is the greatest teacher, and rest is the best medicine.'

It was an unexpected introduction, but it had a brand of honesty and wisdom that I immediately trusted.

'I guess I'm feeling the benefits of being here,' I said, 'most of what I need is here, and a lot that I don't, isn't.'

'Good. You should have one objective, to achieve happiness through self-realisation.'

'Happiness?'

'Yes—*happiness.*'

I was unsure how to respond.

He continued, as though reading a page from a tome of thoughts. 'Your body is a vehicle, and your consciousness its passenger, together giving you the experience you know as your life, which has been granted for this one reason—to educate yourself into the utmost state of happiness.'

There was a sobering air to this old man, and I wondered if the very reason I got on the plane was to meet him.

'So how do you achieve it?'

'There is only one way—through self-realisation.'

I mustered no response.

As though sensing my unfamiliarity, he kept up. 'Self-realisation is the endeavour to become as highly conscious as possible. It's by journeying inward that we find true peace and happiness, and we learn we are in fact, perfect. Stop creating traffic and you'll see the road is impeccably clear. *This* is the objective of spirituality, and it need be your only goal.'

Our impromptu meeting was turning into quite an education,

and although his words were above my intellectual grasp, I found them of great comfort.

'Ninety percent of the human race tries to achieve happiness through external and material endeavours;' he resumed, 'especially in the west. India might be dirty and chaotic, but in terms of the heart, the west is a mess of epidemic proportions. Everyone is in such a damn hurry, trying to acquire this and that, working a job they hate. All as a means to find happiness. But it cannot be achieved externally. The west encourages indulgence, and its authoritative figures—parents, teachers, and mentors— teach their young to be better than the next person: to seek power, wealth and material possessions. But they're teaching through fear, not love, and probably through the same fear that was embedded into them by their own mentors. It's distorted beliefs and nothing more, and it's your task to break the cycle and journey into the limitless wealth that's within you. You are your greatest guide; you alone know what you need. No one can know it *for* you, let alone impose their beliefs *on* you. That can only cause obstruction of freedom.'

I felt a concurring anger rise within me.

'The west is a culture of expectation and false urgency,' I said. 'It encourages you to break your back. It's how it measures success. Everyone is stuck under a cloud that rains *shoulds*; "should be doing this, should be doing that". If I had it my way that word would be publicly executed.'

'Your days aren't supposed to be lived out like a jail sentence. They're a gift—the most precious of gifts. Each one is here to be embraced, used eagerly as a chance for self-realisation, not filled with busyness and fruitless endeavours that lead to nothing but dissatisfaction and further pain to heal in the next life. There's nothing noble about routine that poisons the present in the hope of a more secure future—time is the only commodity. Each day passed is a day lost. Speaking of the expectations of others, people who criticise so as to distract themselves from their own pain, if you get caught by them, just think of an elephant.'

'An elephant?'

'When an elephant walks down the street, all the dogs bark and growl, but instead of reacting, the elephant just continues his journey, relaxed in the knowledge he's too big for them to bite. This is how to deal with those who judge, dictate, and control. Furthermore, their opinion needn't serve you; if through them you're encouraged into money, power, and other perishables, all you'll ever feel is sorrow and discontent, as these things have no actual substance. Take the concept of money; as a material object not remotely subject to the laws of nature, it's excused from its quantities being managed by her boundaries. Primitive man would slay not two beasts but one, because a second would decompose before the tribe could consume the first. The danger of money is that it's constrained by no such nature. It's just an inherited belief system where the more you get, the more you need, and the more accumulation of distraction, the further from self-realised you become. After food, shelter, and medicine if needed, money has no meaning. None.'

Although he'd been talking for some time, his morning voice was equally croaky. I found its paternal timbre familiar and comforting. I'd never believed in the notion of a guru, but I was starting to enjoy the idea. Although I was listening to him, my mind couldn't but turn to one of his countryman: the doctor in the dorm room in Dublin.

'So how do you move into self-realisation?' I asked.

'Just surrender everything you *think* you want, and you'll be filled with the joy of simply existing; a feeling most have lost touch with due to so much external distraction. Self-realisation is obtained through increased consciousness, which is like the light that transmutes the darkness of ignorance. Reject the illusion of power, and focus on what is permanent, not what is perishable.'

Still surveying the river, we both fell to silence as I digested his words.

'I hear the word *consciousness* often, but I'm not so sure what it is.'

'It's the omnipresence from which all life stems. It knows no death or time, and it can be destroyed—or even affected—no more than all world's warheads can scratch the sky.'

He paused for a few seconds, running his fingers through his beard as though playing a long-loved instrument. 'Do you suffer from feeling alone?'

'Never. I'm very comfortable in my own company.'

'Good,' he said, 'for the true nature of spirituality is *in* aloneness. Those who constantly need the company of others because they cannot bear to be alone still have a lot of work to do. The company of others is impermanent, and will pass like migrating clouds, for the time will come where we shall ultimately *have* to be alone. No one held your hand when you entered, and no one will be holding it when you pass back. The more comfortable you are in your aloneness, the more you're progressing towards your spirituality.'

I was sitting so far forward that I nearly tipped off the bench.

'Death is a porthole that only consciousness can pass, and if in life we were attached to material possessions, death will bring our ultimate separation from them. Those who've spent the journey immersed in social status, sexual gratification, and distractions like workaholism, alcoholism, or by whatever means have failed to become self-realised in this life, will be reborn with the same level of consciousness, and met with the same challenges until they've faced that which needs facing. *All* are subject to this highest of realities; there is no escape, or way around it other than journeying inward and finding true peace and happiness through self-realisation. No one can give it to you—only you can give it to yourself.'

'So how do you measure self-realisation?'

'People who are truly self-realised know it; they *feel* it. They're so filled with the simple joy of existence that the thought of external validation would humour them. Imagine the entire human race standing unclothed in a giant field, all as equal in their vulnerability as each other; there are no external comforts and no social statuses, nothing to hide behind. Those with less self-realisation—dependent on their externality—will feel utterly threatened without all they need. Those with greater levels of self-realisation—invested in their internality—will feel no loss at all.'

Although it was an interesting analogy, I couldn't but respond with a reproachful look.

'You may think this illustration is extreme, but it's a barometer that effectively deciphers the weak from the strong, the *realised* from the *unrealised*.'

A troop of monkeys scattered past. 'Be careful of the red monkeys, young man. Never look them in the eye.'

Still gazing across the valley, we sat quietly for some time.

'Hear that?' he asked.

'What?'

'That mental static you're full of?'

'As in, my thoughts?'

'Yes, that static you hear when you sit in silence—which is often subconscious—is the barrier between yourself and clear consciousness. Identify what you're full of in your emptiest moments and address it head-on. This is how you find true liberation. Be reminded that your life is a vehicular opportunity granted to attain self-realisation, and you are your only master.'

'I find the notion exciting, but equally daunting.'

'Just start by managing the devil at the door.'

'What devil?'

'The mind—it's the devil's workshop. When you buy into your thoughts you let him inside. But, if you ignore it, like a child kicking and screaming, it goes away. Your job is to distract your mind any way you can. Some people paint, others do exercise, some play music.'

'I play music, but wouldn't ambition like that be considered a distraction from self-realisation?'

'There's a big difference between being in the moment, and ambition. Whether or not it provides a distraction from self-realisation depends on how attached to it you are. Ambition, because it too often becomes the endeavour to get out of one's own skin, is a dangerous trap indeed, but creativity is born not through ego, but through the celebration of itself, which is limitless in its altitude. If you want to span your wings then free them from expectation, and be creative not for the glory of art, but for the simple fact that through you it is compelled to exist.'

We sat talking for an hour more, and as though encouraging me back to my own instrument, all throughout he ran his fingers through his long white beard. 'Celebrate the gift of creation,' he said, standing up at a protracted pace, 'it's a spiritual door, and those who have a key do well to open it. Above all, pursue happiness through surrender and self-realisation.'

I woke early the next morning, feeling a definite urgency to hop back on the music horse. It was a brand of anxiety I knew well, but I wished, in line with his advice, to come at it from a detached angle.

For over two years I'd let my love for songwriting slip through my fingers. I'd written little more than the odd fragment of a song, and my confidence had diminished to zero.

To suffer from writer's block is a legitimate condition, but one that can be founded in nothing more than loss of belief—for to say that I had no more songs in me would be to say I had no more feelings or words with which to think and speak. My fresh objective, without attachment if possible, was to reflow myself creatively, to change the stagnant oil in my seals and get things moving again.

I felt more armed against the self-doubt, but it was worth little unless I physically picked up the guitar and got on with the job of reacquainting us. Aside from the odd gig-fix, we'd become virtual strangers. For the ashram duration, it had been leaning against the wall in the corner of my room. I lay on my bed, gazing at it apprehensively, when for the first time in weeks I reached over.

I walked onto the balcony, sat down and began having a mindless strum. While gazing across the valley, I noticed—about a mile in the distance—a derelict temple on the other side of the river. It was a white dome-shape structure, so tall its pointed top stood above the jungle treetops. It might have been an old ashram, but my thoughts, like passing clouds, soon tumbled onto something else.

I sat there tweaking the guitar, trying to find a musical seedling to water and raise. Along with any ideas arose the nit-picking voices in my head, wishing to criticise and throw their spanners of discouragement into the works. It was an ensemble I'd heard before, but where I'd normally lay down the guitar, I made a conscious effort to silence them and let myself flow, like the river—mindless, with no objection, no judgment, and nothing at all to hinder the stream.

The day with the guitar drew on. Some crappy ideas led to some decent ideas, and some decent ideas led to one particularly good idea. I focused as much as I could, warding off restlessness and false hunger.

By the time the red sun sank behind the Himalayan foothills, this one little songling was on its feet. It was the first full song I'd written in two years, and little did I know it was barely the first ripple in a wave of new writing.

<u>BREATHE</u>

(♪ featured on the album *Journeyism*)

As soon as I stopped searching
I was hit by the wave
An endless river flows
From my head to my heart
Keep out of its way

As soon as I stopped burning
I warmed to the flame
Now you run run run
To get to that place
Where nothing never hurts

Breathe out, breathe true
Free from the drag that tows you

As soon as I stopped wishing
Then everything came
There's a rise within my veins
That drags you along
In lust and in chains

As soon as you stopped dancing
Your feet led the way
Move along long long
To get to that place
Where nothing never hurts

Breathe out, breathe true
Free from the drag that tows you

Well come on now
Just run with it
Spiritful, spiritless
And where are you?
When you say
That nothing never hurts

As soon as I stopped searching
I was hit by the wave
An endless river flows
From my head to my heart
Keep out of its way

Bang! the next day came and the Italian bloke slammed the door of the yoga hall. Standing in the doorway, fidgeting as though it were a way to aid digestion, still he looked surprised it'd happened.

After lunch, I bumped into Pramesh outside the eating hall. 'Good afternoon, Mr Kerrigan. How are you?'

'Fine thanks, Professor. Lovely day for it?'

'For what?'

'It.'

'What's *it*?'

'Whatever you want it to be.'

It was a common occurrence for a troop of red monkeys to gather outside the eating hall door. Giving no thought to the potential danger, Pramesh and I sat on a nearby bench.

Quietly we'd observed them. 'How's the size of the nuts on this little joker?' he said, leaning over.

I looked towards his reference, noticing up a nearby tree a

scrawny monkey armed with what looked like Siamese coconuts.

'Poor little bugger, he looks like he's yet to grow into them.'

'What?'

'Like school shoes at the start of a new year.'

'Where do you come up with these twisted analogies?'

'That's no analogy, when I was a kid I was made to wear shoes so big they made Ronald McDonald jealous.'

We lingered on our bench, further observing Captain Crackers. It was perhaps via our imaginations, but the skinny subject was wearing a noticeable frown.

'He looks quite weighed down by them, doesn't he?' said Pramesh.

'They certainly challenge the weight of the world being on someone's shoulders.'

'They must be a serious cause for lower back pain?'

'Maybe they're a natural form of anchor? So he doesn't get picked up by a strong breeze?'

'The fact he can boost himself up a tree; he should get a gold medal for weight lifting. Anyway,' said Pramesh, rising to his feet, 'that's enough primate watching for me.'

He walked off, and as I sat there, still observing the subject, several other monkeys jumped up the same tree. Scratching and fidgeting, their behaviour was not unlike their kind, but when the alpha male leapt up, the troop began to scatter and screech.

He had box shoulders, long fang teeth, and a large mane. In his eyes was a cyclone of hate, and he jumped from branch to branch, thrashing the tree as though to dominate even it. The other monkeys cowered in his presence, and if somewhere in a tree this lot had a telly, it'd be fair to assume he had control of the remote. The ashram residents knew him as Big Daddy, and it was perhaps from being owed peanut money that he gave Captain Crackers an out-of-nowhere smack in the mouth.

It was on, and with the two of them biting and beating, I

jumped to my feet. But just as I did Mr Teen Tang—holding a stick of bread—came limping around the corner. Big Daddy lunged down the tree in pursuit of the old dog, and I threw my rice bowl at the ape. Like a vanquisher of the Matrix, he dodged the bowl with frightening ease, and with our sights now locked, I remembered the words of Mamma Sharvari: 'Never ever look them in the eye.'

He flashed his teeth and charged.

*****

Dear Manuel,

It's been some weeks since I've been here, and it has to be said that life in India is the greatest contrast I've ever known. It's an assault on the senses, but amid the spinning kaleidoscope, life seems to flow as opposed to grind. It's vegetarian and alcohol-free. Although I'd never chose it, I'm feeling lighter for it.

In other news, a monkey attacked me last week. Let it be carved in old stone, there are few things as petrifying as a primate charging with your groin in mind as the entrée and your face as the main.

I'd been warned to refrain from eye contact, but in a lapse of concentration I did just that. I had two items in hand—a small bowl and a large tray. I threw the bowl, but missed, and with my knees shaking like those of Elvis, I secondly threw the tray.

The world slurred into slow motion, much like in grade four when I was fielding in cricket and the batter smacked the match-deciding ball high and long my way. Myself famous as *the kid who couldn't catch*, my best mate—standing at least 7 kilometres away—ran towards me as though intending to push me out of the way and save the universe from certain peril. My blood rose. Although blinded by the sun, I cupped my hands, and—*bang!*—I caught the ball, threw it at him and—*whack!*—hit him in the thigh. His tears were so beautiful I could have drank them, and just as I did that day—*whack!*—I hit the monkey with the tray.

I've since learnt there's a bloke in Rishikesh, who, much like a U.N. of the primate world, provides a service to disarm terrorist monkeys. He's got two of his own, trained up as hired goons that are brought in to rough up your problem monkeys. I'd like to think their names are Emilio and Tony, and when they're not on the job they sit around playing cards and smoking durries, and when they get the goon-call they extinguish their smokes on each other's foreheads, bash out twenty push-ups and make a sign-of-the-cross.

Well, I best be off to visualise mowing the lawns. As for my stance on the ashram, I'm starting to wonder if I'm ever going to leave.

*****

Splash! the next morning came. As naked as all partakers at the point of conception, I crouched down and poured a bucket of cold water over myself. 'Jesus, Mary and the whole barnyard!' I jumped up and shook off, but having endured this many mornings before, I was starting to find it vaguely tolerable.

I arrived a fraction late to 6 a.m. yoga. The teacher was already sitting cross-legged on his platform. His eyes were closed, and the hall was silent, until he stirred. 'Today we'll be doing noli yoga.'

'What's that?' thought I, hoping it wasn't a more loathsome version of karma yoga. The teacher rose to his feet and instructed us to follow him outside.

We gathered in a large circle on the grass area. In its centre were a number of industrial-sized vats, full of what looked like soapy water. 'What's with the vats?' I asked Pramesh, standing beside me. 'Is this a type of karma yoga so awesome we get to wash this joker's car? Or shave his legs? Or pluck his—'

'—Shut up!'

'So what is noli yoga?' asked the teacher to all 30 people; who gazed around as though wondering if each was as ignorant as the next. 'Noli yoga is when we cleanse our internal systems. These vats are full of warm salty water. You're required to drink six to eight cups as quickly as you can, then induce vomiting so as to purge your digestive tract.'

'I think I'm starting to better understand that stalk analogy,' said Pramesh under his breath.

'I can't see how I can be expected to perform this without rotten chops and Victoria Bitter.'

'Victoria what?'

'It's an Australian substitute for oxygen.'

But to be or to not VB, ralph yoga began.

The first horrible salty cup was, as the Scottish would say, 'nay bother', the second, as the Irish would say, 'a right pain in the arse', and the third, as the mentally sound would say, 'best left to graduates of the Neptune Academy of Underwater Arts'.

Still we sculled, cup after cup we did, and with his eyes bulging come his eighth cup, Pramesh ran to the handrail and spewed his life's worth. Be it from the sight of my friend fingering his tonsils, or by my own saltwater overdose, five seconds later I joined by his side.

All joined in. 'Que sera, sera, whatever will be, will be...' seemed a fitting tune as the air filled with the sounds of 30 wretched souls inverting to the heavens—blokes, usually as graceful as peacocks, and girls, once magnetic in their attraction, all wiping away the snot and innards from their indignant faces. I hadn't felt this bonded in ralphhood since graduation eve 1992.

It ended soon after. We congregated back to the hall and everyone sat in their places one by one. The hall was peppered with the sounds of snivelling and coughing, and as my guts settled back into their old selves, I felt oddly terrific.

The curtain of night drew over, and the half-moon hovered on a heavy angle. It was late, and I sat on the balcony in search of a songling.

By this point I'd written several finished songs. Some days I was writing up to ten hours, others more, and always while watching the river flow—as in it came and out it went, ever taking the old and bringing the new. I tried to simulate the same fluency in my writing—with no objection, no judgment, and nothing at all to hinder the flow.

After exercising this over a period of time, I felt a freshness sweep through my writing. It gave rise to a surprising quantity of music—some stuff good, some stuff less good, but through allowing myself to simply *write anything*, I was starting to clear and access my better material. I finished, on this night, a song I'd been working on for some time, and I recorded it to my pocketsize dictaphone.

Dreaming somewhere between the gutter and the stars, I sat there marinating in the songwriting afterglow. Aside from the dull roll of the river, there was not a sound in the sparkling night. I again noticed the derelict temple, lit by the pale moon, on the river's other side. With its white pointed top protruding from the trees, I was always curious of its story, but my interest would usually expire by the next round of thoughts.

I'd been sitting alone for some time when Pramesh opened his door. 'Good evening, Mr Kerrigan. Lovely night for it?'

'Yes it is, Professor.'

'What are you doing awake?'

'Just sitting up and getting to know myself.'

He pulled up his seat beside me. 'What are you listening to?'

'Just some music.'

'Is it Hindu?'

'No.'

'I'm not very familiar with western music,' he said, eying the dictaphone, 'can I have a listen?'

I filled with hesitation, but I handed it over, figuring if I failed to inform him it was me I'd gain some unbiased feedback.

He pressed play and began tapping his foot. 'It's ok, but it's very different from Hindu music,' he shouted, having no idea how to judge the volume of his voice against the headphones. 'Who is it?'

My ears became hot. 'It's me.'

He removed the headphones. 'I've heard you plucking your guitar, but I didn't know you could compose. It's pretty good for an Australian.'

'Thanks,' I said, mostly unsure how to take his comment.

'I wanted to be a singer when I was younger, but I was too ill at ease.'

'I feel that way all the time, but if Rod Stewart can strut onto stage and rip into *If You Want My Body* without a flinch, then why should the rest of us hold back?'

He put the headphones on for a final listen. From this point, each time I wrote a song I'd sit him down and have him review it. It was a confronting experiment, and his ease with stating the truth was impressively unchecked.

'So when did you write this one?' he shouted.

'Tonight.'

'I would have never guessed this voice to be you. What are you going to name it?'

WHAT IS SLEEP BUT THE FEET'S SURRENDER?
(♪ featured on *Journeyism*)

Rolling in like a tired wheel
Looking to slow down
Fading in like a silhouette
From the darker side of town

Coming in like a hurricane
Running rather late
Call it love but in my veins
It feels a lot like hate

Rolling in like a tumbleweed in the wind
Bounce across the desert then just start again
Burning down like a cigarette in the dark
Crackling a melody from end to start

What is dark but the lack of light?
What is blue in your reddened eyes?
What are words without their ink and voice?
What are greets without goodbyes?
What is time but the tick and tock?
Again and again and again
What is sleep but the feet's surrender?

Lazing about like a Labrador
Full in love with the fire
Watching all you folk I adore
Acting rather wired

Rumbling like thunder in the wind
Sheets are blowing, thrashing, I should bring 'em in
Belting down like a sky that warned you so
Lighting up the night for free don't miss the show

What is hate but a twisted love?
What is law but your say-so?
What is life but a long laid walk?
Between the sky and the ground you know?
What is tired but a battlefield?

> *When your eyelids are looking for war?*
> *What is sleep but the feet's surrender?*

I woke the next day just in time to see the morning star wink its farewell. I was sitting alone in the gardens when from around a corner limped Mr Teen Tang and his faithful master, Mamma Sharvari.

She stopped on the cobblestone path, and she sat beside me at a pace compensating the aches of an old lady. 'Good Morning, David,' she said, sounding frailer than usual. 'What's news in the life of a young man?'

'Well…' I paused. 'I was charged by a monkey.'

'Did you look him in the eye?'

'S'pose.'

'Ah yes, young people can be so brave and witless.'

'Perhaps, but I was helping the old dog. He was being charged by the red alpha.'

'Oh that wretch! He must owe a lot bad karma to have been born such a miserable soul. Big Daddy. He's the one who mauled Mr Teen Tang's leg.'

'At least he didn't get another one the other day.'

'Good, if so we'd have to call him Mr Do Tang.'

'Meaning *two legs*?'

'Yes!' she said, and although I wondered if when the monkeys happened to take to him with a tattoo gun and write *I Love Fish 'n Chips* on his forehead, if she'd switch his name to *Mr Grilled Flake and Minimum Chips*, I smiled in response.

He was lying by our feet as we talked, and he gazed up and blinked away.

'He looks like he's getting thinner.'

'Yes,' she said, 'he's very old. I really should make him a dog jacket before he's claimed by the cold. The light is fading for both of us. When he dies, I'll die too.'

I gathered her comment referred to her belief that he was the reincarnation of her husband. Although I could have discounted it, I couldn't but be stirred by the loyalty. She appeared shorter of breath, and her face, framed by her long white hair, looked heavier with age.

'Help me up,' she said.

I did, and as she hobbled up the path, I couldn't help but wonder if that was our last goodbye.

Mr Teen Tang stayed by my feet. I knelt down and patted him around the underside of his neck. 'Maybe I should get a jacket made for you, old bloke?'

He rolled onto his back, with his red rocket in glowing agreement.

'Ah for farck's sake! Put it away, ya dirty old…' I said; standing quickly up, where from this aerial angle he looked less like a dog with a dick, than a dick with a dog wrapped around it. Either way, it proved there was life in the old fella yet.

Some nights later the moon was full, marking a month since Ange had left for Pondicherry. I spent the night, like a spellbound insect, following the moon along the banks of the Ganges.

Without intent, I reached Haridwar, an ambitious slog southwards. I crossed the river on a narrow footbridge. While walking along the eastern bank I could hear a crowd singing up ahead. It was dark and I quickened my pace, at which time a young kid rode up from behind—'Namaste, mister!'

'K-farcken-rist!' I gasped, putting my hand to my chest.

'Where are you from, mister?' he asked, slowing his riding pace to match my walking.

'Ahhhr… England.'

'Oh, well you mustn't like Australia very much?'

'And why's that?'

'Because Australia is number one at cricket and England is some other number.'

'Actually, I'm from Australia.'

'Yyyaaayyy! Australia is number one! Australia is number one! Do you know Ricky Ponting?'

'Sometimes. So what's all that singing up ahead?'

'It's from Har-Ki-Pauri. There's a burning funeral tonight.'

I stopped walking and he skidded his bike around me in a cloud of gravelly dust.

'Can you give me a lift?'

He nodded keenly and I jumped on the carry frame of his bike.

After a couple of minutes of peddling with his every ounce, we reached the ghats. There were hundreds in attendance. Most were standing on the river steps, and others stood knee-deep in the water. Many were chanting indolently; their voices weaving together like the threads of a common rug.

'It's a prayer to Lord Vishnu, the protector,' said my little mate.

We entered the crowd, and having had a difficult enough time working our way through, we stood near the river's edge. The sky had fallen hostage to the siege of a million stars, and with the glow of the full moon on its surface, the river appeared bluer and more luminous than usual.

In the crowd's centre was the focus of the ceremony. Laid out on a burning table was the body of an old man. The head was exposed and the torso and legs were wrapped in white cloth. The throng kept murmuring its song, creating a continuous drone that seemed without need to break for breath.

Standing by the body, presumably the family, were three men and a woman. One of the men hollered aloud and the crowd fell silent. He produced a large stick, thoroughly ablaze. He stepped forward and held it to the body and the others stepped back.

It was perhaps because I was attending the funeral of someone I never knew, or, seeing a body being disposed of in a way I'd never seen, but as it engulfed into flames I felt suddenly a long way from home. With the strong wind proving means less of extinguishment than enhancement, the flames lashed into the night sky, and the man with the stick, presumably the eldest son, struck the stick forcefully into the head.

'It's to release the spirit,' said my mate. His words were of some comfort; it not being every day I'd seen a son abolish his father.

As though the smashing of the skull was also their cue, the crowd resumed its drone-like singing, and we stood for a few silent moments before he turned to me again. 'Goodbye,' he said.

'Thanks for the lift, mate.'

'What is *mate*?'

'It means, *friend*.'

'It was my honour for you to ride on my bike. You are my god!' He slung himself onto his pushy and tinkered back up the dusty road.

I felt him referring to me as *god* a little too rich a compliment to accept, but having found this sort of idolising treatment was how Indians generally regarded westerners, I felt the popular belief of Indians being dodgy and untrustworthy to be an outright fallacy. Perhaps I'd grown biased, but having observed, so far, that Indians had great senses of humour, wit, and in massive contrast to the west, *time*—time to talk to you, time to give you their full attention, and time to have a laugh with you if you were willing— my verdict was they were amongst the most open-hearted people I'd met.

I stood on the road as the disbanding crowd poured upwards from the riverbank, and although in the company of strangers, there felt between us a tangible air of union. I was the only westerner present, until, just ahead—the view of her being compromised by the passing by of countless souls—I spotted a western girl.

I admired her from a safe distance, but as though feeling my gaze, she turned and our eyes met. I looked away, but my neck muscles were no match against my curiosity, and when I turned again she offered a faint smile.

As did I feel in this moment, I've always found it mysterious that in situations of the like I can go from a young man mostly comfortable in his own skin, to a trembling kid picking his imaginary nose.

'Should I go over? Shouldn't I? Should I? Shouldn't I? She loves me? She loves me not...'

I advanced, and it was perhaps via my ego's design, but I was certain the illumination in her eyes grew. 'What am I going to say? What am I going to say?' She grew bigger into view. 'What am I going to say? What am I going to say?' I was almost upon her. 'What am I going to say? What am I going to say?' I arrived. 'Excuse me?'

'Yes?'

'Do you watch M*a*s*h?'

'Why?'

'It's just... you look a bit like Klinger.'

'Pardon?'

'Ya know, Corporal Maxwell Q, later Sergeant.'

The ground opened up, giving me the option to cannonball in. 'I mean, hello?'

'And you are?'

'David. I mean, Dave.'

'Hello, I'm Kayley,' she said in an aristocratic accent.

Kayley, with her dark wavy hair and smouldering green eyes, was so excruciatingly magnificent that the thought of kissing her was more heartrending than a teaspoon of water after crossing the desert naked while carrying a bar fridge full of dead wombats—

or something like that. And offering me a partway-responsive smile, my delusions of grandeur were beginning to set.

'So where are you from?' I asked, still picking my imaginary nose.

'England.'

'England?' thought I, wondering if she was lying to me as I had to my little mate. 'And what are you doing here?'

'I'm on holidays, and you?'

'I'm staying at an ashram in Rishikesh.'

'So you're a spiritualist?'

'Part-time.'

'And what do you do for a living when you're not being a spiritualist?' she asked, prompting my mind to go for a little imaginary wander into *Shit-That-Blokes-Say-To-Impress-Girls-Land*—that close at hand place where like dirt on the sidewalk cometh the rain, truth and rationale are simply washed away. A place where a man, despite if being able to distinguish the first difference between the sun and the moon, could feasibly pose as an astronaut, or a wine connoisseur that grew up in a 16th century château on the French Riviera, or a Brazilian billionaire struggling to do away with his billions, or a—

'—Ahem?' she coughed, 'so what do you do for a living when—'

'—I'm a dolphin trainer.'

'Reeeally?'

'The guide dog training previous was getting old.'

With the two of us strolling along the riverbank, I was very much enjoying our chance meeting, until—'David, I want you to meet someone.' And walking then out of a nearby shop, was an older lady.

'Mummy—'

'—Mummy?' thought I, my inner LP scratching hence.

'This is David. He's Australian!'

Mummy, adorned with more jewellery than I knew the Earth possessed, was even more aristocratic than her daughter. And all I could really do—as I stood opposite—was try to look intelligent.

'Hello, David,' she said in a deeper version of her daughter's voice, 'and what do you do for a living?'

'I'm a dolph—'

'—Sounds interesting,' she said, turning back, 'now Kayley-darling, we must go get a facial, a tweezing, a manicure, a pedicure—that lovely young man at the clinic is just to die for.'

'Mummy and I have flown to India for a flagrant shopping spree!' said Kayley, obliging me to do that thing, where, pretending to care more than one does about the price of shite in Shiteland, the subject raises their eyebrows.

My head began to whirr like a war siren. 'I can't fuse with a lass who refers to her old girl as *Mummy*, I feel like I'm trying to ping Prince Charles.'

'Joining us for a facial, David-darling?' asked Mummy.

'Ahhhr… no thanks. I only brush my teeth on special occasions.'

'Come then, Kayley-darling, our driver is waiting.'

An awkward silence arose, but was broken, to my surprise, by Kayley clasping my hand into hers. Filled with equal measures of embarrassment and delight, a sum total of zero words made it from my brain to my mouth. Mummy, looking positively baffled, stepped back. 'Well… I guess he's quite clean for an Australian,' she said, a remark to which all I could really do in response was equalise my blinking to my frowning. 'And Kayley?'

'Yes, Mummy?'

'Watch your footing now.'

Kayley's face grew heavy, stirring my curiosity as her mother turned and departed.

The moon had grown brighter, and the sky hosted an immeasurable explosion of stars. The crowd had all but dispersed, and we strolled along the river in virtual seclusion.

'So,' she said.

'So,' I returned.

'So were you really a guide dog trainer?'

And it was then, with the timing of someone with a particularly bad sense of timing, that my bike-riding mate went rattling past. 'Namaste, Mr Mate! Australia is number one and England is some other number!'

'Ssshhh!'

'What'd he say about England?'

'Ahhhr… nothing.' I said, as he stopped just ahead in a cloud of gravelly dust. He spun his bike around and approached. I gave him a loaded look, hoping he'd discern from my eyes my attempt to balance fraternalism with caveat not to rain on my parade.

'Where are you from, miss?'

I shook my head, subtly.

'England.'

'Oh, well you mustn't like—'

'—This is my little mate from earlier, he took me to the burning ghats!'

'I see,' said Kayley, 'so what mustn't I like?'

'Aust—'

'—He did a real top job of explaining the ceremony!'

'That's nice, but what mustn't I—'

'—Anyway, mate, you better get going before your parents start worrying.'

'Australia, miss, you mustn't like Australia?'

I hung my head.

'And why's that?'

'Because Australia is number one at cricket and England is some other number.'

'Did you put him up to this?'

'Definitely not.'

'Bless,' she said.

'Bless?'

'Don't worry, my lovely. It's a term of endearment.'

'And my lovely?'

'It's not meant literally, in England we call our plants my lovely.'

'You are both my god!' he said, circling his bike around us before lastly departing.

We crossed back over the footbridge, and she dragged me into a small jewellery shop on the other side of the river. The merchant's eyes dilated at the sight of us, and I was just about to tell him I was an Australian cricketer before remembering my current vocation of dolphin training. She bought something and we stepped back onto the footpath.

'What did you get for yourself?'

She stepped toward and reached her hands around the back of my neck. 'It's not for me.'

With the languid pour of the Ganges filling the air, we stood facing each other, and when she rested her arms around the back of my neck, I wrapped mine around her waist. This really was the brand of romance any traveller hopes to find when they buy the ticket. Despite that she lived on a diet of caviar and three pedicures a day, she, with her dark wavy hair and smouldering green eyes, was undeniably gorgeous. Our lips were parted by no more than an inch, and with the anticipation more than I could handle, the lion in the grass stepped forward for the kiss.

'Not here,' she said, her eyes lending to longing thoughts.

The ashram was gender segregated, and with its entrances manned by eunuch guards whose primary objective was to make sure none partook in anything that led to a smile, going there was out of the question.

'Where are you staying?' I asked.

'In Agra.'

'Pardon?'

'Our driver brought us here just for the day.'

'Right, but where are you staying tonight?'

'In Agra!'

'But that's 400 kilometres away!'

'I know, I have to meet my mum back at the car.'

'When?'

'In ten minutes!'

'As in, you're leaving in ten minutes?'

'Yes!'

'But… but…' I couldn't believe it; it was like being handed a hamburger, and where all I could think of was the mess I wished to make with the choice of sauces, being denied a mere bite.

I walked her back to their car, where so loaded from credit card hunting that she looked more *of* bag than woman, her mum was waiting. 'Hello, darlings! I hope you two had fun now. Come Kayley-darling, our driver is waiting.'

'Dear me…' I sighed, wondering if the car was going to depart to the clearing of silver trumpets.

'I really did want to get to know you,' said Kayley. 'Shame we didn't meet yesterday?'

'Shame indeed.'

'Maybe you should come see me in England sometime?'

'Is this an attempt to condemn me to eternal curiosity?'

'Perhaps.'

'Perhaps?'

'Well, you never know what the pages of the next chapter might read.'

'David-darling,' said Mummy, 'I think you should come to

England sometime; my daughter likes you.'

'Can I have that in writing?'

'Kayley-darling, he has quite a sense of humour. Marry him!'

The driver opened Mummy's door and in she hopped.

I turned to Kayley. 'Maybe you'll come back to Rishikesh sometime soon?'

'I would, but we fly home out of Agra in three days. Though?'

'Though, what?'

'Though you could come see me in Agra before we leave!' she said, kissing me on the cheek and handing me her hotel business card.

The car's engine started, and like Charlie Bucket with his golden ticket, I gazed at the business card in my hands.

'I'll be staying at this hotel until Thursday.'

'I'm not so sure… it's a long old way…'

'Bless, I really did want to get to know you,' she said as she hopped in the car.

It was cruel, and as the car faded into the night, the lion in the grass lay down and died.

I arrived back at the ashram feeling a lot heavier than when I left, and I can't have laid on my bed for a second before the obvious question rose—'should I? Or shouldn't I?' The sides of the coin flipped in my head, and rocking in a cradle of indecision, I fell asleep somewhere around then.

But long and restless the night it proved, for knowing that if I didn't go, the whole what-might-have-been curiosity might never let me rest; thus I tossed and thus I turned. The small hours stretched like a rubber band near its breaking end, and for the one wink of sleep I'd got, 39 were getting away. 'I can't go through life wondering on this. Even if I go to Agra to discover it's a waste of time, at least I'll be satisfied in knowing, and won't spend eternity adrift in uncertainty—like an astronaut farting in space after eating a bowl of bran the night before lift-off.'

And thus it was, as the dawn sun saturated the new day, the decision was made. 'I'm going to Agra.'

10. The Next Chapter

The journey was going to be no short trip, about seven hours of hard time. I hopped on the tin can bus, and the surrounding seats soon filled around me. The driver started her up, and with some people nursing baskets of fruit—and others cages of flapping chickens—this bus felt less disconcerting than the very paramount of life.

'I hope she won't think I'm some sort of halfwit stalker?' I thought, sucking on an Everlasting Gobstopper of hope.

But as we pulled onto the rutted highway, I knew in my heart I'd made the right decision. Gazing out the window my mind went for a little imaginary wander into *Romance Land*—an amiable place where I could picture us waltzing through fields of pheromone daisies. And snacking—for the one reason they were the only low-fat food source available—on aphrodisiac marshmallows. And horizontal dancing—for the sole purpose that in this cordial world there was but no other form of exercise—the morning, noon, and—

'—Hello, sir! Can I be sitting next to you?' my dream, still a kernel, was terminated by an inquiring Indian.

'So where are you from?' he asked, settling as much into his seat as the idea of interviewing me for the next seven hours.

'Greenland.'

'Oh! I have a cousin from there.'

'No, you don't.'

'Yes, but lying is good for your health.'

'How?'

'Because it stimulates the imagination.'

'Do you reckon that would hold up in court of law?'

He laughed freely, too freely, and even more freely than that, he rested his hand on my leg.

I felt the sweat gathering on my brow, and having fallen in love for about a second, maybe two, two and a half tops… I then just felt really weird.

Regardless, I knew his statement wasn't sexual, as it was common to see Indian lads walking down the street with their arms slung over each other, even holding hands. Nevertheless, minus the upshot of breaking his heart entirely, I wished for the removal of his hand to take place tremendously soon.

I considered sticking my finger in his ear, or serenading him to death with the vacuous tunes of Westlife, but proceeded, instead, to cough and beat on my chest.

'Are you all right, sir?'

'I'm on my way to Agra to get some tests done; the doctors here couldn't get to the bottom of it.'

'Oh,' he said, withdrawing his hand.

But nothing was going to silence him completely; as for his next trick he became painfully forthcoming about his cousins, his goats, his chickens…

'Sorry, mate, I've got some daydreaming I need to finish.'

He went quiet, and my mind drifted back to *Romance Land*, where again I could see Kayley and I waltzing through fields of chocolate, and the two of us spending long hours eating each other's edible clothing. And be it motivated by lust, cocoa bean intake or other, we were just about to perform imaginary canoodlisation when, 'Hello, sir!' my neighbour said, 'do you know how to milk a cow?'

'No!'

'Why?'

'Because I'm as much a farmer as a taxidermist.'

'If only I could remember, it would be my great honour to teach you.'

'If only.'

The bus rattled up the pot-holed highway, and with the bus windows magnifying the sun, I sat there panting like a dog in a car.

The hours of the dusty day were melting into a sun-bashed blur, but while sitting in privacy of my thoughts I could hear a song idea forming in my head. Welcoming it with delight, I sat quietly—both listening, so as to let it reveal itself, and pushing, so as to go further into its culmination.

Like a blurred image sharpening into view, I could hear a vocal melody, a chord progression, and even the beginning of a drum line.

At this delicate stage, though, the idea was just a spark—a mere seedling at most—and the slightest distraction could cause me to lose it forever. I wished I'd brought my dictaphone, to at least hum it to disc, but having left it at the ashram, I sat there playing it over and over in my head—trying to record it to memory, when, 'Hello, sir!' my neighbour begun. 'It is to my great relief that I've remembered how to milk a cow!'

'Listen, mate, that's all very nice, but can we save the cowology for later?'

'So first you must pat the cow… and then you must comb the cow… and then you must sing some mantras to the cow… and then you must pray to Shiva for the cow… and then…'

Trying to block him out, I frenziedly scanned my head, but like a knot beginning to slip, the songling was starting to weaken.

'Mate, please, can we save the cow-stuff for another time?'

'And then you must paint the cow…'

I dove into my head, but with the idea fading further, my grip was growing oilier.

'And then you must have your wife put some make-up on the cow…'

In a last attempt, I clutched toward, but the knot slipped and was gone.

I sat there massaging my eyeballs into a pulp, as my neighbour concluded in a contented tone. 'And that, sir, is how you milk a cow.'

'Thanks, mate, that's just super-tops.'

The sky had dropped to darkness by the time we neared the peripheral haze of Agra. Sighting, for the first time, people by the million, cars, rickshaws and buses by the more—I near had to rub my eyes to instil their belief. We pulled into Agra bus station soon after. Having been the passenger of baked bean tins more luxurious than this bus, I considered throwing a disembarkation party.

I stood on the side of the highway, looking as lonely as Bob Dylan on an album cover, and a rickshaw pulled up like a mozzie to a vein. I showed the driver the hotel business card and he signalled me to get in.

He drove on, and after driving on, he drove on a little more, and having driven this far he concluded, that, since I was a paying customer—one who having zero knowledge of Agra would be none the wiser if taken to his destination via Dallas, Texas—he might as well drive on a little further.

The traffic was an eighth wonder, with each vehicle like a droplet in an endless river of headlights. A million inharmonious exhaust pipes spewed their filth, and for each one died a thousand environmentalists.

I arrived at the hotel, and I was now not only daunted by the situation, but the stark proof of our class difference. This place—a tall white building with gold eves—looked more like a casino than a hotel.

I stood out the front, feeling less like the lone ranger than the lone dickhead. She was the rich kid, and I was not, but as I begun up the marble steps, I willed myself to believe that love could melt all monetary boundaries.

I looked as dirty as a dung beetle after a day on the job, and where my disposition would have been fittingly scored by Slayer, Megadeth or Black Sabbath, the lobby was perfumed with the inane tingle of *The Girl from Ipanema*.

The lobby was laden with staff, all leaning on the reception desk. None seemed to notice me enter, as they were transfixed by the telly. I assumed it was some breaking news story, and I walked around to get a clear view, where the matter so utterly-riveting-it-couldn't-but-induce-hypnosis was revealed—a shampoo commercial. 'Fair dinkum, homo sapiens would be crawling in his remains.'

It was 10 p.m., quite late enough for unexpected guests to drop in.

'Hello, sir, is there a girl staying here by the name of Kayley?'
'What?'
'Is there a girl staying—'
'—No,' he said, failing to break eye contact with the telly.

'I was told she's here. She's with her mother—the two of them English?'

'What?'

'A girl, ya know? An iny as opposed to an outy!'

'Oh yes,' he said, tearing himself away from the advanced hair technology climax. 'I'll be ringing them in their room.'

I leaned on the counter, but just as I did a thought like lightning shot through my mind, 'what—*the farck*—am I doing here?'

'Sir, madam is on the line for you.'

He handed me the phone and I put it to my ear.

'Hello?' said a tired female voice.

'Ahhhr… hi? It's… ahhhr… David, funnily enough, I'm in the lobby. You see, I couldn't help but be lured by the curiosity of our situation, and to quote yourself, "see what the pages of the next chapter might read". Whether our story is something substantial, or not, or we show each other our—'

'—Sorry, this is Kayley's mother speaking, who is this?'

An orchestra of ten thousand chimpanzees starting clapping in my head. 'Ahhhr… hi… it's David…'

'David who?'

'David-the-Australian-knob-you-met-yesterday-who's-now-unsure-if-he's-mistaken-your-daughter's-flirting-as-a-fallacy-he's-created-in-his-head—David!' I, for the duration of my hesitance to respond, thought.

'Oh! You mean, David-darling?'

'Yes, I think.'

'How did you get here?'

'I had a driver,' I said, failing to clarify that mine was for a bus.

'Let me get Kayley.'

After a succession of clunky phone-handling noises, the phone skimmed across a fresh ear. 'Hello, Kayley speaking?'

'Ahhhr… hi? It's… David, I'm in the lobby. You see, I couldn't help but be lured by the curiosity of our—'

'—David who? I don't know any David.'

It now felt like that nightmare when you turn up to school dressed as Santa Claus—only to find out that the Christmas fancy dress day is next week—was happening live in the lobby.

'David, the Australian..'

'Oh, *you*?'

'Yeah… *me*,' I said, feeling pretty far from endeared to be addressed with such regard.

'Wait there, I'll come downstairs.'

Phone hangs up.

By this point the telly-watching-staff had peeled themselves away from their shampoo commercial. They were gathered in a circle of friendly intrusion, to which all I could really do in response was whistle a casual tune. 'G'day, Jack.'

'Your country, sir?'

'Gooseland'

'Where's that?'

'West of Mooseland.'

The elevator binged, and out walked Kayley, wearing a complimentary dressing gown—that, or she'd just flown back from an evening with Hugh Hefner.

I stood before her as vulnerably as the day I was born. 'David?' she said, shuffling over and offering the world's lightest peck on the cheek, 'what on Earth are you doing here?' She may as well have been holding a tray of stale donuts, as I could see in her eyes my coming Agra was, plain and simply, a fuckup.

Desperate for backup, I glanced back at the staff, and although the image existed in my mind, if they'd broken into an exchange of money I wouldn't have been surprised.

The elevator binged again.

'Can we just get something straight?' I asked.

'Yes?'

'When we were walking on the footbridge, and you gave me the necklace by the river, were you—'

'—Kayley-darling?' said Mummy, popping out of the elevator. 'Look, David is here.'

'Hhhmmm… I can see that, but he's looking quite dirty now isn't he.'

Not that I expected to be exempt from having to earn Kayley's interest, but if there were a bus going back to Rishikesh right then, I'd have opted for it gladly. But it was too late, and standing there listening to them talk about me as though I weren't in attendance—'and he did this, and he did that, and he…'—I had to do some career-quickest thinking.

'David-darling,' said Mummy, 'tomorrow morning we're going shopping! Fancy joining?'

I was 99.9% sure this Agra-endeavour was a complete waste of time, and although the 0.1% of subsisting hope was likely comprised of 99.9% delusion, my brain calculated I still had a 0.0001% chance.

'I'd love to, I think.'

The decision was made, but finding this hotel to be more of a laxative than a luxury—the likes where your morning newspaper is brought to you by a maître d' accompanied by a violinist—there wasn't a chance I was going to stay here.

'Well, the pages of this chapter seem quite read,' I said to Kayley, 'I guess I'll get going now.'

'But you're coming shopping with us tomorrow?' she asked, seeming anxious about it being otherwise.

'Yeeesss…' I said, studying her. 'I'll come for a bit.'

There was more going on here, and it was my intention to find out what.

I trounced up the road and checked into a hotel more

befitting to a man of my disposition. I closed my eyes and dreamt of *Romance Land*, but the imaginary figure with which I'd shared the dream had blurred to a vague silhouette.

The next morning came. After praying to *Visa Aphrodite*, the God of Shopping, I went back to their hotel.

The staff were gathered at the counter. Again they were immobilised by the telly—the subject of hypnosis this time being a nappy commercial. 'Fair dinkum, the human race is just about around the s-bend.'

The elevator binged, and out rolled Mummy, dressed in an outfit made of so much fur that if she tripped over it would have yelped. 'Good morning, David-darling!'

'Ahhhr… good morning,' I said, 'and where's Kayley?'

'She's away for the morning getting a quick manicure. Please, let's have something to eat.'

I took a seat, but for the simple, yet, profoundly true fact, that coming to Agra to hang out with the mother hadn't been part of the plan, I felt as awkward as the laws of awkwardness would allow.

'So, David-darling, tell me about yourself.'

'You first.'

'No, no, it's important I find out some things about you.'

'It is?'

'Yes.'

'Like?'

'Like what it is you want to do.'

'Well, I wouldn't mind doing something boutique.'

'Like?'

'Like being a funeral director for the burial of funeral directors.'

'Bless, so Kayley tells me you are staying at an ashram?'

'Yes,' I said, looking not at all forward to where this was going.

'So are you a spiritualist?'

'An amateur one.'

'Do tell!'

'Well, I'm not blind or submissive, just distantly interested.'

'I don't see much in it myself.'

'It's not for everyone.'

'David?'

'Yes?'

'Are you troubled?' The interview entered the stage where the interviewee finds the questions less motivated by a genuine interest, than a means to dig up critical dirt—like when a reformed donut addict is asked if they were jam or ring inclined, or an Evangelist about their heathen days in telemarketing. 'I mean, what is it you're truly looking for?'

'Self-realisation.'

'Self-what?'

'It's the endeavour to become as conscious as possible.'

'Hhhmmm… sounds difficult. I seek salvation through shopping. I've always encouraged material things for my children.'

I glanced over at the staff. Breakfast between the old girl and the Aussie proving a higher rating show than anything on the telly—or someone had tripped arse-over its cord—all were gazing over.

Kayley came parading into the lobby. She sat beside me, catching her breath. 'Bless, I'm so sorry!'

Mummy rose to her feet and cracked her fingers. 'Come now, darlings, are we ready?'

We hailed a rickshaw and got in.

With Kayley on the left and Mummy on the right, I felt like an inmate in transit. 'So where are we going?' I yelled over the engine.

'To the Sadar Bazaar market, it has hundreds of stalls!'

'How many do you expect to look at?'

'Every one!' she oozed, 'and be warned, Mummy gets a bit twitchy when she goes shopping.'

We arrived, and our driver made the rookie error of asking Mummy for a fee higher than he'd quoted. 'Don't you try and rob me young man or I'll call the police!' she barked, to which he shrunk like a blow-up doll playing with a dart.

'Hello, sir, hair comb for you?' asked some merchant.

'No thanks, mate.' I said politely, the three of us walking away.

The market was mostly undercover. Like a den where all the world's material, leather jackets and fugitives hid out, I wondered if we'd ever again see the light of day. There were as many hanging rugs, and pairs of jeans, as woodcarvings and baskets of mangoes. For every item on hand were a dozen hysterical merchants, some going so far as to physically haul you into their stalls.

Driven by some primal hunting force, Mummy barrelled ahead, while Kayley and I moseyed a nice distance behind.

'Does it bother you when I hold your hand?' she asked.

'Legally, yes. Physically, no.'

'You've got quite nice hands, long fingers.'

'Thanks, some say I'm a well-hung lesbian.'

'Ah, you're so funny, and such a good friend for coming all this way to see me.'

'Dear me...' I sighed, few things deflating a boy as much as when a girl strikes with the f-word.

'Hello, sir, hair comb for you?'

'No thanks, mate.' I said, this time with a hint of irritation.

Mummy dragged us into a leather jacket stall. Its staff twitched before her like an assembly of cadets before an inspecting sergeant.

With an item in hand, she approached one of the younger guys, and her breathing grew heavy. 'How much for this leather jacket?'

'Two thousand rupees, miss.'

'Two thousand!' she barked, her eyes bulging. 'I'll give you five hundred and not a rupee more!'

'But miss, this jacket has been handmade in Kashmir and—'

'—You listen to me, young man! I am a businesswoman, and if you think that I'm going to fall for that twaddle then I must look a lot stupider than I am! Are you telling me I look stupid? Are you?'

'But miss—'

'—Enough!' she barked, grinding him to silence. She inhaled long and deep, as though gathering her strength for the next attack. But just when one felt its volume would exceed the attack prior, she scaled it to a whisper as she leaned in, 'and it's *Mrs* to you.'

'Hello, sir, hair comb for you?'

'I've got no f#&k'n hair, mate! What am I going to do with it? Comb my—'

'—Now now!' said Kayley, 'it's just Mummy's influence! Never look her in the eye while she's shopping.'

It was too late, and her mother—in terms of merchant slaying—became to me over the next hour what Obi-Wan Kenobi was to Luke Skywalker.

'Why don't you two darlings run along back to the hotel, my business is with these men…' she said, turning back.

We left her to her kill, and a man was less than sad to finally be minus his love interest's mother.

After another rickety rickshaw ride through the rumbling streets of rubbish-strewn Agra, we made it back to the hotel.

We went up to her room and she closed the door behind us. Regardless, I chose to neither invest, nor take heart, in a stock of 0.0001%. 'Well, it's been interesting,' I said, 'but I best be getting back to Rishikesh.'

'Are you sure?'

'Shouldn't I be?'

'It's just…'

'Just what?'

'Just… nothing.'

I took a step forward, and she sat backwards on the bed.

'David?' she said, coyly. 'Can I ask you a question?'

'I guess you just did.'

'Surely you wouldn't have come all this way for a shag?'

'My dear, man builds skyscrapers, man puts himself in tinfoil spaceships and flies to the moon—some stretch themselves to acts as outrageous as becoming ballet dancers—all in the pursuit of impressing women. So forgive me for finding you attractive, but yes, of course I would have come all this way for that.'

'Ah, you're so funny, and such a good friend for coming to see me.'

'Is that what a girl really thinks?'

'What?'

'That a bloke travels for seven hours on a bus to come see a girl he fancies so the two can be *friends*?'

'Well?'

'Kayley, I didn't come here expecting anything, but I don't fare well you taking the piss. I should have never come here. I feel ridiculous. I'm going to leave.'

But just as the laws of attraction would typically confuse it, all a boy's admission equalled was a girl rising to her feet, walking over, and it was just as she leaned in that—'Hello, darlings!' Her mother walked in.

'Ok, that's me done,' I said, picking up my backpack.

The two of us walked down to the lobby, and the staff were once again drooling around the telly—the subject of hypnosis this time being a toothpaste commercial. 'Good on ya boys, dentists recommend it.'

Kayley and I turned to each other. The final page of our final chapter reached at last.

'So,' I said.

'So,' she returned.

'Kayley, can I ask you a question?'

'I guess you just did also.'

'That night in Haridwar, as your mum was biding us farewell, she said, "watch your footing"?'

Her gaze dropped to the floor. 'Well?'

'Well, curiosity is killing the cat…'

'And?'

'And meow fucken meow…'

She still offered no response.

'The fifth amendment?'

'It's just…'

'Just what?'

'It's just…' she stopped and exhaled forcefully, 'maybe you should come see me in England sometime and we could finish what we started?'

'Bless, my lovely, I think we just did.'

I hopped on the bus for what was to be another seven-hour dust-scuffling mission back to Rishikesh.

As we pulled onto the highway my mind was quick to turn to the Kayley experience. I felt considerably foolish, and in hindsight, rather embarrassed, but knowing, too, that rejection would prove a shorter-term sting than regret, I was glad I came and for that reason I felt mostly resolved.

Some kilometres passed, when in a bump and thump the bus pulled over to collect more people. As I sat there, gazing out the window, I felt someone sink into the seat next to me, and, to my great dismay, a hand rest on my leg. 'Hello, sir! How did your test results go?'

I turned to see, and my eyes, to my brain's disbelief, filled with the sight of the cowologist-bloke-from-the-bus-trip-coming-*to*-Agra.

'So,' he said, 'after you milk the cow, you then must…'

'Ah for farck's sake! Of all the million-billion people!' I thought, massaging of my eyeballs by default.

Sitting there, trying to block out the reprisal of his drivel, my attention couldn't but be drawn to his hand on my leg.

'Mate?'

'Yes?'

'About your hand on my leg.'

'Yes?'

'I come from a cruel world where our main religion isn't called Hinduism, but Circumcision-ism, where anything unwanted is simply cut off.'

'Oh,' he said, withdrawing his hand. 'So where are you from?'

'Haven't we already been through this?'

'Yes, but I can't remember. So, where—'

'—Ikea.'

'Oh! I have an uncle from there.'

'Is he a foldout chair or a do-it-yourself table?'

'Both! So do you play cricket in Ikea?'

'I'm from Australia.'

'Oh! I love Australia! And I love all the things Australia makes! Like the cricket, and crocodiles, and *Indiana Jones and the Temple of Doom!*'

'I think, mate, you'll find that movie was made in America. Unless there was an Oz-grown version called *Indiana Bruce and the Temple of Draught* that I haven't heard of?'

'So, do you know Ricky Ponting?'

'He's my granddad.'

'Australia is number one at cricket! Much better than England, South Africa—and Ikea!'

'I don't think Ikea have a team, mate.'

'That is correct.'

'Then why would you profess Australia to be better than a team that doesn't exist?'

'Because lying is—'

'—Good for your health. I know, you told me last time.'

The bus rattled up the pot-holed highway, but it was while sitting there, counting sheep and imaginary naked things, that the fragments of a song began to form in my head. I could hear a vocal melody, a chord progression, and even the beginning of a drum line. But this time, like a forgotten face coming forward through the fog, I recognised it as the songling I'd lost on the bus trip coming *to* Agra.

I sat there as nervous as excited: both listening, so as to let it reveal itself, and pushing, so as to go further in.

At this delicate stage, still, the idea was just a spark—a mere seedling at most—and the slightest distraction could cause me to lose it once more.

'So,' my mate he dared, 'I will now be telling you how to wash a cow!' But explaining to him then that the fastest track to enlightenment was to hold your breath for the sum total of forever; he inhaled and fell to silence.

I pulled back into my head, talking myself through it. 'Perhaps it could go from G to Em?' I could hear everything—the guitars, the vocals, and the chorus melody—like an organised cyclone the idea spun. But my greatest challenge was to *a.* retain it, and *b.* find it on the guitar and fish it into the external world.

I started to write some lyrics. There was an image of stairs, but the theme, as I fleshed it out, grew to be more about the struggles between two people than those between myself and artistic longing.

I sat in my seat, playing it over in my head, and playing the drum line discreetly on my lap. Long after the dark of night had stretched across the sky, the bus rolled into Rishikesh.

I ran up the ashram's long ramp, sat on the balcony, and recorded—along with the sounds of nearby wildlife—a first-draft seedling version.

WHEN YOU CALL ME
(♪ featured on *Journeyism*)

This is it I swear
No longer will I scale endless stairs
In the hope that I might reach some higher grace
And fly away

So why are we so tense?
When at least we're catching every second breath
Let us stop this dance of restlessness
We're blood red

When you call me
Hear the story
Don't implore me
Or ignore me
When you call me

Struggle to connect
No longer will I hunt around in bed
But she only listens when I'm talking head
She's heaven sent

You only love or hate
You never like or merely tolerate
When you're coughing up words of expensive taste
My heart eats away

When you call me
Hear the story
Don't implore me
Or ignore me
When you call me

Relax now
Your panicked paces
Relax now
There's no sense
On panicked faces
Relax now
Panic stations

This is it I swear
No longer will I scale endless stairs
In the hope that I might reach some higher grace
And fly away

11. Plan A

Dear Manuel,

It's been two months since I've been here, and time seems to have withered into itself. Although this life of yoga and meditation has lent to the most productive period on record, I'm reinstating the plan to ride a motorbike north to south. It's ambitious—and definitely a detail I'll be sparing Mum and Dad—but the date is set and the mode decided.

May the road rise to meet you. May the wind be at your back.

*****

The next day all Christmases collided, as the day to buy a motorbike had come. I hadn't ridden for years, and although I came from a background of riding dirt bikes in the Australian bush, I'd in fact never ridden a road bike at all.

I'd heard through the grapevine there was a bloke in Rishikesh's industrial centre who built bikes for the Israelis. I made my way to his workshop, which was little more than a corrugated shed set up on the roadside.

I couldn't have been standing out the front for ten seconds before the young proprietor approached, 'סולש חא' he said, wiping his nose in his hands and his hands on his jeans.

I gazed at him blankly.

'Oh sorry, my friend, you looks like an Israeli. My name is Lucky. Are you looking for a bike?'

'Well, yes, but I just want to scope it first.'

'But, my friend, I already have the bike for you!'

'Nah, I just want to—'

But before my words reached his ears, one of his apprentices came strolling around the corner pushing an old black motorbike. It was a Royal Enfield Bullet—the darling motorbike of India. (Originally of English design, they're like the smaller brother of a Harley Davidson.) This bike, however, looked as tired as a pair of Mike Tyson's punching gloves.

'So what do you think?'

'I dunno, mate, it looks a bit rough.'

'No no! We'll rebuild it. This is just the start. Look, the frame is good, and it has a new piston and back brake.'

'Nah, I really don't want to muck around with rebuilding, I'd rather get something that's clean and ready to go.'

His face turned oily, and he put his arm around my shoulder, 'trust me,' he said.

Because, when money came into the picture, Dr Jekyll often turned into Indian Mr Hyde, he may have just given me seven reasons as to why I shouldn't trust him. 'It might need some tinkering along the way—' he kept up, 'a timing adjustment here, a carburettor tuning there, but I'm sure you can handle that.'

'Of course,' I said, concealing I was as mechanically inclined as a hand cream model.

I stood there, chewing my imaginary fingernails, when an actual Israeli—also a customer—approached. 'שלום חא' he said.

'Sorry, mate, I'm Australian.'

'Oh good, very good!' he said, taking a lengthy drag of his cigarette. 'My brother has been to Australia, he liked Melbourne the best.'

Although I offered a faint smile, I was instantly wary of him, as I wondered if Mr Lucky had, for a discount in his fee, put him up to sweet-talking me.

'Trust me, Lucky is the best. This is a good bike, and he will totally rebuild it for you. New tyres, new seat, and even a new paintjob, any colour you want. Come, look here,' he said, leading me over to his own bike, which, by word of the horse's mouth, was near the completion of its makeover.

It too was an Enfield Bullet. It had high chrome handlebars, a fat back wheel, and for reasons better known by its' new owner, it was iridescent purple.

'Please, have a seat,' he said, and when I hooked my leg over and sank into its seat, my soul filled with the music of AC/DC. I sat there feeling tough, and with a stiff upper lip, dreaming of highways to hell.

'You see,' he said, showing me photos before its metamorphosis; where it looked even less loved than the bike I was being offered.

'Are you sure you're not working on commission here, mate?'

'When I first came here I wasn't sure either, but Lucky took this bike from a turd to a diamond, and he speaks Hebrew! So all us Israelis love him!'

'I speak seven languages actually, Hindi, German, Italian, French, Spanish, Portuguese and Hebrew.' It was Lucky, standing behind us. 'But I don't know how I learnt Hebrew; it just seeped into me.'

'Well, mate, I wish I had the same absorbency problem.'

'And you're speaking English to us.'

'Oh yes, so eight languages. How many do you speak?' asked Lucky, turning to the Israeli.

'Ahhhr… four.'

'And you?' he asked, turning to me.

'Ahhhr… yeah. So if I go ahead with the rebuild, how long will it take?'

'Five days, maybe less?'

'And you really speak eight languages?'

'Yes.'

'I'm in.'

'So what colour do you want it?'

'Blue, I reckon.'

'And what name?'

'Name?'

'We give you a personalised plate.'

'You must give it a name!' said the Israeli. 'It gives soul to the bike!'

'Well, I'd like it to be something Australian, like an Aussie insect, like Mozzie…'

'Or Stinger…'

'Or Blow Fly…'

'And the bike's going to be blue, so… *The Blue Fly*.'

Over the next few days I sat around Lucky's shop with a group of Israeli lads getting bikes built. The days were filled with the smoking of durries and many a heated debate about our bike's transformations. If it was good dirty fun, then no part was more so than at the completion of a bike, when all—with a cup of chai in hand—would be summonsed for a send-off toast to the next man leaving. Most were heading south to Goa, but it was my intention to ride further, possibly to India's southern tip, or to see Ange in Pondicherry.

After just three days, what was once a bodgy-looking heap with a bent exhaust pipe, a torn seat and a dented tank, was now a sparkling blue beast with chrome wheels, baggage racks and a number plate that read: *The Blue Fly*.

I hopped on and sunk into its leather seat. When for the first time I started it up and it idled meanly—*buda buda buda*—I could hardly wipe the smile off my dial. The boys circled around, dragging their smokes and nodding their heads.

It was time for my sendoff. 'All the best to you,' said Lucky. 'Ride defensively, there's nothing crazier in India than the roads.'

And looking out to the highway—with its trucks, cars, buses, rickshaws, cows, motorbikes, and donkeys and carts—I felt I had to agree. I clicked the bike in gear and took off for its debut thump.

'Ah… freedom at the flick of the wrist!' I sighed, as the long-forgotten feeling of being on a bike flowed through my veins like a reformed alcoholic reunited with the bottle. The feeling of motion, of the wind on your face, and the ability to escape from anything at will. It seemed to me in this moment that no amount of yoga could ever simulate this high.

I figured I should take the bike for an introductory ride around the Rishikesh area; to first get a feel for riding it, and to second scope out any mechanical discrepancies before heading off on the big trip.

I rode straight from the workshop up into the high mountainous terrain that framed the Rishikesh valley. *Buda buda buda*—the bike rumbled beneath, and with the sun on my face I hugged it hard while winding around corner after corner of steadily climbing road.

As I ascended into the forest area the sun became masked by the trees, causing the temperature to drop to a disquieting cold— that, myself wearing only shorts and a t-shirt, I was less than equipped for. The views as we climbed were nonetheless worth their weight in breathlessness, and while riding on a particularly sheer ridge, I was so high up that the Ganges beneath looked like a thin vein running through a flesh of landscape. I hadn't felt this awake since forever, yet the riding experience was such like a dream that the money I'd paid for the bike felt worth it even for this one day.

Falling deeper in love with my new toy, I continued to snake along the mountain road, until—*buda buda buda putt putt putt*—its engine cut out. 'No cause for alarm..' I wished to believe as I clicked it into neutral.

I rolled the bike over to the roadside, and the surrounding silence, cut occasionally by a far-off bird whistle, seemed to land squarely on my shoulders. I tried to kick-start the patient, but to no avail. I tried again, but no luck… and again, but with the engine sounding sadder by the attempt, I hopped off.

I stood there in my shorts and t-shirt, feeling decidedly colder than when I was riding. After a few minutes of dedicated shivering I heard another motorbike approaching. Its sound increased through the trees, and when the bike came burling around the corner its rider was so gargantuan they looked less like a person than a bald giraffe. I waved out, and when the figure pulled over I realised, to my surprise, it was a girl.

'So where are you from?' I asked.

'Austria. What is the problem with this bike?'

'I can't seem to start it. Do you reckon it's the spark plugs?'

'No.'

'Do you reckon it's the timing?'

'No.'

'Do you reckon it's because the Theory of Relativity was devised by a German?'

'No. Move aside.'

I flapped clear out of the way.

She hopped off her bike, and her fully erect height was such that if she were a netball player she'd surely have to kneel down to score a goal. She held the bike by its handlebars, put her foot on the kick-starter, and with one giant kick, booted it in the guts and it roared to life.

'Here!' she barked, handing it back.

This was truly one of life's more emasculating moments, like when a man fails to find reverse in a manual car, or when the unfortunate need arises for him to ask his mum to remove a stubborn jam lid.

I took back my bike, and if she turned to her own bike, yelled *start*, and it roared to life, I wouldn't have been surprised.

She hopped back on and disappeared up the road. It was the least romantic experience of my life.

Later that afternoon I spent time in my room doing something I was only just finding my feet in—*writing*.

Having up until this point never considered myself a writer, nor, by attending creative writing classes, having taken active steps to become one, my capacity as a writer was mostly unrealised. My self-perception was slowly starting to change, though, as I'd met several key people along my travels that'd encouraged me to *write down the things I say*.

I was flattered to be considered worthy of such praise, but felt that if my turn-of-phrase was remotely engaging, then it was by no means from being the English teacher's pet.

As a first-generation Australian, I was the son of a Maltese mother and an Irish father (still am). From the passion and emotionality of the Maltese, and the sentimental and poetic tendencies of the Irish, my perceptions, conduct, and tones of communication were shaped. Save for the odd loud email, I'd barely channelled this through the medium of written word;

neither had I felt, thus far, that I had a particular story to tell. On the canvas of this trip, though, I became the middleman of many meetings between pen and paper—writing down reflections, one-liners, lyrics, rants, and anything else that wanted *out*.

This day was no exception, and it was while sitting cross-legged on my bed, happily scribbling away, that the door of my room creaked opened slightly. I barely took notice, thinking it to be no more than the wind, until a hairy-hand-with-long-spidery-fingers appeared around the door's edge.

My heart rate rose.

The door groaned opened another inch, and the hairy-hand-with-long-spidery-fingers soon became two hairy-hands-with-long-spidery-fingers, both gripping at the door.

In chance need of a weapon, I reached for my guitar, when the door opened further and joining the hairy-hands was a hairy-face with inquisitive eyes—it was a monkey.

But this chap wasn't a red Bandar, a compatriot of the Big Daddy clan, but a grey Langur, known as a mostly passive creature. He was tall and slender, and he had a lengthy tail and a black face.

Regardless, he was an alpha male, and I less than fancied the prospect of a primatological headlock. His beady eyes were brimming with curiosity, and they were fixed firmly on me as he pushed the door wide open.

My heart rate rose further, but in a don't-mind-me-ol'-son cockney manner he just casually sat himself in the doorway.

With my guitar in hand, I began to quietly play a few chords. The sound seemed to arouse his curiosity, and he slid himself into the centre of the room. 'Should I play you a proper song, Boris?'

Blinking away, he'd paid me his full attention, until he spotted the bin in the far corner and dragged himself over. Although he didn't speak English—and I not a word of Grey Langurian—it took little imagination to hear his thoughts—'old chewy, bits of paper, crappy pen, cotton swabs…' And all throughout the ransacking, he kept checking in with me over his shoulder, as though mindful of causing offence.

Bored with the bin, he turned back to me, and as though hesitating to leave for the sake of politeness, he sat for a minute before making a deep sigh. 'Well, that's me off then, say hullo to the wife for me.' I could hear him say as he let himself out. He was so human I nearly asked if wouldn't mind shutting the door behind him.

I walked onto the balcony, and while standing there eating a packet of chips—*bang!*—a loud noise thudded from behind. I turned from the fright, and sitting by my feet was Boris. He'd jumped down from a nearby tree.

He was this time not alone, having brought his mates, neighbours and in-laws—a plenteous troop of males, adolescents, and females with clinging babies. I was nervous to be so outnumbered, and I could only hope he'd described me in favourable terms. They circled around, like an undulating wave of fur keen for its lime and chili-flavoured prize.

I began to throw them the chips, to which the littler ones proceeded to tug at my pants. Through fear of any breaking into *What About Me*—or dacking me at that—I tried to be as even-handed as possible.

I gradually grew more confident, and began to hand the chips directly to them, to which each monkey picked the chip out of my hand as politely as when receiving holy communion. There was one baby at the back, however, that all throughout the service just couldn't reach the altar.

I threw some chips directly to him, but he was too little to outgun his peers. I could see the maths ticking in his eyes, and he leapt into my arms without warning, soaring over the other's heads like a furry Superman. I caught him like a kid coming off a slide, and he clung to the arms of my t-shirt. My heart was flying in my ribcage, and I worried he might bite or scratch, or that the other monkeys would catch on and do a stacks-on-chip-man pile-up. But he just clung on and blinked innocently as though wondering why the hold up. Having experienced the terror of the red Bandars, and this companionable moment with a grey Langur, I felt I'd officially graduated with our evolutionary cousins.

I gave him his tangy prize, and he jumped out of my arms as quickly as he'd jumped in them. Boris cleared his throat like your average Uncle George, and if in a cockney voice he bid farewell I wouldn't have been surprised. 'Well, ol' geez, that's us off then innit, see ya next Mondee if not before.'

During the small hours of the next morning I was awoken by a strange yowl coming from outside. I tried to defy it by way of a pillow sandwich, but too unyielding I rose to my feet and opened the door. Aside from the vague silhouette of swaying trees, it was pitch-black outside, still in the darkness could be seen the gleam of two lonely eyes.

I switched on the balcony light, inspiring all the universe's moths to dive into it kamikaze-style. Revealed also was the shadowy beast. It was Mr Teen Tang. He was a pathetic sight: blighted by the cold, and there was little more to him than ginger fur stretched over old bone. I brought him inside, and clearly ill at ease, he lay on the floor as flat as a pancake. I wrapped him in a green blanket and placed him by the foot of the bed. I turned over and fell back to sleep within a second.

Some hours later the sun did its rising thing, and the birds did their chirping thing. I lay on my back, having forgotten I had a guest until I heard him swallowing on his gums. I rolled over, and he gazed up with an embarrassed look.

It was about 5 a.m., and when I opened the door I was met by a parcel on the balcony. It was a tin, with a note: *To calm your nerves from the Bandars. Never look them in the eye again.*

Pramesh was already sitting out. 'Good morning, Mr Kerrigan.'

'What are you doing up so early?'

'I had a bet with the sun.'

'I like that metaphor, Professor.'

He eyed the tin. 'Is that a chutney from Mamma Sharvari?'

'Yes.'

'She's a darling, that one.'

'She is,' I said, sitting beside him.

'Do you know what her name means?' he asked in the fixed tone of a quiz show host.

'Can I phone a friend?'

'It means, *Mother Twilight.*'

Having often spoken in terms of *light*, feeling brighter or fainter, having more or less, I found it distantly interesting. 'I like that Hindu names have actual meanings.'

'Hindus are a particularly embracive bunch.'

'I guess western names do too, but no one really cares. So what does Pramesh mean?'

'*Master of Accurate Knowledge.*'

'Are you sure?'

'Yes. What does David mean?'

'Son of parents who at the birth registry were short of coins for the parking meter so had to think of something quickly.'

Mr Teen Tang, the superstar all-rounder of the Arthritic Olympics—winner of gold medals for the 100-metre limp and not-very-high jump—came hobbling onto the balcony. 'Morning Rex, how's your javelin?'

'What's he doing in there?' Pramesh sneered.

'He was turning into a three-legged ice cube.'

Ogling up whenever the topic, the dog performed his morning stretch with great difficulty, fighting against the rigidity of his spine. He limped over and sat by Pramesh's feet. In the cat man's eyes was enduring reserve, but when he reached down and the tail of the old pup wagged, a fleck of canine love appeared.

'It warms me to see you've come round to the ways of dogs, Professor.'

He looked at me curtly. 'Maybe David means, he who loves to gloat?'

'You know she believes he's the reincarnation of her husband?'

'Hindus.' he jeered.

'It's certainly different.'

'Reincarnation and unity of all form is the basis of Hinduism. Guilt and dismissal of responsibility seems to be the Catholic code.'

'You say it like you expect me to disagree.'

'Perhaps, I just find the concept of heaven and hell absolute tripe.'

'And my infantile scone was irrigated in the name of it.'

'When heaven is depicted as cloudy place with white bunny rabbits and white lambs bouncing around playing white harps, where—*the fuck*—am I as a black man supposed to sit?'

'A fair question, but I find the idea of hell even more ridiculous—an eternity of being on fire because a man washed himself with a fraction too much passion?'

'And some men are cleaner than others!'

'My idea of hell is living in a world of Wally's that love the term ASAP.'

'Yes! That's almost as annoying as—'

'—When someone finishes your sentences for you?'

'At times you can be such a—'

'—Ssshhh…' I said, taking the lid off the tin and tasting the chutney. 'Have some of this stuff, mate, it'll make you believe in Jesus.'

He did, and he made a faint sign-of-the-cross. 'Let me get some bread out of my room.' He stepped over Mr Teen Tang, and the old dog shuddered as if someone had walked over his grave. I spent the intermission observing the dog, grappling with the depth of his sad eyes.

Pramesh returned, 'here,' he said, handing me a piece of bread and sitting back down.

We observed a moment of silence while tucking in. The dog's gaze failed to relent, and I gave him a small piece of bread. 'Mamma Sharvari and this dog certainly have a unique bond,' I said.

Pramesh raised his eyebrows, as though feigning interest.

'And they certainly seem to be fading together.'

He leaned over and helped himself to a large scoopful.

'Time is against them, I suppose, especially for him with winter coming.'

He proceeded to suck at his teeth.

'You know she wants to make him a dog jacket?'

He raised his eyebrows again, this time much higher.

I mopped the tin with the last of my bread. 'You know what, Father Professor?'

'What's that, my son?'

'It's time I returned the favour.'

I rose to my feet, lifted up the dog and carried him down to the main drag. He was lighter than a budgie, and although I was nervous if I dropped him he'd smash like a porcelain husband, I wore him around my neck like a fox scarf.

I hailed a rickshaw and we hopped in, placing the old dog on my lap. The driver, seeming to forget his job entirely, sat there grinning and facing us.

'To a tailor, please. Any one is good.'

'Yes, yes, I know the one!' he said, hitting the pedal.

Mr Teen Tang, no doubt feeling the bumps in his bones, looked a very worried version of his usual self. I tried to conduct an ambush interview, but he was refusing to comment until his publicist was present.

We arrived at the tailor's, and, assuming I was the patient, an old man approached with a measuring tape in hand. 'Good morning, sir. Suit, vest, pants or shirt?'

'No thanks, but can you make something for this dog?'

'Suit, vest, pants or shirt for him?'

'A jacket, if you can.'

'Hhhmmm… lift him onto the table.'

I did, and with the dog being measured up like soldier signing on, from here on the process got very serious.

True to India, there were a million souls walking past the shop front, and with no such spectacle having a fart's chance in a hurricane of going unnoticed, the shop was soon flooded with a crowd of young guys. Some had their arms slouched over each other, and most, consumed with entertainment, were covering their mouths as they laughed.

One such guy spoke out. 'Why are you making a jacket for the dog, sir?'

'Because he's getting married.'

'To who?'

I didn't answer, but if ever there was a more fitting placement for a *your mum* comment, then I'm not a Libran who enjoys fruit, swivel chairs, and asthma.

'What about his penis, sir?' asked the old tailor.

'What about it?'

'Do you be needing his penis to be exposed, so he can be

doing some wee wee?'

'Ahhhr...' I said, taking a second to appreciate the dog's predicament. 'I suppose that would be good.'

And so cutting around the old fella's old fella, the other old fella kept at it.

After an hour of the cutting of material, and the stitching of thread, he was done.

'One hundred rupees, sir,' said the tailor.

'No problem,' I said, handing over what was just three dollars Australian.

Mr Teen Tang looked over and blinked sadly, positively conscious that he looked like a chicken drumstick wrapped in a potato sack.

After another luxurious rickshaw ride we made it back to the ashram, and figuring that with no word of who, where, or why the jacket, I'd leave him on the balcony, I walked up Mamma Sharvari's steps for the last time.

I laid him by the doorstep, and turned to walk away, but with Harry the Parrot on duty—'Hari Om! Squaaaaaawk!'—no such discretion could be executed.

'Oh! What have you done to him?' said her voice through the fly screen door.

'He's ready for his first day at school.'

'Please, David, come in and sit. I've just made some chai.'

I went inside and she handed me a cup.

'I hope it's not too sweet? I've already put three or four sugars in it.'

I closed my eyes and hoped for the best.

'How is it?'

'Just right, thanks,' I said, having actually grown to love the obnoxious sweetness.

'I'm leaving tomorrow morning.'

'Where are you going?'

'I'm not sure exactly. I've bought a map of India. I'm planning on riding south.'

'You're on a motorbike?'

'Yes.'

'Then be very careful.'

'I know, the roads are pretty crazy.'

'It's not just the roads, it's the police.'

I sat up.

'They'll get you for anything they can, and not in the interests of the law, but your money. It's called *baksheesh*. They're particularly corrupt in Goa, targeting tourists on motorbikes, especially young men on their own. They work in pairs, and when they pull you over, one will talk to you from the front, while the other plants drugs in your baggage. If caught, you'll have to pay an amount of money so extortionate you probably wouldn't have it, or, go to jail.'

'They'll have to catch me first.'

'Ah yes, you are brave, but young and witless.'

I smiled.

It was time to get going, but knowing I'd never see her again, words of parting failed me. I stood there feeling faltered, and so I knelt down to the old dog. 'See ya, pup, I hope the other school kids don't laugh at your jacket,' to which his previously worried expression seemed to dilate to one of fondness.

The old lady rose to her feet. She looked older than when we first met, and yet her face, framed by her long white hair, still glowed with its trademark radiance. She stood short, but proud, and her large brown eyes were charged with meaning. 'Goodbye, young man,' she said, palming her hands into prayer position, 'we'll never meet again. Always follow your light.'

The sun began to sink for what was my last night at the ashram. With guitar in hand, I walked onto the balcony, just in time to savour the dusk lightshow.

I sat there day-dreaming, dusk-dreaming, and probably even Ganges-dreaming, just as I had for many long hours while writing music on the balcony—always while watching the river—as in it came and out it went, mindless, with no objection, no judgment, and nothing at all to hinder the flow. I'd been at the ashram for over 70 days, and having inadvertently honoured my favourite songwriting analogy, that, like an antenna, a songwriter should simply *receive*, I'd written my best stuff to date.

With the evening star having snuck in, I scanned the full expanse. With neither a tree out of place, nor a hole in the great river, the scenery was in perfect starting position. The last of the light was almost spent, and as I sat there gazing across the valley, I again noticed the white derelict temple on the other side of the river. I'd spent many hours gazing its way, curious of the old soul fallen quiet.

Pramesh moseyed out and took his seat at the right-hand of mine. 'Good evening, Mr Kerrigan, what are you up to?'

'Just taking it in for the last time.'

'You're leaving?'

'Tomorrow morning.'

'I see,' he said, his tone dropping, 'but whom now shall I rely on for ritual annoyance?'

I gazed downward and smiled.

'So where are you going?'

'West to Rajasthan, then south to Goa.'

'That's a long way by train.'

'Even longer by motorbike.'

'Cross-country, ey?'

'Yes.'

'And why, my Australian friend, do you subscribe to such foolish pleasures?'

'To give the bloke doing my eulogy something to tell.'

'Planning on being killed?'

'Hopefully not.'

'Well, travel is the best form of education, as they say. I travelled all through the south as a younger man, perhaps by more conventional means than certain spiritual heroes of mine, but I was out there nonetheless.'

'What heroes?'

'Most notably, Swami Vivekananda, the wandering monk. He walked the entire circumference of India, having set two rules—that he would neither touch money, nor ask for food. People were so inspired he was showered with provisions, and by the time he returned to the coastal town where he'd set out, he was a national hero.'

'And a good story lives forever.'

'It does. So will you head further south than Goa?'

'I think so.'

'The south is a magical place. For the north's mountains and deserts, the south is a place of green forests and white beaches. You'd do well to visit the Guruvayoor Temple; there was once an elephant that lived there, by the name of Kesavan. He was known for his devout behaviour, especially as he got older. One evening, after fasting for the day, he knelt down in front of the temple and died with his trunk raised in worship. His tusks are still at the entrance.'

'It certainly sounds worth a look, mate. Anyway,' I said, finally thinking to ask, 'what's the story with that white building on the other side of the river?'

'It's an abandoned ashram; just ruins overrun with monkeys. Have I ever told you not to look the red ones in the eye?'

'No. But thanks.'

'It's a very famous place actually.'

'Famous for what?'

'It's where the Beatles stayed in 1968.'

So it was here the penny dropped. I'd known the Beatles had come to India, but had no idea that it was to Rishikesh. How uncanny it felt that we'd shared the river for inspiration. They'd stayed at their ashram for about eight weeks—during which they'd written about 48 songs. I stayed at mine for a similar length of time, during which I wrote about 18 songs. Give or take 30 songs, I was well happy!

Splash! the last morning came. As naked as Bill Clinton working overtime, I crouched down and poured a bucket of cold water over myself. 'Jesus, Mary and Bill himself!' I jumped up and shook off, but having performed this baptismal every morning, I by now found it quite invigorating.

It was 6 a.m., and I made my way up to the yoga hall one last time. The large breezy hall was already full of students, some sitting cross-legged and others doing their warm-up stretches. I chose a mat at the back and sat down.

The two-metre tall yoga teacher soon entered. He stepped onto his raised platform, and folded his gangly legs into sitting position. He scanned the room intently, before he closed his eyes and proceeded to meditate. The class, to style, followed his lead.

The hall fell quiet, and despite the monkeys screeching outside, it entered a tranquil state. I sat with eyes closed and legs crossed, and reflecting on my time at the ashram, I waded into nostalgic waters—to the stirring conversation with the old swami, to playing cricket with the kids on my birthday, to the failed Agra experience with Kayley, when—*bang!*—the hall door slammed shut. I opened my eyes, and standing in the doorway—just as he had every day for over two months—was the Italian door-slamming-champion-of-the-universe. But, where I'd generally wished for him to be sent to a door-less island, I'd developed some sort of patience, as although he stood there, fidgeting for Italy and wearing that same blank face, I did nothing but grin.

It was 7:30 a.m., and sitting on my bed and gazing around my prison cell, I grew suddenly anxious about leaving. 'Like Brooks Hatlen, I'm an intuitional man now.' I stood up, and knowing if I didn't leave now, I might never, I began strapping up the Blue Fly.

I said an extensive round of goodbyes, to the teachers, security guards, and even the prayer-singing-chef, but as he walked alongside as I pushed the heavily-loaded bike to the ashram's back gate, my most significant was to Pramesh. Although I didn't confess, I knew when out in the big wide world of motorbiking thrills and spills, I was going to miss our balcony sessions more than anything.

'So,' he said.

'So,' I returned.

'I love goodbyes.'

'What?'

'I love goodbyes.'

'Don't you mean you hate them?'

'No, especially in this case, where I get the balcony back to myself.'

'Mate, at least you're original.'

'Joking, of course, but I will say that the pleasure, Mr Kerrigan, has been all yours.'

'Thanks, Professor, yours too.'

'You're going to have quite an adventure out there. You're probably going to see more of India than I have.'

'I like to think it'll be like your mate who threw his life to the wind and said he wouldn't touch money or ask for food.'

'It's just… you have money?'

'Yes.'

'And a fancy blue motorbike?'

'Yes.'

'Making it quite different in fact?'

'Yes.'

'Fair enough, I'll allow you your piety this once. Remember, a job is better than no job, a career is better than a job, but a calling is better than them all. Goodbye, my Australian friend,' he said, putting his hand firm into mine as we reached the large metal gate, 'until our paths should ever cross.'

The security guard opened the gate, with a loud jangle of his keys. He performed a reverent bow, and I reciprocated as best I could without dropping the bike. Big Daddy scattered past, and with the two of us making firm eye contact, he stopped and flashed his teeth. If ever I wanted to give a monkey the middle finger, the bike only furthered the itch. I stomped it in gear and thumped it up the road.

12. Hail the World of Two Wheels

Day One on the motorbike:

Like a prison escapee having just scaled the wall, my mind wasn't on the finer details of my free life ahead, but to first just get out of there. As I went from 0 to 100 kph up the wide-open road, I couldn't quite believe I was doing it, or that I was allowed. In some juvenile sense I felt too young to be taking on such a thing, and I dared not imagine how long I'd be sent to my room if Mum and Dad were in the loop.

As much without a checklist tour of predetermined places, as without the desire to have anything of the like, I'd set out on the trip having planned it very little. Armed with no more than a shitty little map—and at least some of the determination required in riding it—I was more interested in coming face-to-face with the spontaneous nature of things. More than anything I wished to run my fingers through the sands of adventure, to attain the polar-opposite feeling of life in the office, and discover things without warning but of my own dirt-inducing accord; the gritty in-between towns with names too long to pronounce, to encounter social situations fit for campfire telling, and to exhale the soul-decaying poison of routine and inhale the freedom of unhindered existence.

I cruised along, and judging by the bugs in my teeth, I must have been smiling. The road was as wide and straight, as the sun was high and blazing, and after riding south even for this first hour, the climate felt warmer than the leafy valley of Rishikesh.

I was in full riding attire—black jeans, black vest, and probably even underwear. I had as much of a motorbike licence as a degree in astrophysics, and I was wearing as much of a motorbike helmet as a latex Batman suit. But this was the way of legalities in India, and all I was guilty of was trying to fit in.

I thumped along until the dustiness inspired the need for a cup of roadside chai. I spotted a place on the highway's side and pulled onto the gravelly kerb.

'Hello, sir, where are you from?' asked the merchant.

'Vladivostok.'

'Oh! I have a sister from there.'

Having hoped the question was a Rishikesh-special, I smiled.

As I sat there, drinking my debut cup of roadside chai—and discovering the gallant need to wipe the road-induced dirt off my face—a bunch of kids swarmed around. I fished my camera out, and their faces fell to a hesitant look.

I took the photo, and they circled in, many possibly not having a mirror at home. Such social encounters were nothing new, but when I showed them the screen and they lit into a sea of laughing faces, experiencing them on the road felt especially uplifting.

I began to have a flick through the pages of the map, quietly wondering what the little *N* stood for. Despite having no idea where I was—and even less where I was going—I was concerned on no level; for how could the notion of being lost exist without the desire to be somewhere specific? And seeing that I had no point of desire, and I was on the planet regardless, I in fact felt perfectly *un*lost.

The merchant, standing at my shoulder, poured me a second cup. 'Where are you going, sir?'

'I'm not sure, but what do you think of this place?' I asked, pointing.

'Oh no, sir, that is a very bad place.'

I handed him the map, and he gave me a few dos and don'ts of probably shoulds and definitely shouldn'ts. I slung myself onto the Blue Fly and pulled onto the dusty highway, figuring I'd ride until I could be arsed no more, or pull in before dark.

The day was clear, but after several hours of riding into the unknown the honeymoon-high was wearing thin. Perhaps from the hypnotic sound of the wheels, I entered some sort of default survival mode. It dawned on me as plain as the sinking sun, that the only person that was going to find me a hotel each night, and keep the bike in running order each day, and keep me from becoming a vulture's delight, was *me*.

As the scarlet of dusk began to line the horizon, I pulled into a small town by the name of Meerut, in the neighbouring state of Uttar Pradesh.

I rode slowly through the litter-strewn high street, dodging rickshaws, kids on bikes, cows eating cardboard boxes, stagnant pools of oil, and miserable-looking donkeys pulling carts of rubble. I could feel the cold stare of a thousand eyes, with more people present than should ever have to live in such abhorrent conditions.

The evidence of environmental neglect was too visual to go unnoticed. As someone with a reasonable degree of love for the planet, I couldn't but feel repulsed. Although my stomach turned, I felt I understood—for without the luxury of weekly rubbish collection, where but on the street was the litter to go? Before the modern production of plastic and glass, India's eating utensils were made of clay, which were turfed into the gutter and sorted by the rain. With the continuance of this mentality—and the western introductions—the contemporary problem developed.

This theory didn't make me favour this place any more than I already didn't, and I could only hope that if aliens invaded they'd dock their spaceships overhead, be put off, and hyperdrive it home for a lamb roast.

It was now dark, and although my sense of standards urged me to keep riding onto any other town, it was too late.

I did a few laps of the main drag, in search of hotels, but as though there were reason to consider me suspect, I seemed to be getting the old sorry-we're-all-full vibe. It felt quite ironic, as though the slur should run the other way around.

Having no choice but to cast a wider net, I rode down an adjacent laneway. It was narrow and snaking, and the defective pipework of the fire escapes above dripped as though to add to the unwelcome.

I spotted a neon hotel vacancy sign blinking up ahead. I pulled in by its tawdry door, and as though coming from out of the pipework, a group of three guys circled around. 'Hello,' I muttered, as I parked the bike. They didn't respond.

I entered the hotel. Perched behind its reception counter was a big twitchy and terribly sweaty man being sandblasted by a deafening fan. He was the proud bearer of a cluster of gold fillings, and he grinned like a Bond villain as he wiped his brow with a small red towel. 'Good evening, sir, what are you doing here?'

'I'm looking for a room, please.'

'Are you sure?'

It was hardly the welcome I needed, but to the brand of night that lay ahead, it would prove to be an entirely fitting one. He slung me a key, and I marched up the creaky staircase to my room.

As I put the key in the hole, a terrible smell and feeling of suspicion consumed me. I stepped back from the door, and was hit by a wave of certainty that the bike was under harm's way.

I ran back into the laneway, to find my dear friends still loitering around the bike—one playing with its throttle, another leaning on it, and the last sitting on its seat. My blood pressure duly rose, as did they to straightened postures. Thanks to being stained with the dirt of a day's ride, I appeared ominous enough to make some degree of a threatening impression, and they backed into the darkness like street dogs bored with the fight. A little less green, I made very sure to lock the bike.

I walked back past the big-twitchy-sweaty-bloke behind his counter, eying him keenly.

I traipsed back up the creaky staircase. I was just about to open the door of my room, when the door of the neighbouring room unlocked from the inside and out walked an older western guy.

'G'day!' I said.

'Hej,' he mumbled.

'Where are you from?'

'Sweden.'

He had short dyed white hair, sculpted into an 80's flattop, and no stranger to a protein shake, he was wearing a red muscle tee. Although conversation fell shorter than Danny Devito, I was thoroughly relieved to sight an ally.

I turned back to my door, but as I began to push it open I was again hit by a horrible smell. I pushed it carefully, and as it creaked fully open, lying there, dead, was a body.

Comprised not of arms, shoulders, and a back with an optional tattoo, this was not the body of a human, but with a tail, beak, and crumpled feathers, it was a yellow canary. Naked and undignified, it was lying upturned on the floor of its cage, and adding to the grisliness, in the cage was another live canary—probably the deceased's husband or wife, my eyes not quite bionic enough to discern the working parts of a canary.

I called down to the big-twitchy-sweaty-bloke, who after giving the staircase its routine punishment, entered. 'Oh Freddy,' he sighed.

'Freddy?' I thought, unable to justify why a canary should be named otherwise.

He picked the bird from out of its cage, noticing its food and water trays were empty. 'This is suspicious!' he barked.

I looked at him blankly.

'I gave them water last week!'

I looked at him *more* blankly.

'The previous guest must have emptied it!'

Like an airborne referee, it was then that a fly started orbiting around his head. Its buzz grew to fill the room, and I took sincere delight in watching the sweaty bloke's face mutate into a generous shade of crimson. The fly drew closer to his forehead, and, like a helicopter pilot spotting his mark, it, however politically incorrect, landed on the dot between his eyes. His sweating reached a new high as the fly began to rotate, hither and thither, and the dense silence was soon replaced by the sound of a passionately slapped forehead; so moist he was it sounded like colliding slices of wet ham. 'Aren't you going to say something?' he yelled, as the sodden fly fell to the floor.

I coughed. 'Mate, let's save Gil Grissom the trip. Either *a.* the water evaporated, *b.* the canaries finished it last Tuesday, or *c.* they tipped it three days ago.'

Another fly entered the room.

'In India, everything is possible!' he snapped, saying it as though it were a national slogan to dismiss all responsibility. I opted for the summit of passive aggression—a return to perfect silence. He stormed out. He was angry with me, and I was angry with him, and Freddy, having been used as a lecture stick throughout, probably would have been angry with us both if he were alive.

Less concerned with the bloke than the surviving canary, I filled its water tray and put some bread in its cage. Squabbling, it soon relaxed into the state of ruffled feathers. I wondered how it felt about the loss of its better half, but figuring the perks of a two-second memory might lend to it thinking its mate went down the shops for some smokes, I chose to worry no further.

The room, comprised of little more than four timber walls and a broken window in its top corner, should have had a negative star rating. The bathroom, with a hole-in-the-floor dunny and a cold-water tap for all else, was even less exotic.

Resigned, I crouched down and had a much-needed wash, making sure to keep my lips pursed so as not to ingest any water. I brushed my teeth with bottled water next; trusting little that it was much better than from the tap. I collapsed onto the hard bed, and I could have fallen asleep in a blink, but a dispute flared out in the corridor.

Lying where I was, I had little choice but to listen, and I could make out that the roused voice was that of the Swedish guy. 'I've been staying in this hotel for eight fucking months!'

'Eight months?' I thought, wondering what sort of imp would stay in a joint like this for more than eight hours.

'And whatever little thing we had going on is fucking over!'

Where I'd been relieved to meet him, he proved to be the greatest danger present—as with his voice rising to all-out yelling—*bang!*—one of the contestants was slammed against the reverse side of my door. Nude, I jumped to my feet and locked it in a flash. I felt little safer, though, for the hysteria rose such that if a gunshot pierced the air I wouldn't have been surprised.

I turned off my light and lay on the floor, bathed in the faint orange glow of the streetlight outside. As I watched the ceiling fan barely do its job, I struggled to believe it was only 24 hours ago that I was sitting on the balcony with Pramesh. I thought about Mamma Sharvari as well, and if tonight she was making her coconut chili chutney.

The dull rumbling of the fight continued in the corridor, and with his once relaxed feathers contracted with fear, the squabbling canary had fallen silent. I wanted my mother, and for her to make me some apricot chicken and read me *Scuffy the Tugboat*.

I never left my room all night.

*****

Dear Manuel,

Tonight, in neon lights in my head, the quest to become story-rich features just two words—Fuck. This.

*****

I woke the next morning at first light, unable to get out of Hotel Resident Evil soon enough. I strapped up the bike and slung myself onboard. I was about to start it up when a good-willed, yet risky, idea came to mind.

Its success would be determined by my ability to be catlike, and I stood in the laneway, thinking it through, before walking back inside.

I snuck past the big-twitchy-sweaty-bloke strewn asleep across his counter, and, wishing not to wake any of the resident contestants, I toed it up the creaky stairs. I opened the door of my room, in which I'd left the key, and I closed it quietly behind me.

I approached the birdcage next. I figured this here Tweedy-bloke had endured his fair share of the horrors, especially after losing his husband or wife. I opened his cage door and off he flew out the window—possibly head-on into a truck, or a giant cream pie that happened to be outside. But my intention was no less noble.

Somebody stirred downstairs, and I froze. The motioning settled, and I toed it down the staircase, each stair creaking an inharmonious melody. The big-twitchy-sweaty-bloke snored like a hibernating bear, until I misjudged my footing and the stairs cracked. 'Good morning, sir,' he said, 'leaving so early?'

My heart stopped, emptied, refilled, rebooted, died and along with its mate Jesus, rose again.

'Are you ok, sir?'

'Yes… I'm… ahhhr…'

'You look as if you've seen a banshee?'

'I must… ahhhr… get going now.'

Like a champion race-walker, I walked into the laneway as quickly as my legs would take me. I slung myself onto the bike, knowing I had seconds before he walked upstairs and discovered the misdemeanour.

I kicked the kick-starter, but there was no response. I kicked again, but nothing… and again, but still nothing… 'Come on, ya bastard!' I whispered through gritted teeth, watching him sitting at his counter through the hotel window.

Kick! Kick!—nothing. *Kick! Kick!*—nothing, and it was then that he rose to his feet, stretched, and proceeded up the stairs.

With sweat teaming down my brow, I kicked again, but with the engine sounding sadder by the attempt, I jumped off, stomped it into neutral and began wheeling the awkward bike down the laneway.

I reached the main drag and a crowd of locals swarmed around. 'Does anyone know how to start an Enfield?' I pitched with life-or-death importance.

'Yes' said a man, stepping forward, 'but do you know Ricky Ponting?'

'—Can you please just start it?'

He smiled, and spent the best part of his life expectancy climbing onboard.

I stood there twiddling my thumbs and jumping up and down like a kid busting for a wee. He turned to me and smiled again, and, as though the touch of god was within his leg, he booted it in the guts and it roared to life.

'Excuse me!' a voice hollered, and when I turned to see my eyes filled with the sight of the big-twitchy-sweaty-bloke speed waddling towards.

I turned back to my aide. 'Ok, thank you! I must get going! Quickly now!'

His smile remained, as did his arse in the seat.

I choked on any available words, until, like Basil Fawlty at his wits end with Manuel, they chose themselves. 'Please understand before one of us dies!'

He hopped off and I threw myself onto the bike.

'Stop that man!' yelled the big-twitchy-sweaty-bloke.

Something in the eyes of my aide changed, and I stomped the bike in gear and gunned it up the highway. I exhaled long and hard as the road drew out, the only imaginable addition to the victory being if the Tweedy-bloke landed on my shoulder and cracked me a thank you beer.

Day Two on the motorbike:

I coasted along the highway with the wind on my face, more than content to watch the dawn lightshow introduce the day.

I was growing more confident with the bike, and was hoping to make it southwest to the city of Jaipur, the capital of Rajasthan.

Although it wasn't that far, my aim was quite ambitious.

Even at this early stage, I'd discerned there to be a significant difference from covering distance on western roads and Indian roads. Where in the west—on its smooth marvels of asphalt marked with legible lines—a motorbike could realistically cover a 1,000 kilometres (621 miles) a day, if in India—on its patchy and pot-holed affairs—300 kilometres was covered, then it'd been a very good day indeed.

Another mildly endearing, yet mostly annoying factor was the road signs. They were perhaps the most dangerous element of all, for if a traveller was to take their inexactness as gospel, they'd find themselves coming undone.

An example was to see a sign that reads: *Delhi 99 km*, and after riding 20 kilometres see another: *Delhi 98 km*. It was baffling, and the best you could use them for were as ballparks, distantly trusting that slowly but surely, but, blindly, you were chipping towards your destination. *Why* was a mystery, but settling on the theory that the bloke doing the measuring—using the old technique of counting his footsteps with pebbles in a bag— must have worked as a juggler who dropped a few on the side, I eventually became accustomed.

It was high noon, and the white sun cut down like a diamond. I was nearing Delhi, but figuring I'd save myself the pollution-induced asthma attack, I pulled off the highway and onto the bypass freeway.

Streaking with road trains, buses, convertible sports cars and more, the freeway was an enormous triple-lane thoroughfare at a standard as top-notch as those in the west. All vehicles were moving at a pace far greater than India's average, and aiming only to match, I opened up the throttle.

I initially felt nervous to be riding so fast, but soon settled in as a member of the stream. Another tourist, also on an Enfield, came riding alongside. 'חא שולם' he yelled over the traffic, revealing he was Israeli. I was too slow to respond, and he scuffed me off and sped into the distance.

Be it from the heat of the day, or the passion of my throttle hand, the bike growled like a werewolf proud to show its teeth. I was at the height of my riding confidence, and nothing near or far could make for a pebble of hindrance. *Buda buda buda*—the bike rocked beneath, and unsure whether *it* or *I* was in charge, I held on tight. My eyes watered behind my sunglasses, and seeing, then, the Israeli guy return into view, I salivated further and caned past him without a whiff of acknowledgment.

This was it, the most polar-opposite feeling of life in the office—speed *vs.* sterility, open space *vs.* four grey walls. It seemed in this moment that no net, trap, or lasso could hold me back. But it was then—when a large truck compromised my pace—that I pulled out into the overtaking lane, where, up ahead, and no further away than the length of a few vehicles, was a bus stopped in the middle of the freeway.

A bolt of fear near struck me down, and my heart rate mounted such that to my ears there was no longer the sound of the bike, but only internal beating. If this were at home, or in any country where responsibility was considered that of oneself, the bus would have had its hazard lights on. But this was India, and I was fast learning the concept of responsibility seemed something of a national allergy. I was travelling at about 90 kph, and calculating I had about three seconds before I would likely be in a fatal collision, my teeth gritted and my body tensed.

Three seconds was all I had—just three seconds—but regardless of any measure of time, there felt no past or future, just the present, and all too present at that. Yet in the same airless breath, time drew out like a line with no end, and like a plane coming in for the crash, my mind rattled with a wallet of thought-to-be-sorted-before-death.

In an instant it shot to the seat of life's juncture—family, mates, kids not had, mountains not climbed. The words of Ange featured—'whot sort of numb-nut would wannae take on these roads?' As did those of Pramesh—'planning on being killed?' But on top of this flurry was a feeling of great embarrassment, that, unbeknown to my parents, and, destined for the crown of Sir John Doe, *this* was how I was going to die.

I was moving so fast, that, convinced any attempt to brake or manoeuvre around the bus would equal further loss of control, I could reach for the brake lever no more than I could imagine jumping into a net when standing on top of a burning building.

Two seconds was all I had—just two seconds—and frozen with fear I braced to cop the collision. But it was then that the freeze somewhat thawed, and causing the ill-tipped twist of fate I couldn't have needed less, I pushed the footbrake.

On Enfield motorbikes, the foot-operated *brake lever* and the foot-operated *gear lever* are on opposite sides to each other than the design of all other motorbikes in the universe. When riding in a relaxed state, I could manage the unfamiliarity, but when startled, I'd default to using them the traditional way around.

And so it was on this day, when in a life-or-death situation, instead of pressing the much-needed brake, I, putting the bike into a higher gear and causing more of what I couldn't have needed less—*acceleration*—hit the gear lever.

One second was all I had—just one second—collision was near, metal and glass *vs.* flesh and bone, there was to be no contest, I was going to die, right here, right now, in India, and at such a young age.

But instinct took over, and as a result of my gear-changing blunder, I employed every lever available—two feet pushed down, two hands squeezed tight. I had little understanding of what I was summonsing the bike, but it went into a curving skid, and when it straightened back up into a speed wobble that caused us to swerve and miss the back left-hand corner of the bus by little more than a couple of feet. I missed the bus! I missed the bus! I missed the *fucking* bus!

With my eyes still wide with fright, I pulled over, jumped off, and jumped up and down. 'Fffuuuuccckkk! Fffuuuuccckkk! Fffffuuuuuuucccccckkkkkk!'

It wasn't skill that saved me, but a twist of fate where if I hadn't have stuffed up the initial braking, I would have slowed down to a marginal extent but likely hit the bus at a critical speed anyway. As a result of the braking bungle, though, I put the bike into a speed wobble that caused us to swerve and miss.

I sat crouched on the side of the freeway, pale, silent, and staring into the nothingness. With the sound of my heart still flying in my ears, never did I feel so lucky and unlucky, so simultaneously.

'Where's a newsagent? I should buy a lotto ticket.'

13. The Desert State

I must have sat there for half an hour, and even if I had a cigarette in hand, it would have taken me far longer to keep my hands still enough to light it. I gradually stood up, inched back on the bike, and began up the road at a tortoise's version of a hare's pace.

Shortly after, I reached the state border, where standing proudly on its behalf was a large sign: "*Welcome to Rajasthan. The Desert State*." Pakistan, a place I'd been advised to avoid, was bordered on the state's far west side, but it was here that I crossed over the less-dubious eastern border.

After just a few kilometres, the desert state description proved to be no lie. The high sun bashed down with an even harder-core commitment, and the land relapsed into a rocky wasteland. The wind was as dry as I'd ever felt, and the line of the horizon fluttered nervously. Some of the rock formations were like a trick of the mind. With long rows like stone caterpillars edging in the distance, large boulders appearing to balance on a rock half the size beneath, and tower-like spikes near and far. In fact, if Wile E. Coyote and the Road Runner zipped past, I'd have done nothing but try to beep in time with them.

I rode slowly along, spotting a scatter of men working in the distant fields. Their attire looked as though it were from a thousand years back—large red turban headwear, fawn-coloured tops, and loose white pants pulled up into what looked like a nappy. I watched them from afar, wondering how they survived the heat and dust. There was something dignified about them; as though harbouring an underlying pride that their hereditary line survived such hostile conditions. They were the *Rajputs*, the men of the desert, and in days past were known as great horsemen and swordsmen.

Picking up the pace, I kept cruising along, when in the distance could be seen a group of animals absorbed in the blur of the horizon. They seemed to be in a road train formation, and they were creating a long trail of dust. I rode toward until the blur sharpened. They were camels: an entire herd, spitting, moaning, and stirring the dust.

But unlike the *what up bro* leisurely meander of your average camel, these fellas—employing the walk one does when dashing to the next room for toilet paper—were ambling with small awkward steps. I wasn't sure why, but as I rode closer, I could see that their feet were hobbled by rope. I guess it was so they couldn't run off from the shepherd, but bearing in mind they were en route to the Pushkar Camel Fair 150 kilometres away, the toilet paper hostage knot was a brutal disabler.

Much to the satisfaction of my plan for the day, later that afternoon I reached the capital city of Jaipur, *The Pink City of Rajasthan*.

I entered its web of traffic, and composed of more dusty

animals than grimy vehicles, it was like a bottlenecking face-off between fur and metal. Its pace ground down to the point of nearly going backwards, and as if riding through traffic that included a zoo's worth of camels, horses and donkeys wasn't unusual enough, up ahead was a wannabe stuntman standing on his motorbike's seat and riding it no-hands.

Despite the chaos of the traffic, I was starting to understand the harmony behind the disharmony. Amid the muddle of trucks cutting you off, rickshaws letting you in, dodging this ox and watching that camel, there was some sort of synchronisation where everyone was actually *thinking*. Interestingly, too, never was any offense taken. Where in the west we drive by such rigid rules that if a car makes a wrong move then some hot head jumps out of his pickup armed with a bazooka, in India nothing came as a shock. In fact, judging by the locals, driving was a mind-sharpening exercise to be treated as a sport, or PlayStation game—it's just, you only got one life.

I sat idle at a large intersection, engulfed in a sea of motorbikes, and with guys reaching over to shake my hand, and others beckoning from a distance, with each vehicle was a company of bright faces.

With the bike in gear, I sat waiting for the traffic lights, when a deafening trumpet-noise blared from behind. I turned to see, and standing directly behind me—hairy legs considered equal members of traffic as shiny wheels—was an elephant. I gave a faint nod to the guys perched on top, to which less worried than I that their leathery friend may or may not pick me up and use me as a toothpick, they waved down.

The lights changed, and determined to get swiftly out of the elephant's way, I released the clutch too abruptly and stalled the bike. I yelled to the guys to halt their beast, but if they were trying, I couldn't tell, for the elephant edged forward to the point that it nudged my bike while making a deep growling noise. I kicked the kick-starter, and with the bike having thank-*farck*-fully roared to life, I got us out of there.

Feeling like I'd slipped into some ancient world a millennium back, reaching Jaipur felt like the first real reward of the motorbiking endeavour. This strange medieval city sat nestled in a desert valley, and while riding through its wide boulevards I noticed an old fortified palace high on a distant hill. I fancied riding up there, so I pulled over to get some info.

One second passed, fifty people gathered...

Two seconds passed, a hundred people gathered...

Three seconds passed, two hundred people gathered...

And when at the five-second point there were more people amassed than numbers knew, I spoke. 'Hullo!' I said with a slightly Indian-adapted accent (for to say it in brazen Australian would sound to their ears like *how low*).

'Hello, sir, where are you from?' asked a man. I gave him the answer, to which of course he referred to Ricky Ponting, without the first inkling that the topic could at this highly-accumulated stage cause irreversible toxicosis.

'What's the name of that fort up on the hill?' I asked.

'It is the Jaigarh Fort—a very special place. It's 500 years old!'

'Can I ride up there?'

'Yes, and no, there's a path, but it's very steep and winding. And—'—*beep beeep beeeep*—there was a truck behind me wanting to get through, giving me no choice but to ride on.

So it was established I could get up there, but still having no idea how, I stopped again. 'Ok, sir,' said the next man, 'first you will be coming to the second traffic circle on the third time, and secondly you will be going for the first time around the fourth traffic circle, and after the fifth time...' I tuned out somewhere around then, concluding the legend to be true—that when it comes to giving directions—the theory being that even if they have no idea they'll make something up to save face—the good people of India can be absolute rippers.

Having figured I'd let my nose do the leading, I twisted and turned through the city's laneways. When I reached the foot of a large thorn-scrub covered hill, I came to a long-winding path that led up to the fort. I sat idle at the bottom, feeling awfully daunted by this thin cobblestone path that looked more suitable for walking than riding. With the sun in the latter stages of its descent, I proceeded up, where the first matter of concern established was that the bike tyres were slipping on the smooth cobblestones, giving the path a personalised ice rink-feel. Pulling deeper into my denial, I continued, where the second matter of concern uncovered was that the higher the path ascended, the narrower it grew, making it impossible to turn around even if I wanted to. Yet despite admitting that this was officially one of those best-not-look-down jobs, upwards I pressed, where the third, and, without question, most frightening, gruesome, and utterly terrifying matter of concern realised was that all of a sudden—I really reeeally needed to go the toilet.

But when I reached the summit in one piece, the view felt like it had been worth the risk to come see. Cradled in the haze of the desert, the expanse of Jaipur unfolded beneath, and with its scatter of sandstone buildings creating, from this great height, an overall pink tinge, the fable of the Pink City was proven true. I hopped off the bike and sat on a nearby ledge, feeling strangely filled with a sense of home. I thought about Dad, and wondered if tonight he was putting newspaper on the kitchen table before cooking his brew. I thought about Mum, and wondered if today she'd watered her garden with that same piece of hose she's been using forever. I thought about their third-born son, too, and how he ever came to be on a hilltop in India, so terribly far away.

After making my way back down into the city, I found a hotel, and already knowing that with every Indian hotel was a man standing behind its counter with a loud fan blowing in his face—and, in conjunction with his reception duties, watching an even louder telly—I was less than surprised to find this one of no exception.

'Hello, can I get some toilet paper, please?' I asked, to which with a look that suggested he was disappointed he didn't have a water pistol full of urine beneath the counter, he broke gaze with his telly. 'What's that?' he asked.

'What's *what*?'

'Toilet paper?'

'It's ahhhr...' I stopped, spending a second trying to imagine a world in which one has never heard of it.

The cuckoo clock mounted on the wall behind him chimed rowdily, playing the part of a cerebral jumpstart. 'Actually, I know what it is,' he said, 'but why go to the bother of wiping and smearing, when you can simply wash your troubles away?'

'And what would I be washing them away, with?'

'Your hand.'

'And come breakfast, lunch, and dinner, what would I be eating with?'

'Your hand.'

'I see,' I said, walking back outside using the inane melodic charm of *Twinkle, Twinkle, Little Star* to disremember the topic.

I unpacked the bike, and with the last fragments of my energy carried my bags, spare petrol and guitar, up to my room. It had been a massive day, and although I'd nearly been killed twice; by the foot of an elephant and a head-on with a bus, the love affair with the Blue Fly was in official bloom.

The room was simple but clean, and much to my delight it had an upright shower. Happy to be home, I stood in front of the mirror. Excluding a machinegun, I was so blackened from the road that I looked like a poor man's Rambo. I hopped under the shower and scrubbed to the beat of a new obsession.

I finished up soon after, but with the grime having proven too difficult to remove from around my eyes, I was left with what looked like road-induced eyeliner. 'From Sylvester Stallone to Simon Le Bon?'

Too numb to care, I lay down for a thousand and one years.

The next morning, a peculiar sound beat my alarm to the beep. But unlike a rooster crowing at the dawn, or the delicate chirping of birds fading in with first light, this wasn't your everyday contributor to the morning soundscape. Tantamount, instead, to a herd of tap-dancing draught horses fed on lager and laxatives, it was a group of local guys out in the corridor; hocking, spitting, and blowing things by no means only out of their noses. I was less appreciative of the disruption than quietly impressed with their coincidental rhythm, which was such that I wondered if they were about to break into a choreographed routine from Stomp.

The bike was parked in the hotel laneway. Having had a last-minute, yet failed, attempt to remove my road-induced eyeliner; I put on my full hero suit of black jeans, black vest, boots and the rest. The Blue Fly, however, like a ham-fisted groom unable to do up his own tie, needed twice as much attention, and having strapped it up with A to Z, I lastly slung myself onboard.

I kicked the kick-starter, but as per the morning previous, there was no response. I kicked again, but nothing... and again, but still nothing... 'Lucky I'm not in a getaway situation today.'

Kick! Kick!—nothing. *Kick! Kick!*—nothing.

'Ah come on, ya _ _ _ _!'

With the engine sounding sadder by the attempt, I hopped off, clicked it into neutral, and figured I'd walk it along the main drag until I found someone who could help.

'Hello, sir, where are you from?' asked a nameless man.

'Uzbekistan. You don't happen to know how to start an Enfield, do you?'

'Yes! My cousin has one at home. Do you like cows?'

'No,' I said, standing back.

He hopped on the bike, and, as though the touch of god was within every Indian's leg, he booted it in the guts and it roared to life.

'Thanks very much,' I said, feeling this matter had officially reached the point of boredom. 'Do you know the road for Pushkar?'

'Yes!' he said, pointing in multiple directions.

I was soon out on the open desert road, Pushkar-bound; my understanding being that it was the main tourist hub of Rajasthan, full of Europeans, Israelis and more. I'd also heard it was a place highly regarded for buying shoes.

An hour on the highway passed, and making the desert ripple like *Tatooine*—the home of the Skywalkers—what was once rock-strewn had fined down to an orange-coloured sand. The horizon wavered restlessly, and with the high blurry sun looking even wearied by itself I couldn't ride for ten minutes without needing a swig of water. The desert men—still wearing their red turban headwear and loose pants pulled up into shorts—were working in the outer fields, and some, with tall walking sticks like wizard's staves, were ambling through the dust with flocks of goats.

The Blue Fly was in fine highway form, but like a dog having eaten too much grass, it started to splutter and spit.

When I pulled over, I noticed something up ahead, lying in the middle of the road. It moved, and from the distance I could make out it was some sort of large animal. I hopped on the bike and rode closer, wondering if it was a camel having suffered the cruel fate of the toilet paper hostage knot.

It was a donkey. It was lying in a pool of its own blood—having obviously been hit by a vehicle—and it kicked wildly as I stood over it. I knelt down, at which time a group of local staring enthusiasts popped out of the sand and swarmed around. 'Hello, sir, why are you watching the donkey?'

'I'm figuring out what to do with him.'

'Why should you care? It's the donkey's problem.'

'You believe in reincarnation, don't you? In a past life he might have been an American president.'

I grabbed the donkey by two of its legs, at which time my comrades—going to heart-warming lengths to be as unhelpful as possible—stepped clear out of the way.

With enough difficulty being unaided, I dragged the donkey to the roadside, whereupon the lads broke into raptures. Some, attempting discretion, cupped their mouths as they snickered, while others, beaming, slapped each other on the back. In just under three seconds, my mercury rose to a critical level.

There was a thick trail of blood running from the middle of the road to the roadside, and the donkey lay there looking very near its end. Its leg was gashed to the bone, and figuring it'd be claimed by the cold of night, I covered it with some old newspaper lying nearby.

I proceeded to walk away, at a genuine loss, but it was then that the donkey stood up. I turned back to the lads, and they wobbled their heads as one. 'It's a miracle, sir! George W. Eeyore!'

I'd certainly found the Indians to be a gentle-hearted race, a people whose interest in you was almost always deep and genuine. But it was also my observation that when it came to animals their well of compassion ran dry. (I later learnt of a politician from Delhi who became respected simply because he had all the stray dogs of Delhi euthanised—his logic being they made his drive to work look unclean.)

I slung myself back onto my horse, I mean, bike, and kept barrelling along the highway. And as the flat desert landscape buckled into tumbling hills, the once straight road grew winding.

A few hours later I came within the vicinity of Pushkar. After the mission of unfamiliarity since leaving Rishikesh, reaching this western safe haven was a very welcome comma in the story.

Now only a couple of kilometres shy of the town, I slowed the riding pace way down, and with the bike farting like a petrol-intolerant swine, another tourist—himself on a red Enfield—came riding alongside.

'סולש חא' he yelled over his engine, revealing he was Israeli.

'G'day!' I yelled back.

'Oh sorry, my friend, you looks like an Israeli!'

'That's cool, mate, I'm Australian, but I get mistaken as Israeli. It must be the motorbike.'

He gave me a thumbs-up.

'I've heard that greeting before. What does it mean?'

'It means, *shalom ahi* or *hello brother*?'

We shook hands while coasting parallel.

'My name is Lior, and you?'

He was skinny, bordering on emaciated, but like all the Israelis I'd met he was bronzed and toned. He had a tattoo of a fox on his forearm, and on his head was a jungle of dark curly hair so vast that for all I knew it was harbouring a troop of tree monkeys.

I told him my name.

'Your bike doesn't sound so healthy, my Aussie friend.'

'I'm going to have to take it to a mechanic as soon as I get into Pushkar.'

'I know a good one, follow me.'

We soon made it to the mechanic's, and like most Indian workshops it was little more than an oil-soaked bamboo hut. We hopped off our bikes and stood out front.

'You want a cigarette?' he asked, crouching down and stretching his back.

It had been longer than I could remember since I'd had one, and I rather enjoyed the idea of rebelling against my tortured little lungs in their tortured little ribcage. 'Well, I sometimes smoke o.p's'.

'What's o.p's?'

'Other people's.'

He stood up and flicked one over.

I lit up and inhaled; the relief flowing through my veins so wonderful it was surely a thing that money couldn't buy, although, of course, it could.

'So, Aussie brother, where have you ridden from today?'

'Jaipur. Have you come in from Jaisalmer?'

He shook his head. 'Jaisalmer is too deep into the desert, too close to Pakistan, and too far by bike.'

I appreciated the tip, but appreciated its optional nature even more.

We stood leaning on our bikes: one red, one blue.

'I've used this mechanic before,' said my new friend under his breath, 'he's good—a little crazy—but still he's a good mechanic.'

Just as he finished his words, a tense-looking man approached. He was as gaunt as the walking dead, and he wore a red turban so large I couldn't help but wonder if it was against the best interests of his spine. 'Good day, sir,' he said in a paste-thick accent, 'I am being the boss here. How can I help you?'

'G'day, I was wond—'

'—Actually, sir, excuse me for one moment,' he said, turning around and screaming at his three apprentices with surprising ferocity.

'Sorry, sir, how can I help you?' he asked, turning back.

I told him what I thought was wrong with the bike. While half listening and making a series of accommodating noises, he put the bike on a milk crate and began some preliminary tinkering. 'Screwdriver!' he barked, to which one of his apprentices, halfway stooped, came cowering over with the object in hand.

Nervous, the kid handed it to him, but with the tone of a precious artist feeling he could no longer work with such abysmal brushes, the boss slammed it on the ground. 'Not that one! The other fucking one!' The apprentice, like a wounded animal, limped back to the bamboo shed. 'I am sorry, sir,' said the boss, turning back and straightening his turban, 'but I am normally being a very nice man.'

He knelt back down, and with a deep-set frown he recommenced his tinkering. I stood a polite distance away, but although he'd soon pulled the bike into more bits than I knew it was made of, he seemed against imparting any diagnosis.

'So what do you think is wrong with it?' I asked.

'Please, sir, be waiting one moment,' he said, turning again to his apprentices. 'Bring me a fucking oil tray! The big one! The fucking big one!'

I turned to Lior and shrugged, and still leaning on his bike, he feigned assurance with a dismissive wave of the hand.

The boss turned back. 'A thousand apologies, sir, but these boys are my nephews and it's my responsibility to teach them to be men. Cup of chai?' he added, making an admirable effort to force a smile.

In response to the boss's command, the same apprentice came shrinking over, but he was so stooped by now, that, minus the bell and rope, he looked little dissimilar to the *Hunchback of Notre Dame*. He handed the boss the oil tray, but as though bracing to be slapped, the boy twitched like a Greyhound.

The boss, like a surgeon would to instruments being passed

by a nurse, took the oil tray without looking, but when the tray was skimmed by his eyes, I saw in them thunder and lightning.

His face, like a blood recipient left too long on the drip, boiled to a fluorescent purple, and like a sea monster levitating out of the ocean, he rose up and inhaled—'This is not the big one! This is the other fucking one! How many bloody-fucking times must I tell you bloody-fucking boys what to do! Look at the bloody-fucking shit all over the place!' His fury was so climactic, that his voice, like a short-changed eight-year-old on Christmas morning, cracked twice per syllable. 'This is how you fucking do it! First you do *one* fucking works! Then you do *two* fucking works! Then you do *three* fucking…' and he frisbeed the oil tray their way, reducing them to startled animals diving behind bikes and benches.

'Farck me dead!' I thought, happy for his sake he never opted to be an air traffic controller.

The outburst eased as his face morphed from purple to wraithlike white, yet just as he finished wiping the saliva from his chin, a street kid, armed with a large trumpet, came up from behind and blasted it into the back of his head—the trumpet sounding as tuneful as a camel having its udder wrapped around its hump.

The mechanic's turban, like the *Leaning Tower of Pisa*, slanted forward in the trumpet-stream, and with his eyes shrivelling into fine diamonds, he descended into perfect silence as he turned to face his offender.

The trumpet-kid, seeming altogether proud to have delivered such a specialised service, held his hand out for payment. Yet as though mindful of the notion of value-for-money, he inhaled long and broke into a slapdash rendition of Louis Armstrong's *Hello Dolly*.

The mechanic cupped the lad's bugle with his quivering hand, demoting it to a farting kazoo, and knowing full well that distance would be required for the pending eruption, I stepped clear out of the way. My eyes were wide with anticipation, as kilobyte by kilobyte the mechanic came back online. No force of this Earth could have made me look away. 'Anything could happen, anything at all...' and it was then that he reached for a spanner, raised it into the air, and just when one felt the trumpet-kid was about to taste the steel, the mechanic collapsed to the ground.

'Farck me dead!' I thought, concluding the only thing that could have topped this was if the ghost of Freddy Mercury moonwalked past singing *Another One Bites the Dust*.

To his aid, the apprentices scattered around, and the little trumpet-kid stood aside, as though in his heart he knew this was indeed his last bugle call. The scene was sad and sombre, and looking resigned to the fall of his career, I couldn't help but wonder of those he'd claimed before—old ladies carried away on stretchers, and street dogs having a Sunday scratch inverted with fright. Although the *Last Post* would have been the cherry of encores, his lips dared not meet with his bugle again.

Although lying in the dust, the red-turban-wearing-mechanic was to be no such casualty, as after a few short seconds, he inhaled sharply, rose up like a vampire, and chased the trumpet-kid down the street.

'Well, that's him away then,' I said, turning back to my bike, and still leaning on his own, Lior gave another dismissive wave of the hand.

Having failed to catch his prey, the mechanic returned and dusted himself off.

'So anyway, mate, about the bike?'

'Yes, the bike is not fit for riding.'

'Well, I can see that. So what do you reckon?'

'No no, it's not so bad. I don't think we should wreck it.'

'No, I mean, what do you *reckon*, as in what do you *think* we need to do to fix the bike?'

'Oh, you mean fixing?'

'Yes! Fixing!'

'Well, to fix the bike, the something that I reckon we need to do, is something that at this point in time I am not so sure of.'

'I'm afraid I'm going to need a bit more clarity there, mate.'

'It's like when god set out for the mountain, and when he reached the top he learnt there was an elevator he could have used.'

'And how is you not knowing what's wrong with my bike remotely similar to god and elevators?'

'I'm not so sure myself—just like I am not so sure what is wrong with your bike. I'll have one of my apprentices look at it. It may take one day, two days, maybe four. Thank you. Come again,' he said, disappearing into the bamboo shed.

I walked back over to Lior. 'So?' he asked, lighting up.

'Well, he says he's going to have one of his apprentices look at it, but after his faith demo, I'm not sure if constructing Lego is beyond them.'

'I told you he's a little crazy, brother.'

'You're not wrong.'

'You mean… I'm right?'

'Yeah, as in you're *right*,' I repeated, himself having no familiarity with the Australian practice of a double negative equalling a positive.

Bike-less, I stood scratching my head. 'Do you want to give us a lift then?'

'You and who else?'

'Just me, mate, *us* in Australian-English is singular.'

'Yes, of course Aussie brother; hop on, rooms here are cheap, but it's even cheaper if we spilt.'

I hopped on behind him and we headed into the innards of Pushkar.

We soon made it to what looked like a good hotel, small and cheap, and adding to its two-star rating, our room had a balcony with a full view of the famous Pushkar Lake. We unpacked his bike and dumped our bags, and summonsed by our hunger we took to the streets.

With endless restaurants, hotels, clothing shops, and chai and chill houses, the narrow-winding laneways of Pushkar were unmistakably touristy. Maintaining the cultural balance, though, was the threatening racket of trumpets and drums from the Hindu wedding processions scuttling along.

'This place is crazy,' said Lior, 'look at all the girls!'

He was right; for with as many westerners present as locals—and the western girls given, seemingly, little choice from the heat but to parade around less clothed than usual—this place was indeed *crazy*.

'So what do you want to eat, mate?'

'Her!'

'Other than her?'

'Her mate! You?'

'Give me something normal, like a steak sandwich and a hamburger, hot chips and sausages...'

'This country is vegetarian.'

'Well f#&k'n fuck you!'

'What?'

'Sorry, mate, it's just... it's all getting to me, and if I eat any more rice I'm gunna fair dinkum turn into a giant grain.'

'What does it mean, this "fair dinkum" that Aussies say?'

'Ahhhr... I guess it's an expression of authenticity, meaning *really* or *seriously*, for the most part.'

'Is that right?'

'Fair dinkum.'

'Well, if you want to eat something different, why don't we go to an Israeli restaurant?'

Lior took the reins, and soon led us down some stairs and through a beaded doorway of what appeared to be an underground Israeli lair. The room was smoke-filled and dimly lit, and had a dramatically low ceiling. It was packed with people; equally with the sound of Hebrew and the high falsetto laughs I'd grown to know of the Israelis.

We sat on a couch in the far corner, at which time I noticed, hanging on the wall above us, a small flyer: *Traditional Indian Singing Lessons*. 'Could be cool?' I thought, but it was here the thought ended.

'You want a cigarette?'

'Yeah,' I said, subscribing to the airlessness.

'So tell me, my Aussie friend, do you have a girlfriend?'

'No, you?'

'No,' he said. The matter, in standard bloke fashion, opened and closed from one neighbouring second to the next. 'But tell me, my Aussie friend, what does—'

'—סולש חא' said another man, interjecting. He'd clearly mistaken me as Israeli, and I gazed at him vacuously until Lior intervened. They conversed in Hebrew for a few seconds—the only word comprehensible to my ears being *Australian*.

'Oh sorry, my friend, you looks like an Israeli.'

'That's cool, mate, shalom ahi.' I edged.

'Hello, brother, my name is Eval.'

He was tall, tanned, and wearing a red shirt and a blue sarong. And the dark-haired girl standing next to him, wearing a yellow crop top and jean shorts that propelled her into the category of *crazy hot,* was so gorgeous she couldn't but induce light-headedness. I tried to look away, but as though bound by an invisible neck brace, my efforts fell at least 180° short. 'I'm Ariella,' she said, leaning down and giving me an unexpected kiss on the cheek. 'Can we share your couch?'

Lior and I exchanged a knowing look. This was definitely one of those situations where you found another bloke's girlfriend a lot hotter than you legally should, but who were we to deny them respite.

The waiter brought us a round of hot milks, and Lior took charge of ordering food.

'What's this?' asked Eval, clasping his mug.

'It's the juice of the desert,' said Lior, taking a fearless swig. The rest of us shared a look of concern, giving me passage to further check out Ariella.

'So tell me, how do you like India?' asked Eval, sitting forward.

'It's fine, mate.' I said, stifling a sudden hyena-like yawn. I was too road-fatigued for much in the way of philosophical discussion—and, possibly vexed he should be worthy of Ariella.

Lior eyed me over his mug, and when I noticed the dejection in his countryman's eyes, I cleared my throat. 'It's a pretty broad question, mate.'

'Do I seem like I'm in a hurry?' said Eval, sinking back into the couch.

I took an apprehensive sip of the milk. 'So how do I like India? It's a two-sided coin, I s'pose.'

'A love/hate relationship, yes?'

'Yes.' I said, turning to Lior. 'This milk-stuff is alright, mate.'

Lior gave a solitary nod, as though more interested in elaboration than milk.

I turned back to Eval. 'Yes, a two-sided coin; on one side it's a zoo, a barnyard, the toilet of toilets. For all its corruption, never-ending dirt, and the fact that many of the locals would sell you their mother, India is hell.'

Lior shuffled in his seat.

'But, because while I'm here I don't have to stomach the six o'clock news, a cell phone, or laugh at my boss's shithouse jokes, on the other side it's heaven.'

Eval sat back up. 'So why did you come here?'

'It's complicated.' My invisible neck brace assumed default position, giving me a clear view of Ariella. 'To be honest,' I said, forcing back, 'I sometimes feel like a pretentious twat having come here at all; like I'm trying to prove something to myself… or impress girls… or something…'

'Fuck the girls.'

'Ha ha! Fuck the girls!' said Lior. I eyed him over my mug, making him default back to hiding behind his own.

'And tell me also…' said Eval, his voice dropping to a more confidential tone, 'what do you think of us Israelis?'

I clasped my mug harder. 'Honestly?'

'Full honesty.'

'Really?'

'Really..'

'I think you can be a bunch of dicks.'

'What?'

'You 'eard.'

'What?'

'You asked me to be honest, mate.'

The three of them broke into fervent Hebrew—the only words comprehensible to my ears being *Australian,* and, *fuckhead.*

'Look,' I said, 'I've found the few solo Israelis I've met, like my good man Lior here, to be totally cool, but in groups there just seems to be an inward vibe where youse stick together and come across as pretty cold.'

'It's true that we stick together,' added Lior, 'but when you come from a country with such division, it's only natural.'

'It's like it takes a little time for us to warm to outsiders,' said Ariella, now leaning forward, 'but once you're in, you're like family.'

Eval turned to Lior. 'Do you think it's true that Israelis come across as rude?' he asked in a tone that, ironically, sounded less than polite.

'I guess so—but only because we don't use *please* or *thank you*,' he said, turning to me as though feeling the need to explain it to an outsider. 'We don't have these words in Hebrew; to us, politeness is expressed by the melody we speak in. So instead of asking in a dry voice "can I've a coke, please?" we'd ask in a more gentle voice "can I've a coke!" kind of kicking up the end of the sentence with a higher pitch. We don't mean to be rude—we're just framed by our Hebrew habits. Besides, *please* and *thank you* don't mean shit! And the English-speaking world seems to use them like excuses, like it's ok to go through life being an arsehole, as long as you say please and fucking thank you!'

'But as for Israelis playing music too loud in hotels, and smoking a little weed here and there,' said Ariella, 'that's because we want to blow off steam after military service.'

'It's mandatory for non-Arab citizens,' said Eval, making me suddenly understand why every Israeli I'd seen was a picture of fitness and health. 'Straight after high school: guys for three years, girls for two years. So right when everyone is set free, we're thrown into military shackles. By the time that bullshit is over, we want to run like a dog with two dicks. Most Israelis come to India, others go to South America, and some to your Australia.' (I'd previously learnt there could be as many as 50,000 Israeli tourists in India at any one time.) 'So when did you finish your service?' he asked, turning to Lior.

'Six months ago.'

'Exactly, and the first thing you wanted to do was leave that fucking place, right?'

'Yes, but my good heart will kill me in the end anyway. If things at home get worse, and I get the call to fight, I'll gladly do it. Fucking gladly!'

'And what would happen if you didn't go back?' I asked.

The three of them went quiet.

'Then when I return to Israel, as soon as I walk through

customs—*bang!*—I'd be thrown into military prison.'

The waiter arrived with our food, and having eaten more rice of late than I wished to for the rest of my life, the sight of falafel, hummus, and chocolate balls, was a more than welcome one.

We sat around over a few more hot milks, until our guests stood up an hour or so later. 'Shalom to you, brother,' said Eval, handing me his email address, 'if ever you come to Israel, you're welcome in my house like family.'

'See you again,' said Ariella, furthering her spell by giving me another kiss on the cheek before they walked away.

'Ah, man! I think I'm in love!' said Lior.

'Just give me a minute, mate.'

He sank back into the couch as we observed in respectful silence.

'So anyway, mate, you were going to ask me something…'

'What?'

'Before they came along, you were going to ask me something…'

'Ahhhr… you know what?'

'What?'

'I can't remember it now.'

'Don't torture me with that!'

He brushed me off with his trademark dismissive wave.

We made our way back out onto the streets, which, as though by nocturnal command were alive with blokes and girls, and dogs and girls, and cows and girls—and, girls.

'Man, I can't get over all the girls!'

'Mate, I'm in enough pain via my own eyes.'

'Yeah, but look at her!' he said, causing me to turn suddenly and meet eyes with yet another temptress dressed to hurt.

'Fair dinkum, my neck can't handle this.'

'You want a cigarette?'

'Yeah, give me two.'

The next morning I was awoken by traditional music blaring across the lake. It was early, and I lay in bed for a languorous smidge longer before walking onto the balcony. With the piercingly bright sun just sneaking over the horizon, the lake glistened like a crystal of mystery in the barren surround. As a mirror the size of a football field, it reflected each bird flying slowly across the dawn sky, and like frantic players in an otherwise motionless scene, down below were hundreds of long-tailed monkeys jumping across the rooftops.

My lungs felt tight from the smoking; still it was my intention to continue the breathing rebellion.

'Shalom, brother,' croaked Lior, rising to his feet and strolling onto the balcony.

'Yeah, nice hair,' I said, for if ever a man had ever risen to the cusp of a bad hair day, he had to a bad hair life. It was dark, curly, and so offensively expansive that it surely enjoyed a passport of its own. But caring not a jot, he stretched his arms, scratched his under, and emptied his lungs from what sounded like the lower intestine up.

'A bit early for foreplay isn't it, mate?'

He shrugged his shoulders and lit a cigarette.

'So how does this lake exist in the middle of the desert anyway? I mean, it's not as if it ever rains out here.'

'The locals believe it was created by the impact of fighting gods.'

'Like one of 'em dropped his helmet?'

'Something like that, and it's proven to have existed as early as the 4th century B.C.'

'How do you know this stuff?'

'I read, the Internet mostly. I'm almost finished.'

I went back inside and tied my shoelaces.

'Where you going?'

'To see the psycho-mechanic and check on this bike of mine. Can you give us a dink?'

We soon made it the workshop, and although the apprentices were tinkering on this and that, my beloved blue bike was nowhere to be seen.

'You want a cigarette?'

'Yeah,' I said, feeling suddenly nervous.

With his deep-set frown looking as grave as the day before, the red-turban-wearing-boss appeared from around the corner. 'Good day, sir, I am being the boss here. How can I help you?'

'I was here yest—'

'—Actually, sir, excuse me for one moment.'

I was shocked by his inability to recognise me, but before I could explain that we'd met, he turned around and screamed at his apprentices with his trademark malice.

'Sorry, sir, how can I help you?' he asked, turning back and forcing a smile.

'I was here yesterday. You do remember me… don't you?'

He looked at me blankly, as though recollecting a file from a bundle of others. 'Oh yes! The blue Enfield! It is ready, one moment,' he said, turning to his boys. 'Bring me the fucking Enfield!' A hunched lad appeared from around the corner, wheeling a squeaky-wheeled red motorbike. 'Not that one! The blue one! The fucking blue one!'

'A thousand apologies, sir,' he said, turning back and straightening his turban. 'It's just, these boys are my nephews—'

'—And it's your responsibility to teach them to be men. I know, you told me yesterday.'

The apprentice returned with the Blue Fly. On top of fixing it, they'd cleaned it to a spiffy showroom standard.

'So what was wrong with it?' I asked.

'To fix the bike, the something that we did, is something that at this point in time, I can no longer remember.'

'I'm afraid I'm going to need a bit more clarity there, mate.'

'It's like when god set out to climb the tree, and when he

reached to the top he learnt there was a ladder he could have used.'

'And how is you not remembering how you fixed my bike remotely similar to god and trees?'

'I'm not so sure myself. Cup of chai?'

I was beyond caring, and with the day just getting away, I wanted to get a move on.

'So what's the damage?' I asked.

'No, sir, everything went well in the operation. There is no damage.'

'No, I mean, how much money do I owe you?'

'Oh well, let me see...' he said, and counting his fingers, moustache, and the rest, he started mumbling the maths. 'I'm sorry, sir, but the price has worked out to be a bit more than expected.'

'Indeed,' I thought, wondering if this spiel was some sort of oath that every mechanic learns at trade school.

'I'm afraid the final price is three hundred and fifty rupees.'

And quickly counting my fingers, moustache and the rest, I did the maths, realising the price was as a mere ten dollars Australian. Can you imagine that faring Down Under? Neither can I.

I paid him his money, and feeling as re-empowered as a suspended police officer being handed back the gun, I slung myself onto the bike.

I kicked the kick-starter, but there was no response. I kicked again, but nothing... and again, but still nothing... 'Hang on, this isn't good...'

The mechanic backed away.

Lior approached. 'No, brother, you can't just *start* an Enfield. You need to seduce the bike into doing what you want.'

'Mate, I think all this girl-induced tension is getting the better of you.'

'Listen! There is a trick to starting an Enfield. When the bike is cold in the mornings, just put it into neutral and walk it for about ten metres. This sucks the petrol through the carburettor and I guarantee you it will start first kick.'

I did as he said. As it roared to life it occurred to me that each time I'd failed to start it in the mornings, I'd done just that. Put the bike into neutral and walked it while looking for help; setting it up to start first kick for the person helping, leaving me to wonder why the touch of god was in their leg and not mine.

'Bring me the fucking oil tray!' bawled the mechanic. 'Thank you. Come again.'

We sat straddled across our bikes. 'Do you want to go to the Pushkar Camel Fair?'

'What's that?'

'It's the annual gathering of the camels of Rajasthan.'

'And what happens?'

'Dunno, they compete and complain about their back problems.'

'Cool.'

We clicked our bikes in gear, but just as we were about to take off, the little trumpet-kid from the day before came wandering up the street, this time armed with a snare drum.

'I guess he's giving a new instrument a try,' said Lior, and as we thumped it up the road, we heard it one last time. 'Not that oil tray! The fucking big one!'

Having cruised the tumbling desert hills, we soon made it to the festival.

The horizon was a blur of camels growling and flicking up the dust. Where the desert spectrum was typically ochre and submissive, the festival was an uprising of every colour in the rainbow—with men wearing their loudest turbans, and women gliding about in their showiest dresses. Even the camels looked as though they'd been counting back the date on their calendars; donning beaded facemasks and mounted with intricately embroidered saddles. Some were even perfumed for the event, perhaps explaining the financial viability of Old Spice.

The first camel contest began, a stacks-on strength test known as the *Laadoo Oonth*, where the camels were sat down, loaded up with cargo of giggling men, and ordered to stand up. The first camel off the rank looked less than happy, but it—and I— felt strangely better when it turned about-face and sprayed its unwanted cargo with foam.

We wandered around the grounds, during which I caught myself holding my hands together behind my back like a retiree holidaying in Prague. Lior wandered off, leaving me to soak up the prophecy of Pushkar being the Promised Land of Elven Shoes. With stall after stall of red ones, green ones, blue ones—and shoes that even shoes could wear—there were enough on show for a millipede and his mates.

'Hello, sir, camel for you?' asked a man.

'Ahhhr… no thanks,' I said, turning to him and his beast, 'I'm just looking.'

The camel inhaled sharply, as though it were about to sneeze. 'But look, he is a beautiful boy!'

'He is?' I asked, sidestepping out of the way as the beast unleashed the snot of a thousand men. 'So what's his name?'

'Alfred.'

'Alfred?' I thought, unable to think why not.

I approached tentatively, and patted his neck, to which he shook his head and gave a hearty moan of protest. He then stepped forward in small steps, revealing that his feet were tied in the toilet paper hostage knot. I gave the man a meekly disapproving look, to which he wobbled his head and rubbed his fingers together. Begrudgingly, I handed him some rupees, and untying the legs of his friend by no means, he pocketed the money with devastating skill.

'How about some shoes for you, sir?' he said, producing a large tray. As his tone veered into auto-delivery I couldn't help but get the feeling I wasn't the first to hear it. 'All of these shoes are made out of camel's leather… but please understand that none of the camels are ever killed… we only use the leather from camels that die naturally…'

'So these shoes were once Alfred's brother?'

'Yes, his brother was a good man.'

'It's just… he was a camel?'

'Yes.'

'They're about to do the camel race!' said a voice. It was Lior.

Alfred turned to his master and inhaled sharply, cueing our earnest departure.

We made our way to the dirt track and took a standing position. It was smaller than a horseracing track, giving us a clear view of the camels grumbling at the starting line. To their side was a short man holding a starting gun. '*Ready, setty…*'—he stopped to readjust himself—'*go!*'

Umpteen camels took off as though he who crossed the finish line first would be awarded one full day without having to carry a thing at all. I mean, really, what other golden carrot would rouse a camel? The red dust stirred as the crowd cheered, and with the stride of the camels longer than that of a horse, the riders were being bounced like tennis balls. I hadn't time to study the fixture, but assuming the favourite was the hairy one with the hump, he soared across the line in first place. The victorious rider, typical of any triumphant male, pranced along the section of audience most filled with women.

'Well, Aussie brother, I've had enough fur for one day. I'm going to ride back to Pushkar.'

'I'll join you.'

With the dust bellowing off us, we coasted parallel on the highway hills.

'So tell me,' said Lior, stifling a smoker's cough, 'do you have a girlfriend?'

'Haven't we already had this conversation?'

'Yeah, but that was yesterday, things can change in 24 hours.'

'Not that quick, they can't. No, I haven't, and neither do you, right?'

'No,' he said. The matter again opened and closed from one neighbouring second to the next.

We'd ridden a few kilometres, when up ahead on the roadside we spotted a local man trying to fix his motorbike.

We pulled over.

'Hullo!' I said with my crappily adapted accent. Looking relieved at the prospect of assistance, he smiled.

'What do you think is wrong with it?' I asked, to which shrugging his shoulders, I gathered his English wasn't up to the question.

His bike was a little 100cc Honda Hero, a dime a dozen in India. Typically, it didn't give me a teaspoon of response as I tried to kick it over.

'Well, buggered if I know.'

Lior lit up. 'What does it mean, this "buggered if I know" that Aussies say?'

'Ahhhr… it means, "at this point in time, I seem to be falling short of the necessary information required to solve the problem at hand."'

'You want a cigarette?'

'Ssshhh… so have you got any more lovemaking tricks to seduce this little beast?'

He hopped on and gave it a few earnest kicks, to which the bike performed a succession of fading farts.

The man just stood there; the slouch of his shoulders saying it all.

'You've got some rope in your toolbox, don't you?' I asked Lior.

He nodded.

'Do you want to grab it for us then?'

'You and who else?'

'Mate, you're at least at *level two* of Australian slang by now. I've already told you, *us* is singular.'

He handed me the rope.

'You go ahead.' I said, tying it from my bike to the other. 'We're about ten kilometres out of Pushkar. I guess I'll just tow him back.'

He hopped on his bike and smiled sarcastically. 'See ya! Wouldn't want to be ya!'

And as he vanished up the road in a trail of red dust, my shoulders slouched to match those of my new friend. Without word, the man and I slung ourselves onto our bikes and the journey began.

It was the hardest of work, for we were going so slow that if a sloth rollerbladed past and handed me a can of beer, I would have been less surprised than grateful. Slowly we kept at it, and with the therapeutic effect of ticking wheels proving a great source of hypnosis, I soon fell into the chasm of my head, and while down there I started thinking—thinking about things, and while thinking about things, I thought, 'I think I'll just sit here and think for a while.'

The high blinding sun baked the desert below, and if ever there was a time I appreciated not being made out of vanilla ice cream, it was then. I kept turning around to check on my mate, and each time he wobbled his head, as if gently showing his appreciation.

We tinkered forth, at a pace that would drive a snail to drink, and with our squeaky wheels tweeting underneath, at one point a cart being towed by the world's most jaded-looking donkey gradually overtook us.

'G'day,' I said, turning to the donkey.

'Did you know that if you take the peripheral foretelling of when the Buddha backdates his enlightenment, and divide it by the cubic measure of all the world's beer, that you discover the eleven secret herbs and spices in KFC chicken?' said the donkey back.

'Jeez,' I thought.

My face elongated with boredom, as the sun rose and fell like a basketball being dribbled on the horizon. My grey beard grew into the spokes of my wheels and my fingernails into the distance. A hawk, holding cutlery, circled above, and just as I realised the squeak of my wheels was in fact a riveting conversation being had between them, we thankfully rolled into Pushkar.

I untied our bikes, and feeling like your neighbourhood-friendly Good Samaritan, I was expecting him to shower me with thank-yous, flowers and the rest. Instead, he gestured for me to take a seat on a small wooden crate on the footpath.

Although he poured me a cup of chai, I was quite taken aback not hearing the words I was conditioned to expect. Having later learnt that pleasantries were, to Indians, considered impersonal between friends, I eventually grew accustomed.

He soon poured me a second cup, and he sat there, with his face poised with a subtle and dignified smile. I fished out my camera and gestured if it would be ok to take his picture, to which he nodded gently.

I pointed the camera his way, yet right at the juncture where you expect someone to smile or compensate some insecurity, he gazed down the barrel with seemingly zero fear at all.

I took the photo, and with every line on his face as truthful on screen as in reality, it was as perfect as nature wound intend.

I showed him, and he approved it with an apathetic nod, accepting the image of himself without a flinch of self-consciousness. I was in awe of his self-assurance, and I quietly wondered how it was so.

I finished my chai and gestured farewell.

As the last orange of dusk was departing over the horizon, I made it back to the room to find Lior in the house. 'Shit man, I thought you died out there!'

'So did I.'

'Do you want to eat?'

'Yeah! Let's go get a t-bone, a lamb shank, a souvlaki and—'

'—Brother, I've told you, this country is vegetarian.'

'Well f#&k'n… at least I'm not the one who fails to say please and thank you when I ask for things!'

'Man, you need sex.'

I hated to admit it, but he was right. In fact, it'd been so long that I'd surely forgotten how babies were even made, or what to do if given the chance to make one.

'Sorry, mate, it's just… it's all getting to me; this imposed vegetarianism, and state of total girlless-ness.'

He nodded.

'Something's gotta give or I'm gunna flat out do me na-na!'

'What does it mean, this "do my na-na" that Aussies say?'

'Ahhhr… it means, "if I am pushed any further in this unfavourable direction, I'll be rendered no choice but to lose all control."'

'You want a cigarette?'

'Is it bacon flavoured?'

We got ourselves organised and took to the streets, and as per usual, the winding laneways were alive with blokes and girls, and dogs and girls, and cows and girls—and, girls.

'Man, I can't get over all the girls!'

'Mate, you need to learn some new songs.'

'Fuck off!' he hinted.

'So what do you want to eat?'

'All of them!'

I put a hand on his shoulder. 'Just focus on the exhalation.'

'I've got to get out of here, truly. Have I even told you I'm leaving tomorrow?'

'For real?'

He nodded.

'So this is like our Last Supper?' I asked, taking a second to reminisce my own in Melbourne.

'Yes.'

Acting out of nostalgia, we made our way back to the same Israeli lair as the previous night. As we sat on the couch in the far corner, I noticed again, hanging above us, the same small flyer: *Traditional Indian Singing Lessons*. 'Could be cool?' I thought, this time tearing off one of the tags and putting it in my pocket.

'So where are you off to?' I asked.

'I think I'll start riding south to Goa. It's a long way, but it'll be worth it for the weather and beach parties. You?'

'I'm still keen to head west to Jaisalmer.'

'I'm not sure it's so smart. It's deep into the desert, very close to Pakistan, and your bike might not make it.'

'I'm just thinking about it. Anyway, there wouldn't be any particular reason we're sitting in the same spot as last night, would there?'

He shrugged his shoulders.

'Reasons including a potential second coming of Ariella?'

'Don't be ridiculous!'

'Well, to quote the words of a mate of mine back home—she was so bad, she was good.'

'Yes, she was, but she had a guy.'

'So you're not such an endorser of the cuttings of lunch?'

'What does it mean, this "cutting lunch" that Aussies say?'

'Ahhhr… I guess it's a lax term for the unspoken war between all blokes.'

'What war?'

'The Charm Wars.'

'You're not wrong.'

'As in, *I'm right*?'

'Yes.'

'Well done, mate! That was perfect Australian practice of a double negative equalling a positive.'

'Cool, you want a cigarette?'

'Most certainly. You know, I've been meaning to start smoking for ages. Thanks, you got me motivated.'

We marked his farewell over a few hot milks, before making our way back into the bustling laneways. There seemed to be an influx of locals, coupled with traditional music blaring across the lake; both likely due to a Hindu calendar event.

Lior dragged his cigarette with obsessive force. 'So, my Aussie friend, this is it, our last walk together on the streets of Pushkar.'

'I guess it is.'

Aside from the canary I'd set free in Meerut, he'd essentially been my first mate since leaving the ashram.

A western girl walked past and hip and shouldered me. 'Sorry!' she said, giggling and clasping onto the arm of her friend. I smiled awkwardly. Lior shrugged his shoulders.

'So anyway, mate, are you going to relieve me of the suspense?'

'What?'

'Have you remembered the question you were going to ask me last night in the restaurant before Eval and Ariella came over?'

'Oh yes! What I was going to ask you was… what does—' but when a group of girls walked past—one of whom gave him a direct bullet of glad-eye—his mind switched like a TV channel. 'Ah, man! Did you see that? Her eyes were like a laser beam!'

'Well, don't let me stop you.'

'But what would I say?'

The two of us came to a standstill as she stopped in the distance.

'The force is strong in you. Feel, don't think.'

The music escalated, and with it girls seemed to be appearing all around, like a Lynx deodorant commercial. Lior, despite his gains, looked positively flummoxed, and he dragged his cigarette as though he were being hung at midnight 'How did god create such a powerful creature? And where did he get the design idea?'

'Mate, now is not the time for analysis.'

'I mean, look at her, she has an invisible power over both of us.'

'Your clock is ticking!'

'I don't even know why it is,' he said, crushing out his cigarette as forcefully as he'd smoked it, 'but for her I'd tear you apart like a piece of bread.'

Perhaps it was from his comment—or the wounding absence of any incoming glad-eye for myself—but it was then that I felt a primal pilot light ignite within. Lior's cracker-rant ascended steadily, as did my interest in it correspondingly decline. Fanning my internal flames, the music rose into a threatening rhythm, and I started to feel as hot as I did dizzy. Girls seemed to be circling like sharks—as though in some premeditated tactical manoeuvre—and my comrade and I could do little more but spiral in the sea of jean shorts and derisive laughter. Lior was looking less than his best, and his mouth hung as such that the flies of Pushkar finally found a place they could call home. I called out to him—as if through water—to which he turned to me with a zombie-like gaze and grabbed me by the shirt. 'Help me!'

'Let go of me!'

'Help me!'

'Pull yourself together!'

'It's a trap!'

'No one can help you! Do you understand?'

'They're everywhere!'

'We are the weaker half of the species and that's just the way it is!'

'Lord, I concede!'

I sighted his love interest, still in the distance.

'Look, mate, there's just no way a girl could find a bloke like *you* as attractive as you find a girl like *that*. Blokes just can't be that attractive! It's just not physically possible! Personally, I don't think girls are even attracted to blokes at all! They just can't think of anything better to do! And another thing… why—*the fff*—'

'—David?' interrupted a familiar female voice, and when I turned to see, to my surprise, shock, delight, awkwardness and the rest, standing there was Kayley the English girl I'd followed to Agra.

Every word fell from my control, and I turned back to Lior feeling dumber than dumber. 'You see, Aussie brother,' he said, quickly straightening the fist marks out of my shirt. 'I told you things can change in 24 hours—one minute no girlfriend, the next perhaps.'

I failed to respond, but to Lior I must have.

'—Ssshhh…' he said, 'don't let me stop you.' A sudden sense of awareness seemed to come over him; like a dog coming out of anaesthesia. 'Shalom to you, brother,' he said, putting his hand firm into mine. 'May the force be with you.'

I nodded faintly.

He exhaled long, flattened his ridiculous hair, and with hopes of horizontal taekwondo in his eyes, he b-lined it towards his girl. Still, however, without asking his mysterious unfinished question.

I turned back to Kayley, and standing before me with her dark wavy hair and smouldering green eyes, still she was so excruciatingly magnificent that the thought of kissing her was more heartrending than a teaspoon of water after crossing the desert naked while carrying a bar fridge full of dead wombats— or something like that.

I stood before her, as vulnerably as the day I was born, and where I hoped for my opening words to be poised, dignified, and laced with integrity and wit, my voice seemed to have filed for annual leave.

'Aren't you going to say something?'

Nothing followed.

'Well?'

'Fff...'

'What?'

'Fffuuu...'

'Pardon?'

'Ahem... fuck!'

'Come again?'

'Yes please!'

'Feeling better?'

I cleared my throat. 'Weren't you going back to England like two days after we said goodbye in Agra?'

'We were, but we decided to extend.'

'We?' thought I, as the proverbial penny dropped like a bowling ball when her mother came parading out of a nearby shop. 'David-darling! Well, hello!'

'Ahhhr... hello, Mummy,' I said, my inner flower wilting thus.

'Fabulous place for shopping, wouldn't you agree?'

'Sometimes,' I said, noticing over her shoulder a fresh trail of distraught merchants.

'Now Kayley-darling, we must go get a facial, a tweezing, a manicure, a pedicure...'

My head began to whirr with a familiar war siren.

'Joining us for a pedicure, David-darling?'

'Ahhhr... no thanks. I only cut my toenails every February 29th.'

'Too funny, come then Kayley-darling, our driver is waiting.'

But it was then, just as she had that night by the Ganges, that Kayley clasped my hand into hers.

An awkward silence returned, and as though still baffled by the attraction, Mummy's face pored with thought. 'Well... I guess he's looking a bit healthier than when we saw him last,' she said in her trademark tone as though I were absent. Bidding us a much-appreciated farewell, however, she turned and departed.

I turned back to Kayley. 'I just can't believe you're here! I don't know what to say, think, do! It's like you're going to disappear in a puff of pink dust.'

'Crazy, isn't it! We've been in Pushkar a couple of days now.'

'And how long are you here?'

'We're leaving in the morning.'

As though in natural resumption of our walk along the Ganges, we began moseying through the labyrinth of winding streets, and as per the harsh extremes of the desert climate, the scorching day had fallen to an icy night. There was not a cloud in the Rajasthani sky, and with a fogless canvas on which to show off, it hosted a shooting star show worthy of an astrologer's convention.

'So how did you get here?'

'Motorbike.'

'Really? Or is this another one of your dolphin trainer stories?'

'A man does what a boy can.'

'Bless.'

'Bless? Oh I remember, it's a term of endearment.'

We kept walking, and lured by the music blaring across the lake, we made our way down to the water. There were hundreds gathered at the banks, most dressed in colourful attire, and many of whom were seated in large groups—singing and playing percussive instruments. In my time in India, I was never a tourist who learnt the names and exact meanings of each religious occasion, but I did feel I absorbed some of the feeling from them. By the haunting whirr of the crowd, and the sight of floating candles drifting across the lake—their sputtering flames reflecting in the water as they bumped along—this night was just such an occasion.

We walked to the lake's quieter side, and, having taken off our shoes, sat side-by-side on the pebbly bank. I was still very taken aback by our chance meeting, and it having been my experience so far that walking arm-in-arm with her in romantic settings was less an indicator of interest than a means to retain balance, I knew not what she was thinking. The Agra debacle played vividly in my mind, and although the lion in the grass wished to pounce, it wasn't me that was going to initiate any new advance.

'So,' she said.

'So,' I returned, the two of us off to a fabulously dead-end start.

'You know, I missed you after you left Agra.'

'I'm flattered, I suppose.'

'Were you annoyed after you left?'

'Annoyed would be a rich way of putting it. I just felt like a bit of a dill really.'

'Well, sorry.'

'Don't be. At least my curiosity was satisfied.'

'What's that supposed to mean?'

'If I hadn't have come to Agra, I would have been left wondering what might have happened if I did, so I at least got my answer.'

'That's pretty clinical.'

'Perhaps, but I don't know how two people, neither in their own country, could have tested it otherwise. Besides, it was you who invited me to come see you yet was ever so surprised when I turned up.'

She seemed to be cracking it, at least mildly, which I found exquisitely empowering.

'I wanted to...' she said.

'To what?'

'You know...'

'What?'

'You know...'

'What?'

'Don't make me say it!'

'All right then.'

'It's just...'

'Just what?'

'It's just...' she stopped and exhaled forcefully, 'I'm married.'

Like the tide going out, all traces of blood drained from me, leaving me to feel a perfect absence of everything. Until, that was, the wave of offense, in all its fuming momentum, came flooding back.

'Married?'

'I'm sorry, but—'

'—Then why in Haridwar were you acting so *unmarried*? In turn leading me to follow you all the way to Agra?'

'You're not letting me finish!'

'I'm Dumbo I'm so all ears!'

'I'm married, but we're in the process of getting divorced, and I haven't been with anyone since, and it's all a bit—'

'—A bit?'

'A bit—'

'—What?'

'A bit exciting!'

'Glad to be of help!'

'It's just, you were so nice to me in Haridwar, and I wasn't used to the attention, and...'

'And?'

'And… it doesn't matter now anyway.'

She stood up fast and walked up the pebbly bank, almost slipping as she did.

'Watch your footing, ey?'

'I'm fine.'

'I'm talking about your mum's warning that night by the car, now it all makes sense.' I stood up and walked up to her, and she grabbed onto my arm. The music seemed to have died down, and the floating candles were close to burnt out. 'Married, ey?'

She raised her eyebrows cynically.

'You don't hear that everyday.'

'Anyway, I'm not anymore.'

'More information..'

'The papers have gone through.'

And introducing the voice of guest narrator, Sir David Attenborough: 'and with the lions in the grass pouncing simultaneously, they lunged lip to lip. Whereupon the remaining details are not suitable for public consumption.'

*****

Dear Manuel,

As the song says, love is a battlefield, or as the other song says, Old MacDonald had a farm, ee i ee i oh..

*****

The next day unfurled into the sky, and having bid our farewell, where Kayley turned left toward a bus station—that would take her to an airport, that would have a big shiny plane, that would fly her far far away—I turned right toward my hotel.

I made it back, and Lior too had all but departed. I wandered around the room, feeling decidedly lonely, when I found a scrunched up piece of paper in my pocket: *Traditional Indian Singing Lessons*. I'd forgotten all about it.

I decided to sign on.

I walked through the hustling morning laneways with a spring in my step, and having over the course of my footsteps decided I was going to quit my Lior-inspired smoking habit, I was feeling rather exultant. Until then, when just upon the door of the place, my brain kicked in. 'Hang on, I hate singing lessons!'

It was true, for it was in my experience, with the handful I'd had, that enduring some cranky old coach breathing down your neck and trying to manipulate you into sounding like a power tool in need of oil—'breathe, sit, poise, stand up, smile, smile wider, smile wider again, fart, poise, stand straight, breathe, turn around, roll over, shake, hold your breath for twelve minutes, no turning purple allowed, back straight, fart, poise, breathe'— singing lessons were far more of a confidence destroyer than builder.

One particular teacher I had proposed that for that day's lesson she was going to teach me how to sing with *emotion*. I was horrified. I mean, how can you teach someone to sing with *their* emotion when you are not that person hence have no idea of the emotional fibre through which they'd sing *emotionally*? Even more insipid, I think what she meant was that for that day's lesson she was going to teach me the technicalities of how to *fake* emotion, which, for the fact that I sing in the hope of shedding a drop of the ocean's worth I already have, I found it duly irritating.

The single greatest quote I've ever heard in describing types of music was by Flea of the Red Hot Chili Peppers, who, in his wealth of passion and experience, said; 'There are only two types of music—soulful and soulless.' Agreeing that it was such a great way of overviewing *all* kinds of music, I had goose bumps when I read it, and upon reflection since I've often felt this simple, yet powerful testimonial is pertinent in describing the authenticity of many things, including singers.

You can spot the singers that have had too many lessons. They sound as though before having found their own unique dirt, they've been polished to the point of losing their shine, or had their seed crushed before it's even sprouted. And speaking, just quietly, of the work of vocal gymnasts—who, seemingly allergic to holding a note, trill about like a leaf in a hurricane—the only thing I find it *moves* is constipation. I mean, sure, have someone give you a few tips and the like—how to not lose your voice, etc.— but being puppeteered into singing with factory preset emotion is enough to make me choose to hold my breath not for twelve minutes, but twelve days.

I certainly don't profess to be much of a singer. If anything, I think I'm a reasonably good *crap singer* as opposed to a reasonably crap *good singer*. But if I were to credit myself at all, I would by claiming my abilities are not learnt, but self-taught, my feeling being that anything useful attained in life is done this way.

As someone with a voice that could once make a cat shed eight lives per earful, I learnt to sing the old-fashioned way, from being out in pubs, fulfilling my quota of out-of-tune notes, and enduring punters less than gift-wrapping their disapproval. But it was from doing this—and busking when out travelling, and tweaking away with mates back home—that over time I progressed to a level where I half knew what I was doing and my confidence and stamp grew from there. This is how you *find* your voice, and because it comes from *you* and is a product of your emotional catalogue—which is exclusively *your own*—it cannot be handed to you like a crayon with which to go away and draw. It is your experience—no one can give it to you, and no one can take it away. And upon snapping, now, back into the need to continue with not only my opinions, but the narrative, let me just state that the view has been truly spectacular from a horse this high. 〰

But figuring this one in India might make for something different, I rang the doorbell.

'Yes?' asked an old man with a short white beard.

'I'm here to have a singing lesson, if that's all right?'

'Yes. Please, come in.'

I removed my sandals, and after hitting my head on the low door beam, I entered. The man—instructing me after the fact to mind my head—disappeared through a beaded doorway.

I stood in the entrance room of this eccentric little house, somewhere in a faraway northern desert of India. Although I felt privy to be getting such an exclusive gander at its innards, I felt suddenly nervous as to why I was here.

With a tray of hot chai in hand, he returned and stood opposite me, saying not a word, as though studying me before speaking. I gazed up at the clock, needing to know the time by automation.

'So tell me, young man, are you a singer already?'

'Well, I think I am, but I don't really know what I'm doing. It just kind of happens.'

'Singing is not a sport. A real singer is in tune with his heart. Not with knowing what *happens*.'

I was thoroughly refreshed already.

'Come,' he said, 'we will have the lesson on the roof.'

We walked up to the rooftop terrace, where the full expanse of the desert spanned its wings. With its glassy surface mirroring the pale day moon, the roof boasted an even better view of the lake than from the hotel balcony.

There was a small lessons area, complete with an arrangement of large vivid cushions and straw mats. Taking the edge off the hot day, tingling overhead was an array of wind chimes. He ordered me to sit, and I lowered myself cross-legged.

He sat opposite, nursing an Indian *tabla drum*, and as though zoning himself up before commencing, he played it with his eyes closed. I turned my gaze towards the lake, spending a few quiet seconds noticing the sun's rays reflecting off its surface, when, disturbing the serenity with a great thump, two grey monkeys jumped onto the rooftop.

The teacher opened his eyes. 'Ok, let us begin,' he said. 'Sing me a song, young man.'

Stirring in my cushion, I proceeded to give him a sample.

I was understandably nervous. Turning to each other with faces fraught with opinion—their presence not dissimilar to having in attendance Statler and Waldorf, the two old blokes from the Muppets—even the monkeys looked consumed with judgment. Unlike they, though, the teacher gave away little of his thoughts and he just sat there tapping his drum, making not the slightest shift in demeanour.

I finished up.

'So you come from the world of *Do Re Mi Fa So La Ti Do*?'

'What's that?'

'The basis of all western music.'

'I guess so.'

'Well, I come from the world of *Sa Re Ga Ma Pa Dha Ni Sa*.'

He put down his drum and reached for a different instrument. It was like an eastern-equivalent of a squeezebox accordion, and making a loud dissonant drone, it was far from my idea of a cup of sonic tea.

'We will sing through the major scale—ascending and descending,' he said, 'and in-between each note we will make râga-style improvisations.'

'What's *râga*?'

'It's a Sanskrit term for melodic formula.'

'And what's *Sanskrit*?'

'It's the oldest of all Indian languages. Follow me.'

As I followed, though, I was terribly pitch-vague, for unlike when singing in the western scale, I could barely predict the next-coming note. Joining me in my concern, it seemed, the Muppet Monkeys looked less than impressed.

'I'm sorry, but I feel like I'm going for a walk in an unfamiliar place.'

'That's ok,' he said, 'just keep singing with me. I'm not here to tell you what to do, but to encourage you into your abilities.'

His attitude was a welcomed contrast to that of my western teachers, and after about fifteen minutes I felt fairly locked in to the eastern scale. It was quite an exalting experience, in fact, for hearing my voice singing in a style I'd never heard it before, I felt less like a constituent than an on-listener.

The lesson wound up after an hour, and although I wasn't sure if what I'd learnt would be of much benefit in my own musical endeavours, the experience had definitely been memorable.

We stood up to bid our farewells, and he spoke. 'At the beginning of the lesson I thought you were bloody-shit, but now I think you are bloody-ok.'

I was well chuffed, knowing there to be few higher honours than to be revered as bloody-ok. The two of us shook hands, and the Muppet Monkeys broke into a firm round of applause. Actually, no they didn't.

Back to my old state of mateless-ness, that night I took to the streets on my own, and as per usual, the winding laneways were alive with blokes and girls, and dogs and girls, and cows and girls—and, girls.

I walked along, in casual hunt of a restaurant, when I heard what sounded like crows squawking in the distance. I tuned into the sound, and as though it was a long lost, yet inherent, part of my psyche, something in my nature started to stir. The sound grew louder, and my curiosity grew equally, when two blokes wearing Melbourne footy jumpers came wandering around the corner. They were Australians.

'Oi!' I yelled out as they passed.

'Ey Aussie!' said one.

'Farcken g'day!' said his mate.

And as though by automation, we stood about in a circle—playing out our native male habit of folding our arms and talking in voices deeper than natural.

'So where are you two blokes from?'

'Don't the footy tops give ya a hint, mate?'

'Melbourne?'

'Shit-yeah!'

Their names were Alex and Owen, and mine was Dave, but by friendly default we referred to each other as Alo, Davo, and the unforgivably Australian—O'o.

'This place is off its chops, Davo! How's all the girls?'

'Mate, you're fair dinkum preaching to the choir.'

'Yeah, but look at her!' he said, and like a trio of synchronised swimmers, we harmonised our whiplash.

'We're about to grab something to eat, Davo. Keen?'

'Yeah-nah abso-bloody-lutely!'

We walked along the streets, just the three of us.

'So what d'you wanna eat, Alo?'

'Her!'

'Other than her?'

'Her mate!'

It felt as if he was paying tribute to Lior, and while walking along O'o kept himself entertained by tenderly antagonising Israeli girls—'g'day, gorgeous, how ya getting on? D'you know *why* they call it Down Under?'

Sensing no malice, their responses were mostly smiles, and for me, having been without the company of Australians for longer than I could remember, hearing such rustic banter was music to my ears.

We chose a restaurant and settled in on its rooftop terrace. 'Not a bad perch, boys,' said Alo, 'well suited to surveillance.'

A waiter approached.

'G'day, sport, give us a round of your finest apple juices, please.' O'o ordered.

'Apple juice? Bit tender, isn't it?'

'Davo. Just sit back, relax, and learn something.'

'S'pose.'

'So how long you been o.s., Davo?'

'Ahhhr… I've been overseas… for about… ages. Youse?'

'For us, been on for young and old… for about… ages as well.'

'And where in Pushkar are youse staying?'

'Hotel Shonk.'

'Not much chop?'

'Chopless.'

'Why?'

'Coz it's a porthole for all the dunny-budgies of the universe.'

'And the head's up on dunny-budgies?'

'Flies in the toilet.'

'Righto.'

'So where's those apple juices, Jack?'

'Should be any tick of the clock.'

'They're pretty busy in this joint.'

'As flat out as a lizard drinking.'

'What's the g.o. with ordering food then?'

'Dunno, but I'm starving.'

'Love to go a bit of flake.'

'And a pickled onion!'

The waiter returned, and the mystery of the apple juices was revealed. It was beer—foaming, wet, frothy beer. I was astounded, and with a faint wink the waiter poured three glasses and tucked the half-empties under our table.

'What's the go there? I didn't know you could get a beer in the entire country!'

'Apple juice, Davo. Wrap your laughing gear around that.'

I sat there with an unspoiled glass in hand, studying it as though it were once my old lore. 'Ya know, I haven't so much as had a sip of beer since Moses' mum taught him how to strap on his sandals.'

'Well, that decides the toast then,' marked O'o, 'to Davo's inevitable return.'

And upon clinking our glasses—and tipping them down our fat necks—I could do nothing but grin, for the flaccid flower in my heart bloomed once more, and having got it any-old-how, my taste buds, like the *Benzedrine Monks of Santo Domonica*, broke into a choir rendition of the theme music from the old VB beer commercial. 'Dramatic?' Perhaps not, for as a matter-of-fact, I had it right-then, and my return sip was just that emotional.

'So how's that working out for ya, Davo?'

'Mate, there are no words.'

'All in moderation.'

'That's it.'

'Just don't chuck an Alo and end up laying pavement pizza.'

'Spew?'

'Technicolour yawn on all channels.'

'Chunder stopping at all stations.'

'From Coober Pedy to Timbuck—'

'—Ahr-choo!'

I couldn't deny that tasting the long-forgotten tang of beer was like being reacquainted with a lost love, but despite the joy I could feel my I.Q. dropping by the mouthful. 'Boys, I think I'll finish this one glass and leave it at that. I can feel myself morphing into me evil twin brother.'

'And what sort of a bloke is he?'

'One best left in the basement.'

'An honourable display, Davo, but not a track we'll join you on.'

'So if alcohol is illegal in India—' I, in my naivety, began, 'what happens to the waiter-bloke if he gets caught by the cops?'

'Davo, Davo, Davo, you disappoint me, son. The cops are in on it, and the restaurant pays 'em off every month to keep their mouths shut.'

'Like the Al Capone days?'

'That's it.'

'What do they pay 'em in?'

'JB gift vouchers and fried dim sims!'

'I fair dinkum loathe the cops in this country.'

'You're not wrong. Some days it makes me wanna smack someone.'

'Alo, you can't get about always wanting to snot every bastard.'

'If I have to live in a world where Celine Dion enters my head without invitation, I'll fucken deck whoever I want!'

'Back to the cop-thing, I can't get over the blatancy.'

'Yeah, their badge is just a criminal licence.'

'I'd feel less offended being mugged by some poor homeless bloke—at least that's honest. If I get pulled up on the bike I'm gunna ride to the bitter end.'

'Are you on a motorbike, Davo?'

'Yeah.'

'Are you a virtual-Israeli?'

'How do you get about?'

'Buses.'

'Are you a virtual-retiree?'

* *A note to the non-Australian reader:* where our comments may sound harsh, it's clarifying to underline that Australian males measure fondness by the degree in which one can insult the other before offense is actually taken—like a form of testing your intimacy; where the bolder the remark, the greater the love. For clarification of this account, please refer to the *Australian Glossary of Slang, Terms, and Things*.

'Ya know, boys, I must admit bumping into youse has been a rare treat. I feel so normal all of a sudden. Like I can swear and join me words, and clear me throat without covering me mouth.'

It was then that I realised I was speaking through the left side of my mouth. I'd probably been doing it my entire life, but never before had I been conscious of the fact, that, including yelling at and throwing empties at our tellys, wondering if Skippy the Bush Kangaroo actually *did* understand what his mate Sonny was on about, and, tending our lawns not dissimilarly to the good people of the Australian Army Reserve—mowing them with our Victas just one weekend a month—that we as Australians have this habit.

The apple juices flowed late into the night, and having risen to bid our farewell, we once again—with arms crossed and talking in voices deeper than natural—stood about in a circle.

'So how much longer you in Pushkar, Davo?'

'I'm off tomorrow morning.'

'Where to?'

'Jaisalmer, maybe.'

'That's a fair old stretch.'

'I'm still just thinking about it.'

'Righto. Well, we'll shoot through on ya, Davo. Catch you on the glory track.'

'Gents, the pleasure has been neither mine, nor that camel's over there—'

'—But all ours?'

'Get stuffed.'

The next morning came, and I stood on the hotel balcony one last time. Like a jewel in the waterless surround, the lake was as perfectly unmoved as ever, and doubled on its surface was each bird migrating slowly across the cloudless sky.

It was, and, still is, rare for me to feel so much as a teaspoon of self-credit, but as I stood there that morning, I felt overwhelmed with a sense of pride. That if not for having set sail, and if not for the miles travelled, fought and suffered, I would have never found this incredible place that all my life had been waiting for me to discover it. If even for just a moment, I felt an extension in my breath.

In preparation for the ride ahead, I applied the full superstar suit of black jeans, black vest, boots and the rest. I strapped up the Blue Fly too, with bags, spare petrol and guitar, putting an official end to its sabbatical.

I rode through the winding laneways at a swan song's pace, taking a last few minutes to record this place to memory. After saving myself from a near-accident—thanks, of course, to one last case of girl-induced whiplash—I clicked the bluey up a gear and aimed for the highway.

14. Decisions, Decisions

I was soon out on the open desert road, somewhere-bound; for I still hadn't made up my mind if I was going to start heading south to Goa or further west to the far desert city of Jaisalmer. I rode along, and if I were a skilful enough rider I would have controlled the bike with one hand and flipped a coin with other.

Sitting firm upon the grumbling bike, I kept coasting, and after a short time, I reached a road sign: ◀ *Southbound* left— *Westbound* right ▶. It was decision time, and as the sign grew bigger, I began chewing my imaginary fingernails. 'She loves me? She loves me not? She loves me? She loves me not…' and steering to the right, westbound we became.

It was going to be no short ride, but keen to dispel the myth of Jaisalmer being unreachable, it was head up and tyres down. 'I mean, there's a road? And it's all the same planet?' So figuring that unless there was a devil on the highway to whom I had to play the blues, or a mysterious black hole that would plunge me to the whereabouts of the Abominable Snowman—which, just quietly,

I think is *Sesame Street's* Mr Snuffleupagus having got lost and fucked up when out skiing—surely it was reachable eventually.

An hour on the highway passed, and making the desert undulate like a body of water, what was once orange-coloured sand had lightened down to a golden, almost white, powder. The horizon soon fell as flat as a blade, and with the high persistent sun looking disfigured by itself the day was shaping up to be hotter than anything under the roof of an Australian summer. Wheeling through this arid setting was a rider's dream, and feeling high on the silkiness of the desert, so too did my wish for it to never end.

After some time the road slowed down into a small highway town. I was applauded by a crowd of guys whistling and cheering me on—some even running out to offer me drive-by high-fives. It was the closest I'd felt to being a king on a two-wheeled throne, and I knew I better not get used to it.

I pulled up, and as though wondering what on Earth had led me to their remote place of residence, the best part of the entire town swarmed around. If this mobbing had happened on day one of the biking jaunt, I would have been understandably nervous. Pushing out their eyeballs, most stood circled around, but an old man weaved his way forward. 'Hello, young sir, are you riding to Jaisalmer?'

I was struck by a sudden feeling of déjà vu, and by the time his question was finished I realised there was something about the keenness of his eyes that resembled my late Maltese granddad.

'Yes, I am,' I said, 'how far is it, please?'

'Oh Jaisalmer is a very long way, but every story has its ending,' he said, revealing he even had a certain lyricism comparable to my grandfather, a man, who having lived to the age of 97, said that growing too old was like letting the devil get his way. The man produced a neatly folded hanky and he wiped his brow. 'Can

I ask a favour, young sir? Can you give me a ride to Jaisalmer?'

'I would, sir, but my bike is very overloaded.'

'That is ok,' he said, putting a hand to his chest. I returned the gesture by doing the same, but rode away feeling less than gracious.

The midday sun was getting angrier overhead, and although my tan was coming along swimmingly, I couldn't help but wonder if the fire in the sky ever got fed up singing the same blistering song.

I kept riding into the unknown, and the horizon trembled such like a hallucination that on straight stretches of road I'd need to remove my sunglasses to check my focus. This was some serious Mad Max-style touring, and running more on wishful thinking than my abilities as a mechanic, I dared not imagine what might happen if the bike filed for retirement.

On the bike trip, I'd seen countless dead dogs on the road, and whenever I saw one that looked mostly intact, or newly dead as it were, I'd drag it to the roadside. This day was no exception, and spotting another signed-off soul, who, adding to my soft spot looked like my late Labrador, I pulled over.

While I was stopped, sitting on the bike and slaking my thirst, with the sound of the dry wind whistling around me like a ghost, another motorbike pulled up alongside. It was carrying three local guys, and as I dismounted my bike, slowly, from being sore from riding, its burly rider addressed me in a derisive tone. 'Ey! We've got three men on our bike and you've only got one! You take one!'

Less offended by his suggestion than by the tone in which he'd asked, and feeling that if I was going to take anyone I'd rather have taken the nice old man from the town prior, I offered no response.

'Well? You take one!' he pushed. Angered by my lack of response, he dismounted his bike and walked up to me nose to nose. 'Did you not hear me?'

'I heard you.'

'Well?'

'Well, what?'

'Well, you take one man!'

'I told you, I heard you.'

He stepped in closer. 'Are you scared of me?'

'Should I be?' I said, my heart flying in my chest.

'Well, there's three of us and only one of you..'

Still I offered no response.

'Why have you come out to the desert?' he pressed in a graver tone. 'Pushkar is far enough for you tourists.'

Breaking eye contact, I walked clear around him and dragged the dead dog off the road, causing him to burst into laughter. 'You should be more concerned for yourself! Not the stupid dog!' the fat guy gloated, and like a pair of half-witted henchmen, his mates broke into back-up laughter.

To say that I would have loved to see the Earth open up, show the gamut of its teeth and swallow him whole would be no lie. While slinging myself onto my bike, though, I thought of a more satisfying idea. 'I tell you what, mate. I'll take you on my bike.'

'No. Take him!'

'No. You.'

A cocktail of confusion and wariness sprawled across his face, still he, much to my delight, hopped on behind me.

'I hope you can keep up on that tin of a tuna, mate.' I said to my skinny opponent, his bike being a bodgy little 100cc Honda Hero. A look of blankness took him over, and I kicked the Blue Fly in gear and tore it up the road.

A kilometre passed.

'Slow down! We must be waiting for my friends!' my fat mate yelled. But with every intention to leave his chums in the dust, I slowed not a tick. He started tapping me on the shoulder. 'I said *slow down!*'

'The more he asks, the faster I'm going to go...'

It was a matter of principle for which wars had been fought and nations destroyed: if you're going to ask for something, ask nicely.

A hundred kilometres passed, and with significant distance between us and his mates, part one of my plan was in play.

'I need to get petrol!' I yelled back, and spotting a petrol station, I pulled in.

We hopped off, and seeming more than content with his free ride, he stretched his legs and scratched his massive gut.

To my surprise, petrol in India was twice the price than in Australia, so I considered my next question only fair. 'Rupees, mate?'

'What?'

'Are you going to kick in for the tank?'

He laughed aloud.

'So the sun shines through your pockets?

'What?'

'Are you going to kick in for the tank or what?'

'Why should I? You're the rich western boy!'

Wrestling the urge to spend the rest of the day explaining exactly why I considered him the ill-mannered swine he was, I put the nozzle in the tank. With nothing but the sound of a ticking bowser, a few minutes passed.

'Any minute now...' I thought, bearing in mind part two of my plan, and less than a minute passed before he said what I was hoping to hear. 'Wait here, I'm going to the toilet.'

As he walked away, I counted backwards from ten, hopped on

the bike, and with the only price paid being missing out on seeing the look on his face when he returned, I rode off without him. I'd often been torn between sweet, sour, or savoury, but concluded here that revenge tastes better than them all.

Several hours passed, and still sauntering through the dust with their walking sticks like wizard's staves, as always were the desert men working in the far-off fields. As parched as they, I felt overdue for a roadside chai, and, spotting a place, I pulled over.

Like many of these chai stands, it was equipped with a rest area—not much more than a bamboo-framed structure roofed with dry palm leaves. I walked into its shade and sat on a rickety cane chair.

'Hello, sir, cup of chai?' the man serving asked.

I nodded, and he brought over not only a fresh cup but also a tray of water. It was as appreciated as unexpected, and washing up felt so religious that if Jesus appeared crooning his bread-breaking favourites, I might have provided harmonies.

The man's son, about six years of age, came skipping over and sat beside me—his legs swinging like a high-speed pendulum. 'Where are you from, mister?' he asked, looking up with bright eyes.

'Australia. Where are you from?' He gave a hearty laugh, as though understanding the gag, but wondering if he actually knew, I fished out my map. 'This is where we are now.' I said, pointing to Rajasthan, 'and this place is called *India*.'

But as though wondering why I'd want to impose such needless information, he cowered and shrugged his shoulders. I felt like a right killjoy, and it occurred to me then that most of these children probably had no concept of where they were geographically. The light in his eyes dimmed, and, I guess feeling there were a range of ways to better spend his day, he walked away. I was by no means offended, but to the contrary was impressed with his resolve. In fact, I would have loved him to have a word to my old maths teachers—bland characters numbing us with maths involving more letters than numbers. For where would I be today without the countless uses of 1a + 1b?

The man serving poured me a second cup, and it was then that three Rajput desert men joined me under the shelter. They were old, or at least aged to look it, and wiping their faces as though this was just another of many days under the sun, they laid down their staves and sat around me.

Two of them began conversing in a language far beyond my grasp, while the third turned his attention to me. With his English as inept as my Hindi, conversation barely reached a level that allowed us to exchange names. But what I remember, irrespectively, was he had a voice so deep it could have framed Barry White for a Bee Gee. I fished out my camera and gestured if it would be ok to take his picture, and he nodded gently.

Much like the man I'd towed into Pushkar, he gazed down the barrel of the camera as unmoved as a mountain. I took the photo, and with the lines on his face resting like trenches to old tales, the photo was cover shot perfect. I showed him, and he approved it with an apathetic nod, accepting the image of himself without a flinch of unease.

But where last time I was baffled by the coolness, it occurred to me this time as to why. As far as I could tell, these people weren't filled with the fear and self-consciousness that advertising and marketing bombard us with in the west, hence nowhere along their path to adulthood are they robbed of their childhood purity.

A few minutes later the little boy came running back, and with the light in his eyes—and the swing in his legs—returned, he sat next to me. His hands were cupped, and when he opened them and a large butterfly flew from out, he jumped with joy. 'What's life-giving *vs.* life-sapping.' I thought, witnessing nature, not the futility of 1a + 1b, be his greatest teacher. He came running back into the shade a minute later, and sitting on the old Rajput's knee, they looked like a spectrum of contentment young and old.

Time was ticking no less, and figuring I should get going if I was ever going to reach this make-believe city of Jaisalmer, I slung myself onboard the Blue Fly. But just as I was about to pull onto the highway, my three dear friends went buzzing past on their Honda Hero. They'd obviously picked up the abandoned party on the roadside, and having failed to see me, I rode up alongside. 'G'day!'

'You fucker! You absolute fucker!'

'Would I be right in guessing you're angry at me?'

'I'll kill you, you arsehole-bastard!'

'So you are angry at me?'

'You owe me fifteen hundred rupees you prick!'

'Now that hurts my feelings, mate.'

'You foreign arsehole-fuck!' he bawled as his rider swerved their bike into mine, and swerving out of the way and taking off up the road, I better understood that the taste of revenge was even nicer after having time to cure.

With each kilometre tinted redder by my sunglasses, another hundred kilometres passed, and despite contrasting requests, the sun wasn't going to quit singing its same blistering song. The faint line of the horizon kicked and shimmered, and the golden sand planes floated like a sheet in the wind.

This was without question the biggest day's ride I'd attempted yet, and with the bike and I playing the part of a pair of solar panels I couldn't ride for five minutes without needing a swig of water. Time seemed to matter neither here nor there, and I was as much counting the sand in my eyes as the sheep in my head. Although the brilliance of the desert was relentless, I was truly starting to wonder if Jaisalmer existed at all. The highway straightened into a perfect line, stretching as far as the eye could see, and its rise and fall offered a sensation like the gentle rocking of a boat. Adding to the ecstasy, I was the only soul on it.

Acting as a sort of sonic aroma in which the entire visual was engulfed, when riding I'd almost always be listening to music. Music such as (*please feel free to skip this indulgence…*) The Police, Neil Finn, Blueline Medic, Iron Maiden, Wilco, Audioride, Massive Attack, Secret Garden, Johnny Cash, The Cure, Leonard Cohen, Sarah Mclachlan, Jeff Buckley, Andrew McUtchen, Prem Joshua, Samuel Barber, Pink Floyd, Kasabian, Rufus Wainwright, Beastie Boys, Mazzy Star, The Smiths, Carole King, Guns 'N Roses, Augie March, Thievery Corporation, Cold Chisel, Donnie Dureau, Bob Dylan, Foo Fighters, Colin Hay, Bruce Springsteen, Toto, The Psychedelic Furs, Pantera, Beethoven, Groove Armada, Pete Yorn, Velure, Endorphin, The Prodigy, Everything But The Girl, Split Enz, Icehouse, The Band, Radiohead, Hilmar Örn Hilmarsson, Billie Holiday, AC/DC, Chris Isaak, Ricochet, Suede, Fear Factory, Unkle, Richard Ashcroft, Portishead, Daft Punk, Supergrass, Gavin Friday, Neil Young, U2, Dion, The Misfits, Black Sabbath, Crowded House, Oasis, Metallica, Christopher Keogh, Bert & Patti, Weezer, Elvis Costello, The Crystal Method, Burt Bacharach, Frank Sinatra, Ennio Morricone, Nick Drake, My Morning Jacket, Sinéad O'Connor, Travis, The Beatles, Santo & Johnny, Adnan Sami, John Lennon, Elvis Presley, Prince, James Horner, Manic Street Preachers, Glenn Miller, Stevie Wonder, Paris Wells, Justin Timberlake, Kings Of Leon, James Iha, Madonna, INXS, Spun Rivals, Polka Party Time, Beck, Men At Work, Kate Bush, Whitesnake, Ben Harper, Morrissey, The Verve, Goldfrapp, PJ Harvey, Midnight Oil, Johnny Garofalo, The Doobie Brothers, Billy Bragg, Subaudible Hum, David Bowie, Café Del Mare, The Malaka Social Club, Ella Fitzgerald, Ron Sexsmith, Ben Kweller, Michael Jackson, Lamb, The Dream

Academy, Black Grape, The Cardigans, The Chemical Brothers, R.E.M, Tim Reid, Lyle Lovett, Nelly Furtado, Seal, Gaslight Radio, Björk, You Am I, Mötley Crüe, Christopher Cross, Buddha Bar, Placebo, Bing Crosby, Sam Brown, Sting, Julian Senserrick, Rush, Talking Heads, Creedence Clearwater Revival, Little River Band, Andy Summers, Jaye Christopher Hanson, Faith No More, Stevie Nicks, Neil Diamond, Def Leppard, Ryan Adams, Blacklisted, Parliament, Tears For Fears, The Cult, Starsailor, Depeche Mode, Kevin Bloody Wilson, Cat Stevens, Linkin Park, Guernica, Jamiroquai, The Church, Tool, Noiseworks, Bungalow, Smashing Pumpkins, Cake, Josh Ritter, Sime Nugent, Pulp, Passengers, The Soggy Bottom Boys, Snow Patrol, Tim Finn, Chris Brady, New Order, Fleetwood Mac, Foreigner, Mr Mister, The Music, Paul Kelly, Kyuss, Red Hot Chili Peppers, James, Daniel Lanois, Eurythmics, The Stone Roses, Mike Powers, Morcheeba, Kylie Minogue, Eminem, Dido, Sigur Rós, Dread Zeppelin, The Guadalupe Underground, Duran Duran, John Denver, Chuck Jenkins, Stereophonics, Clannad, Living Colour, The Prayer Boat, Doves, Timothy Slater, Jewel, The Clash, ZZ Top, Pixies, Deuter, Something For Kate, Red Cloud, Paul Colman, Death In Vegas, Billy Idol, Powderfinger, Enya, Norah Jones, Yanni, Dan Rockett, Simon & Garfunkel, James Taylor, Tim Rogers, Hank Williams…

…And sometimes my own songs. But on this day I happened to be listening to the soundtrack from *The Lord of The Rings*.

It was perhaps from the emotive stir of this incredible music, or from the soft ebb and flow of the highway, but I could scarcely remember a time when I felt so overwhelmed with a feeling of total freedom.

The highway rose into a crested hill, and with the horizon still jittering in the distance, I removed my sunglasses to check my focus, when there, rising from out of the desert haze, stood Jaisalmer, *The Golden City of Rajasthan*.

*****

Dear Manuel,

I've just ridden 1,000 kilometres across the Rajasthani desert, from its eastern to western edge.

However glorious, this motorbiking thing is no small challenge, and after a full day I'm left walking with a distinct limp. I'm now in Jaisalmer. It's a curious place, and with the desert sun bouncing off its high fort walls, it looks more like a golden sandcastle from *Ali Baba and the Forty Thieves* than anything from this day and age. I think my goal to be as far removed from the real world is well on the way though, for if I so much as do a summersault or drop my compass, that's me off the map.

*****

I rode up the cobblestone boulevard of the fort's tiered citadel. With goats and geese scurrying out of the way I felt like Gandalf entering Minas Tirith on his horse. The fort's innards—still occupied with markets, squares and dwellings—were teeming with life. The lanes soon contracted into footpaths, and unable to ride further, I parked the bluey and continued the hotel search on foot.

I seemed to be getting the old sorry-we're-all-full vibe, perhaps because I was covered in filth, sweat and half the sand of Rajasthan.

Driving me deeper into the fort's maze, my trail of rejections led me to its epicentre, where, as though the last hotel on Earth, was a small doorway with a sun-faded sign that hopefully read: *As Though the Last Hotel On Earth.*

I walked inside, down some stairs and into a tiny underground lobby. Jumping off his stool at the sight of a customer, a young man approached.

'Hello,' I said, 'I'm looking for a—'

But before I could finish, he handed me a hot cup of chai. I could have kissed him, I really could have.

'Are you my brother?' he asked, extending his hand to mine.

'Yes. Brothers,' I said, withdrawing my hand and getting the feeling I'd just validated some desert mafia oath. 'Do you have a room please?'

'That depends.'

'On what?'

'On what you require.'

'Walls would be good.'

'We only have one room left.'

'And?'

'And it has not been in use for over five years.'

'And?'

'And it requires cleaning first.'

'And?'

'And that is all.'

But less than comfortable with sleeping in a room full of ghosts, boogiemen, and other unsolved mysteries, I walked away.

'Wait, brother! Let us clean it first and then you can decide.'

'I think I'll just look for something else, thanks.'

'It will be cheap.'

'How cheap?'

'Twenty.'

'Twenty rupees?' I asked, checking his offer of what was a mere 70 cents Australian was for real.

'Please, brother, the room is good. It just requires cleaning. Why don't you go up to the roof and watch the sunset. Come back in an hour and then decide.'

Figuring I had nothing to lose, I walked upstairs to the hotel's rooftop restaurant, where the last of the sunlight was bleeding across the horizon like red wine into white sheets. Adding to the wonder, the city lay everywhere beneath, as though still marinated by its medieval heyday as a merchant hub for camel routes to Egypt, Arabia, Persia and Africa. I stood there until the last slither of sun tucked itself behind the Pakistani border, and when the first star pierced overhead soon after I figured it was time to check on this room.

I walked down to the underground lobby, and the same man approached with another cup of chai. 'Are you my brother?'

'Haven't we already been through this?'

'Yes, but are you my brother?'

'Mate, if this room is any good I'll be your sister.'

'Come with me.'

He led me down a long hallway, and when he opened the door and I was met by a large clean room with a double bed, candles burning against the sandstone walls, and fragranced with sticks of incense, his brotherly service proved first-rate.

'It was once an old storage room, but I think it's ok for you, yes?'

'Mate, it's tops!'

'No, we are at the bottom of the hotel. The rooms upstairs are tops.'

I made no further comment.

I settled down and scrubbed up, and after the day's mass sunray intake, my freshly-scoured skin tingled with a fraction too much Tabasco to call enjoyable.

I took to the streets soon after, and sore from the day's ride it was I that was walking in the toilet paper hostage knot. The fort laneways, however, seemed to match my pace, as unlike the nocturnal chaos of other Indian cities, Jaisalmer, at night, was a place that breathed as opposed to bustled. The locals left me to it, and even the mystics and jugglers had a much less hard-sell approach.

I stopped to watch one of the street performers, a man squatting with a basket by his feet. Having noticed me, he removed its lid and began playing a flute. After a few seconds—as though sick to death of the same old song—a woozy-looking python rose from within. The man ramped up his playing, and as though trying to get the snake to break into its hula-hoop routine, he flicked it in the head. I was horrified, and having never before felt sided with a snake, I wanted to flick the man back. Beating me to any such thing, the snake, with a loud hiss, bit his master on the hand.

'It's ok,' said the man, mistaking me as an ally. 'Joe doesn't have any teeth.'

'Joe?' I thought, unable to warrant why a toothless python should be named otherwise.

Rubbing his hand, the man smiled at me dumbly.

'Poor old Joe, he's like an old bloke left shuffling for his dentures.'

'Yes. He has a very beautiful smile.'

'But he doesn't have any teeth?'

'Yes. He wears his smile on the inside.'

'Nothing to do with the flicks in the scone?'

'Yes. Flicks.'

'So how were his teeth removed by the way?'

'Yes. With specially-blessed pliers.'

'Specially-blessed?'

'Yes. Specially-blessed.'

I gave the man a few coins, hoping he'd spend it on an operation that would remove the word *yes* from his vocabulary. I walked off, but not before handing Joe the phone number of the police, the army, and my old orthodontist.

It was time to eat, by golly it was time, and having chosen a place outside of the fort's mainstay walls, I sat myself down. But before I could start looking through the vegetarian menu of biryani, lentils and the usual like, a waiter approached. 'You look like a man in need, sir.'

'Is it that obvious?'

'Yes. But don't trouble yourself with the menu you're holding. Be more concerned with this one,' he said, handing me another one that listed a variety of forbidden items, such as beer, wine, and to my absolute delight—*meat*. It had been almost three months since I'd so much as had sniff of something that once lived, and having lost a considerable amount of weight, I happily ordered the lamb.

Some time later he returned. 'Your banquet, sir.'

'Thank you,' I said, wondering if the word *banquet* was a plausible noun for a single person eating a single dish. Still, wishing not to play the part of a strong breeze in a room full of comb-overs, I dared not challenge it.

'And here is your good knife, sir.'

'Thank you.'

'And, sir?'

'Yes?'

'I feel that it is my duty to warn you that...'

'Yes?'

'If when cutting your meat you catch yourself cutting your hand...'

'Yes?'

'It means you're holding your good knife the wrong way around.'

'Thanks, mate, I'll keep that in mind.'

He left me to it, and like when Bruce the Shark from *Finding Nemo* got lured back to the dark side by a single sniff of blood, I felt, upon the first salty mouthful, as if I was morphing back into my old self. My whole body seemed to relax, and without even realising how foggy I was, my head felt surprisingly clearer.

Having made my way through the warren of cobblestone

laneways, I made it back to my room. I opened the door, and with the incense sticks having burnt out, I noticed a distinct gassy smell. I felt, for a second, perturbed, but upon remembering that this was an old storage room—and, noticing the large pipes running the length of the walls—I considered this the source and chose to care no further.

I switched off the light, and too tired to be in much of an occupational-health-and-safety mood, I lay on the bed. I closed my eyes. Just as the fall of sleep began, I thought I heard a squeaking noise.

I woke several hours later, still in the pitch-black, and with the gassy smell having tripled, so did my concern. Dog tired, I lay there trying not to care, but as my faculties returned I could hear a distinct scuffling noise coming from under the bed. Still lying on it, I patted along the wall, trying to locate the light switch, but failing in the dark, I reached for my pen torch. 'The brotherly service indeed!' I thought, as in the dim light could be seen, just by the bed, ten or more rats squeaking and fidgeting about.

Like a little old lady, I stood on the bed and switched on the light. The rat's work was that of art, as all over the floor—and, all through my backpack—was a sea of black rice lookalike.

My chai-giving brother entered the room, wearing Smurfs pyjamas and a sleeping cap to match. 'Oh?'

'This is not so good, mate.'

He extended his hand to mine. 'Are you my brother?'

'No, I'm not your brother!'

'But that's impossible!'

'How?'

'Because you are mine!'

'I expect my money back. All 70 cents.'

Having taken the hint, he moved me to a different room.

I spent the next day wandering around the fort laneways, and my bike-induced limp had healed just enough to be minus the embarrassment.

Checking out the sites—especially the intricately latticed façades of the citadel's golden havelis—I wandered around on my own, until a young lad began to follow me.

Clearly allergic to the *footstep*, he was using cartwheels as his preferred mode of transport. One after the other he spun, in fact, it was so continuous that paired with Mr Ed they could have passed for a Wagon Wheel. I wished he was wearing a helmet, and as charming as we both knew he was, I knew it was a ploy for begging.

'Stop spinning, mate. I feel like I'm being dry-cleaned!'

And coming to a fast-footed standstill, his face fell to a look of well-rehearsed innocence. 'Chapatti bread?' he asked in a tone designed to thaw the coldest of hearts. He was dressed in tattered attire, and I guessed him to be about eight years old. 'Chapatti bread?' he repeated.

I felt I had to comply, and he, seeming happy with his pending score, skipped alongside as I walked.

We soon reached a chapatti pushcart, but just as I was about to buy him a handful, his demands became more specific. 'Chapatti flour?' he asked, grabbing me by the hand and walking me down an adjacent laneway. My suspicion rose.

After a few minutes we reached a thriving shop, and sitting behind its cash register was a well-dressed lady handling fistfuls of money.

'Is this your son?'

Her eyes filled with abhorrence, confirming my suspicion that she was the mastermind behind his street routine. 'In India, everything is possible,' she said, quoting what I'd gathered to be India's slogan to dismiss all responsibility.

I walked away, wondering if the money he made for her would buy back the innocence she cost him, or if someday he'd be president.

Later that afternoon I made it back to the hotel.

'Hello,' I said to my rat-room-giving brother. 'I'll be leaving tomorrow morning.'

'Really?'

'Yes, I should pay up now.'

'Well, if this is goodbye, I want you to know you were the greatest brother I ever had.'

'Thanks, mate. So am I right in guessing you address every bloke who stays here as your brother?'

'Yes. It is good for business to trick people into thinking you like them.'

'I'll try not to take it personally.'

'So where are you going next?'

'South towards Goa.'

'By train?'

'By motorbike.'

'But, Mr David-Brother, Goa is thousands and hundreds and dozens of kilometres from here.'

'Everywhere is riding distance if you have the time.'

'Well, if you're riding a bike, I feel it is my duty to warn you to be very extra especially more particularly careful when riding at this time of year.'

'Why?'

'Because the children of India take great pleasure in throwing firecrackers at people riding bikes.'

'Why?'

'Because of Diwali.'

'Diw-what?'

'Diwali. It's the National Festival of Lights. It starts tonight and goes for five days. All of mother India will be celebrating with fireworks and sweets and things. Children go particularly crazy!'

'And adults?'

'Even crazier!'

'Cows?'

'Not so much, but make sure you go out tonight and see it for yourself. Jaisalmer will be at its most golden.'

It certainly sounded worth a look, but before I was going to do any such thing, I was first going to have a kip. I switched off the light in my new room, and having lain down, I closed my eyes. Though just as they began their fade to black, I once again thought I heard a squeaking noise.

I woke an hour later, still in the pitch-black, and as my faculties returned I could discern the squeaking noise had escalated to a quiet roar. 'Ah for farck's sake!' I found the light switch and flicked it on.

But to my semi-relief, the squeaking was due not to a matinee show of rats unveiling their art, but from people in the next room having sex on a mattress in grave need of oil. Still, not so keen on listening to a game of *oo-ar* tennis, I upped and left.

I took myself back outside, and with the night sky lit by an untold amount of fireworks, *The Festival of Lights* proved to be no lie. The sandstone laneways were lined with hundreds of oil lamps and lanterns. As I walked past the private doorways of the fort dwellings—strewn with mango leaves, marigolds, and a range of coloured powders—their occupants handed lollies to all passers-by.

Filling the sky was a range of professional fireworks, but the streets were equally ablaze from the work of kids setting off crackers of their own.

The array was endless—big red whizzing ones, little yellow fizzing ones, and double banger ones—exploding that one time extra to ensure your tinnitus had returned for good.

It was child warfare, and with the adults just sitting back and smiling, the kids—as though they themselves couldn't believe they were allowed to get away with it—were running about in circular frenzies.

I saw one little girl—about the age of three—holding a lit firecracker in her teeth. Although the drama of being pounced on by a stranger reduced her to a fountain of tears, I snatched it from her mouth and chucked it to the heavens. But even more spectacular were the efforts of one little boy, who, perhaps from having watched one too many episodes of *Australia's Funniest Home Videos,* tied a firecracker to a goose—the goose running off with seconds to live. I was a nervous wreck, and without proclaiming to be the Doctor Dolittle of children, I couldn't let myself think of the injuries that kids all over India were incurring.

The night grew later than it was, and wishing for one last portion of the desert view before hitting the hay, I climbed onto hotel's rooftop.

With the sky still ablaze with fireworks, disappointed I wasn't, and with the sound of the festivities pouring upwards from the laneways, there was not a nook or cranny in which you could escape its fervency. It had been a master-fluke to experience this festival in such a hauntingly ancient place, and fitting beyond anything I could have thought to order, it was, for me, the ideal full stop to my time in the Desert State of Rajasthan. I thought about Pramesh, and wondered if he was sitting on the balcony in Rishikesh, and if tonight Mamma Sharvari was making her coconut chili chutney.

With the smell of fireworks still in the air, I woke the next morning on par with the sun, strapped up the Blue Fly, and was soon back out on the open highway. I rode for a matter of time, quite occupied by the music in my headphones, when up ahead on the road a bus made an almighty swerve.

15. Two is Company

I was behind the bus some 50 metres, and I braked to keep back. 'Was there an accident up ahead? Was something dead on the road?' As I advanced the question was answered, as there, lost and with a parched tongue hanging out as he scuttled up the middle of the road, was a puppy. He was perhaps on a kamikaze mission, or had mistaken my bike as a two-wheeled dog, but as I flew past he ran almost directly under me.

I turned around and pulled over, and kneeling down to him in a foray of clicks and whistles, his tail fired up like a wee little rudder. Seeming altogether torn between fear and delight, he cowered into the middle of the road and rolled onto his back. I stood up and scooped, and once in my arms, he began frantically licking my face. I loved him from the first second.

I stood on the side of the highway, with this wee little dog in arm. He was entirely black in colour, except for his feet having fully built-in white socks. His tongue was hanging as much as it was dripping. I guessed him to be about six weeks old.

We were 50 kilometres from the Pakistani bord
the edgeless sun cutting down with a firm tone of
was such a hostile feel to this place that even the win
uneasy. We were the only souls present, and it was my guess he'd
fallen out of a car, or, sadder, had been dumped. Regardless, the
one certainty was that this little bloke was as vulnerable as it got,
and he gazed up with a look of total dependency.

Perhaps it was from the look on his face, or that I felt he'd
be a first-rate companion, but the decision was the easiest of my
life. From the bleak desert of India's north, down to the southern
tropics of Goa, I was taking him with me.

The decision was final, but the first problem in need of solution
was how I was going to carry him on the bike. For the tour so far,
I'd been wearing a small daypack on my back, and figuring I could
wear it kangaroo-style on my front, I redistributed its contents
into my large backpack and strapped the daypack to my chest.
I lowered the pup inside, and having either been a joey in a past
life—or too exhausted to care—he made not a fidget of protest.

We rode steadily along, and sitting there in the bag, with his
head hanging out and tongue flapping in the wind at 90 kph, he
was taking to his new gig as canine-wingman with the greatest
of ease. It was nice to have his company, and adding to our
bond, any time I took a swig from my bottle—and offered him
a capful—he'd lick it to the point of breathing it in—'little star!'

By the late hours of that afternoon we reached a small
highway town by the name of Sanchor, on the Rajasthan/Gujarat
state border. It was hardly an aesthetic jewel, but with the orange
horizon fast descending into darkness, it was way late enough to
be pulling in.

I pulled into a car park of a small hotel, and figuring I should keep my four-legged secret concealed, I zipped up the bag as I approached the door. It was locked, but as I proceeded to leave an old woman appeared from the dark. 'What are you doing here, young man?'

'It's late. I'm looking for a room, please.'

'Never before has a westerner stayed here.'

I was unsure how to take her comment; that perhaps 'no westerners' was how she wished for it to remain. Adding to her hostile demeanour, her skin was ghastly white in colour, much lighter than my own as Caucasian. But her facial features were characteristically local, making it difficult to tell if she was Indian or not.

'What are you looking at?' she grumbled.

I lowered my gaze.

'I am Indian, you know?'

I smiled awkwardly.

'I have a disease called vitiligo. The pigment has died over time. And far too long a time have I lived.'

I felt at a fantastic loss for words, and although the pup was concealed, I felt little safer for it.

To national order, a crowd of intrigued locals gathered around, and as though sensing an appreciative audience, the pup began to wriggle in the bag.

'What is wrong with your shirt?' grumbled the woman.

'Nothing.'

'What is in the bag?'

I shrugged my shoulders, though just as I did the pup popped out like a rabbit out of a hat. The crowd gasped like an audience satisfied with the show, and I unzipped the bag and lifted him out.

'Vhy like dis?' asked a young man.

'You mean—"Why like this?"'

'Yes, that is what I said—vhy like dis?'

More concerned with the thoughts of the old woman, I gave

him no answer, and clocking her grave stare, I turned to leave.

'Give him to me!' she said. I handed him to her, and she lifted him by the scruff of his neck. The pup stared at her intensely; forgetting his manners before he'd even remembered them.

'Is it ok that he stays in the room with me?' I half-asked, half-cringed.

Analysing the dangling dog, the old woman hesitated for a few long seconds. 'I suppose, as long as he doesn't piss on the bed.'

She dropped him to the ground, raising my inner mercury. She then poured some milk into a tray, and the pup scampered over and obligingly inhaled.

I checked us into our room and he sat flat on the bed with his chin resting on his paws.

'You reckon you're unsure, mate. I dunno what I've taken on.'

As though poring with thoughts of his own, his eyes filled with worry.

'So, Charlie Chaplin, what are we going to name you?'

He responded little.

'Maybe we could call you *Hindi*? Charlie Chaplin.'

He blinked and looked away.

'Well, buggered if I know, Charlie Chaplin.'

It was then that I caught myself referring to him by the nickname my Maltese nana called me. And thus it was; *Charlie* was his name. I clicked my fingers and awarded him his title, to which he rose to his feet and made his debut bark—'little star!'

The time came to get something to eat, and with Charlie on a length of old rope, we walked down the dusty high street. Like the Pied Piper of Sanchor, a crowd of hundreds followed, making me wonder if I was the first ever westerner to come to this town.

I chose a popup eatery, which was no more than a bamboo frame set up on the dirt. I sat at a table, and the crowd sat at those surrounding. I could have let their staring grate me into a fine dust, but chose instead to enjoy the unique social attention.

I placed Charlie on my lap.

'What is his name, sir?'

I told him and the crowd circled in closer.

I wasn't sure what I should feed him, but figuring leftovers were going to be good enough, I ordered up.

It soon arrived, and I placed him on the table. Clearly not in the mood for saying grace, he inhaled his portion like he was in a televised race. Thoroughly entertained, the crowd, in their own language, broke into a rapturous mass ordering—the only word comprehensible to my ears being *Charlie*.

The restaurateur broke into a sweat as he brought tray after tray, and the lads laughed as the pup obligingly scoffed. Like the regulars leaning on the bar at your local, he'd soon acquired a pot gut no belt could contain.

Still his fans kept on feeding him late into the night, some building up the confidence to place him in their laps for an experimental pat. I felt proud to have him onboard, and felt, too, that my wish for the motorbiking tour to bring me face-to-face with stories worthy of campfire telling was officially granted.

We stood up to mark our farewell, whereupon the gullet of Charlie opened up and vomited more half-chewed rice than I knew India possessed. Suitably embarrassed, I covered his artwork with dirt, but the lads, delighted by the prospect of vacant gut space, broke into a second mass ordering.

We sat back down.

We made it back to the hotel some time later. The old lady was asleep on a chair in reception. 'Like I said, make sure he doesn't piss on the bed.'

'Ok,' I said.

The old lady wasn't asleep, I guess.

I walked upstairs to the room, put Charlie at the foot of the bed and fell into a sea of slumber.

I woke the next morning to find him curled up by my feet. 'Charlie, Charlie, Charlie…' I said, and as his eyes gradually opened, his tail fired up like a wee little rudder. 'Now make sure you don't piss on the bed, little buddy!' to which he rose to his feet, yawned, stretched, and pissed all over the bed. 'Ah for farck's sake, Charlie!'

Prepped for the day, he sat there, wagging his tail and waiting for me to do whatever came next.

I rubbed my eyes like a tired soul, and rose to my feet and gazed around the puppy-trashed room. It was a sobering sight, and it was here that dawned the reality of bringing him on the road. On top of packing my bags every morning, strapping up the bike every morning, and paying for the room every morning—*every morning* I was going to have to deal with a little black puppy whinging while I was in the shower, chewing my hands while I brushed my teeth, and tugging at my shoelaces while I packed my bags.

I sluggishly worked away, and when I went downstairs to pack the bike, Charlie started carrying-on and howling his early morning favourites. 'Ssshhh!' I said, having run back upstairs. 'The grumpy old lady is going to come up here and bust *me* for *you* having pissed on the bed!'

But for every word I spoke he barked a dozen eggs, and left with little choice but to get tactical, I reached for the kangaroo-bag, dunked him in, and hung it on the reverse side of the door. Charlie-free, I ran downstairs, paid the old lady, strapped up the bike, ran back upstairs, grabbed the pup-bag, hooked it across my chest, ran back downstairs, slung us onboard the bike, and sat there 100% rooted before having even hit the road. 'Farcken 'ell…'

I thought, 'this is what it must be like having a kid.'

It was to be Charlie's first full day on the road, the farthest he'd been taken away from his place of birth. The proposal to take him to Goa was a several-thousand kilometre ride, and so I was determined to get a barrelling start.

We rode with the wind in our faces, and his tongue flapped for Christmas. He certainly seemed at ease with the bag, and he'd soon developed a revolving schedule of being on watch or burrowing down for a sleep break.

A hundred kilometres passed, and we were now comfortably over the Gujarat state border. Unlike the picturesque tones of Rajasthan, Gujarat had a more grim and industrial feel. Famous for its political tension and religious bloodshed, I was keen to get in and out in as quick as two days.

With the sensation of riding—and the music in my ears—I'd tend to tune way out. Having forgotten almost entirely, when I turned to reach for my bottle I felt a tongue licking at my chin. Charlie was up. I offered him a capful, and he, to style, licked it to the point of breathing it in.

He was a manageable passenger most of the time, but on occasions where he'd start trying to get out of the bag, I'd inspire him downwards by dropping into it a few bits of chapatti. Other times he'd just want to play and would start climbing up my face, which I'd remedy by riding with one hand and dunking him with the other. But on more trying occasions, where he'd pop up as many as twenty times a minute, I'd confine him to pouch-solitary and zip the bag completely.

Technically speaking, riding with a dog was like managing an additional gear stick—'Brake, turn left, clutch, dunk the dog, indicate, turn right, change gear, chuck him some bread, dodge the camel, turn left, clutch, dunk the dog, mind the cow, zip the bag, turn left, brake, clutch, dunk him again.' I'm not sure I could have managed it in the first week of the riding endeavour, but I was feeling pretty adept by now.

Another hundred kilometres passed, during which I caught myself referring to him by affectionate derivatives of his name. Such as Charlo, Charles Charligan, and Charlie the Chapper Snapper. Much like that with my Labrador Tammy, referring to her as Tam Ham, Tam Jam, and her personal favourite, Fat Cam.

The burnt-orange of dusk began to blend across the horizon by the time we reached the thriving metropolis of Ahmadabad, deep into Gujarat. It was everything you'd expect an Indian city to be: ear splitting, as dirty as noisy, and choked with traffic like a tin of tuna jammed with the work of the seven seas.

We sat idle in the traffic's epicentre, and Charlie was leaning forward out of the bag, with his front feet resting on the tank. For a country boy in the big smoke his excitement was justified, and never was it more evident than when two cows walked past and their mooing inspired his debut growl—'little star!'

With the sky completely dark, it was plenty late enough to be pulling in, and with a hop skip and a jump—or closer to the truth, scoping out five hotels, negotiating prices, choosing one, unpacking the bike, and carting all my gear upstairs—I got us settled into a room. But here dawned the next lesson in the Charlie files; that at the end of a day's ride, when I was feeling as crestfallen as a tortoise towing a quarry truck; Charlie was as pent up as a Jeannie freshly out of the bottle.

I lay on the bed, and like a dad feeling so used up he'd rather hand the kid the credit card than contend with the whinging, as Charlie pulled at my shoelaces, barked at blowflies, and jumped onto the bed to chew my head, I was just too tired to fight. I was tempted to reach for the pouch-bag, and hang him on the door hook forever, but I opted instead to lock him in the dunny.

But if it was peace I was hoping to acquire, then I was gravely denied, as with the added projection of bathroom reverberation, he sooked and squealed and probably even flushed his head to spite me. I lay on the bed, denying him a response, but when his squealing spiralled into a gear higher than usual, I opened the door. It was lucky I had, as I found him with his head wedged between the sink pipe and the wall. I released him from his bind, and laid out some cardboard for his leisure: his choice of use to chew it into seventeen million and three pieces.

There was a knock at the door, and when I opened it, standing there was a tall local man with a lengthy black beard. I guessed him to be about my age. 'Good evening,' he said, 'I am staying in the room next door.'

'Hello,' I replied, expecting him to complain about the dog.

'I've come to introduce myself. My name is Kushal. What is your good name?'

I told him, and although it wasn't that good, I couldn't help but notice how refined he was. 'It's not very often I meet a westerner, and you are a most distinguished guest in my country.'

'I am?' I asked, wiping my nose across my forearm.

'Please, Mr David, it'd be my great honour to take you to dinner.'

I struggled not to blush, but politely accepted.

With Charlie in the gang we proceeded to leave, when another man appeared in the corridor. He seemed less than steady on his feet, and he gazed at me as though he were the very definition of elsewhere.

'Is he drunk?'

'Indeed,' said Kushal, 'he's my friend; sadly he'll be meeting us at the restaurant later.'

We made it to the proposed place, sat ourselves down, and within a minute Charlie fell asleep under the table. The waiter brought us some preliminary chai, and Kushal took a long and experienced sip. 'So tell me, Mr David, are you married?'

'Just call me Dave, mate.'

'Yes, Mr Dave. So are you married?'

'No, not yet.'

'What do you mean?'

'I'd like to in time, but not yet.'

He took another thoughtful sip. 'You know, I fail to understand the western philosophy of marriage. I mean, why go to the trouble of looking all around when your father can do it for you?'

Arranged Marriages vs. *Try Before You Buy*—the cultural boundary was set.

'So are you married yourself?' I asked.

'No, but next year.'

'To who?'

'I don't know. My father hasn't arranged it.'

'Doesn't it make you a tad nervous to gamble the most monumental decision of your life?'

'No, Mr Dave. In fact, the notion of all the choice your culture supports drives me to utter madness.'

It was a fair enough point, and if even for a second, I wondered if his way was better; to have your hand put into the hand of another, might, in its own way, have a certain simplistic romance. Not to forget the financial advantage.

'But what if you meet a girl you like of your own accord?'

He then went on to explain the three marriage scenarios. The first being *Arranged*, where the father chooses entirely, the second being *Love Come Arranged*, where the son may meet a girl he fancies and together with his father they approach the girl's father with a marriage plan. And the third, and most controversial, being *Love*, where the son meets a girl and marries her against his father's will—an act that often results in the newlyweds being ousted by both families.

I took a long sip of my tea. 'So tell me, Mr Kushal, have you ever met a girl you've been interested in yourself?'

'No. But I look.'

'So,' I paused, checking my inappropriateness pH balance, 'have you ever had sex?'

His face fell to a look of disquiet, but its recovery was equally fast. 'No. I don't believe in it before marriage. It's authority without responsibility.'

I admired his nobility, perhaps, and sense of decency, but neither was I sure about his expertise on a subject in which he had zero experience. Technically, he was past his sexual peak, and I wondered if he'd find himself racing a three-legged donkey by the time he got the ring on his finger. Despite his piety, too, entirely resilient he wasn't, as with his voice dropping to a devious tone, he leant forward. 'But tell me, Mr Dave, what does sex *feel* like?'

And leaning back in my chair, my eyes strayed adrift, and my mind couldn't but go for a little imaginary wander into *Sex Land*—a licentious place where all souls are accursed with an anaphylactic allergy to wearing clothes, where coconut oil can be purchased only by the gallon, and the sole way in which one can expire is by being masticated with a touch too much passion—

'—Ahem?' he coughed, seven weeks later, 'so, Mr Dave, what does it feel like?'

'Ever heard of the term supercalifragilisticexpialidocious?'

We'd ordered food. To my pleasant surprise, this was another establishment that served meat on the sly, and I'd ordered the lamb. As soon as its smell reached his sleeping nostrils, one Charles Charligan jumped to his feet like a game show contestant about to win the lot. I was delighted to spare him a vegetarian fate, and he tore apart his debut bone like fairy floss—'little star!'

I guessed Kushal to be Brahman—the highest in the caste system—and so figured he'd have a good overview of his people. 'Can I ask you an ambitious question?'

'Yes?'

'Why do Indians stare?'

'I beg your pardon?'

'I'm not sure if you can notice it like an outsider, but whether we're doing something genuinely interesting, dolefully meagre, or lying in a puddle of our own death, Indians will just stand around and stare.'

'I've never before noticed,' he said, staring by default. 'I guess we stare because we're interested.'

'Well, where I come from staring is considered very confrontational.'

'I do apologise.'

'No need, but now that we're getting down to it, can I ask something else that has bugged me much of the bloody time?'

'What is a bloody time? Is that when there's been bloodshed and fighting?'

'No, in my language that would be a bloody shit time.'

'Which is when there's been bloodshed, fighting and shitting?'

'No, in my language that would be a fucking shit time.'

'Which is when there's been bloodshed, fighting, shitting and fucking?'

'Mate, I don't believe anything I'm telling you is to your benefit.'

'Yes—' he said, 'but can I ask a question in return?'

'Sure.'

'Why do Australians swear so much?'

'Because we've got nothing else to do, now can I ask one back?'

'Yes?'

'Why, like a toy, do Indians wobble their heads?'

He leant back and laughed. 'Ah, that is very good, Mr Dave! Because we've got nothing else to do also. Or have an obsession with retaining our balance.'

We were near the end of the meal when someone collapsed into the seat next to me like a puppet having its strings cut. 'I'm sorry,' said the person. It was Kushal's drunk mate.

With India being an alcohol-dry country, I'd never before seen an Indian tanked, but when it came to camels this bloke didn't know if he was smoking them or riding them. The heat emitting from his head was a sensation to behold, and I felt almost sad I didn't have handy a bag of marshmallows.

Kushal twisted in his seat, but if he was embarrassed on my behalf he needn't have been, as I wasn't that bothered by his mate, until, when Charlie sat under his feet, he kicked him hard out the way. From a dark place, the weather in my head rolled in, and only just keeping check of the storm, I picked up Charlie and placed him on my lap.

'Why is this stupid little dog here anyway?'

The storm blackened.

'He's Mr Dave's dog, you idiot!' said Kushal, to which Sir James Boag grumbled something under his breath, probably about that long lost lotto ticket.

'So tell me, Mr Dave,' he said, 'where do you think you're taking this dog?'

'Goa.'

'Ha!'

The storm blackened, and the thunder rumbled.

'Something funny?' Kushal asked.

'His pipedream!'

'And why is that?'

'Because a dog on a motorbike is not reality!'

'Not reality?'

'Yes, not reality!' he said, using the word *reality* as though he'd recently learnt it.

'So what is this dog's name?'

'Charlie.'

'Ha!' he laughed again, and in a clatter of dishes, he rose to his feet. 'Charlie is not reality! Why don't you leave Charlie dead on the road where he belongs? *That* is his reality.'

The storm blackened, the thunder rumbled, and—in my mind's eye—lightning struck him plum between the eyes. 'Well, mate, if I get him to Goa I'll send you a photo of him sipping cocktails on the beach.'

He slumped back into his seat and handed me his card. 'Ring me then and I'll believe it.'

The candle of night had burnt to its end, and when we made it back to the hotel, Kushal turned to me with a bothered face. 'I'm very sorry about my friend, Mr Dave. He brings much indignity upon himself.'

'That's ok, mate, we all do in some way or another.'

We stood in the hallway for a few minutes, and having bid our farewells, we departed to our rooms.

Charlie was as worn out as I, and when I kicked my shoes into the corner, he buried himself in them for the night. I lay on the bed, and spending a last few seconds marinating in my determination to get him to Goa, plunged into a hollow of sleep.

I woke the next morning to find him curled up by my knees. 'Charlie, Charlie, Charlie…' I said, and as his eyes slowly opened, his tail fired up like a wee little rudder. 'How about you be a good little bloke and don't piss on the bed this morning!' to which he rose to his feet, yawned, stretched, and pissed all over the bed. 'Ah for farck's sake, Charlie!'

Primed for the day, he sat there, wagging his tail and waiting for me to do whatever came next.

*****

Dear Manuel,

So I'm riding along the highway the other day when up ahead a bus swerves to avoid something on the road. I'm behind some distance, and as I ride I see the object of concern. It's a puppy. I snatch him off the road, and in an instant I'm raging with a paternity I didn't know I had. Maybe I need to reacquaint myself with my feminine side, and have a night in with *Steel Magnolias*.

So the bike tour has changed, and so has life for my little mate. Not a bad gig for a dog on course to be food for the crows. I've since named him Charlie, and although I can't see it; I'm seeing this story through.

I've stayed in some dubious joints, towns dark and grim, with names almost as long as the alphabet. At the end of a day's ride, I try to pull in before sundown, but having horribly mistimed it the other night, the sun was long gone and I was still on the road.

The night was set in, as cold as it was dark, and in the cracked state I'm in by the end of a day's ride, I roll into a town called Bardoli. I cruise up the town's main drag, filthy, wide-eyed, and as though summonsed by some instinct, I'm nervous.

I park the bike, and walk the litter-strewn streets doing my least favourite thing—hotel hunting. With all showing me the door, the pickings are proving slim. I'm dirty and getting dirtier, and Charlie is wriggling in the bag just enough to inspire hives.

So I'm standing on the street, wondering what to do, when from out of the shadows approaches a disreputable-looking man. 'There's a Hindu temple down the road,' he says. I swell with suspicion. 'It houses people for free. Perhaps even your kind.' And standing there, wondering what kind I am, he offers to take me there personally.

'Everything is wrong about this.' I think, but feeling I have no choice, I follow.

So I walk into this holy place, feeling even less holy than I look, when from out of the cracks of the temple walls, some 30 of his henchmen circle around. With a cigarette hanging from his mouth, the leading man steps forward and explains that the accommodation at the temple is *not sufficient for a westerner.*

'So why was I brought here?' I think. 'And why has he changed his story?'

'But—' he says. 'There is more fitting place. If you would come with us?'

Everything is wrong about this, and screaming 'don't do it man!' every hair on my arm is standing on end. But like a pre-bloodied victim knocking on murder's door, I feel I have no choice but to enter and I hop on the bike.

To the snap of his fingers, the henchmen disband, filing themselves into a convoy of cars. And stamping out his cigarette, the leading man instructs me to follow their lead.

'It's a trap!' my arm hairs scream, and as though suspecting my intention to flee, the leading man hops on behind me when I start the bike.

'Where are we going?' I ask over the engine.

'You will see,' he says, signalling the convoy to move 'em on out.

I follow the fleet into the gloomy night. It starts to rain.

'The web is sticky, and I'm caught in its outer. I'm walking into a trap, what's the motive? What's the catch?'

And as we're barrelling along the highway I remember that I'm in Gujarat—famous for its political tension and religious bloodshed. With my imagination running like a horse on fire, words like *kidnapping* and *hostage* are shooting within.

The web is sticky, and I'm drawing into its centre.

The highway is an orgy of offense, with as many screaming trucks as mosquitoes in my face, flashing headlights and a pending fate. Then, creating a sensation like a dull punch against the chest, Charlie starts wriggling in the pouch.

Like a television satellite receiving a frenzy of information, there's too much for my brain to handle—the leading man behind, the convoy in front, the cars, the rain, the wriggling dog. But as though not enough in the palette of mayhem, a large truck, beeping its horn and flashing its lights, comes boring up behind us.

I accelerate hard, trying to gain clearance, but drawn by the need to feel included, it's then that Charlie jumps clean out of the pouch. For the first time, he's managed escape—and while barrelling along the highway at 90 kph, he's standing on the tank.

I wish to grab him, but like an octopus juggling eight things, my hands are otherwise occupied. If he falls, he dies. His heart is racing, my heart is racing, and nervous—like a daunted surfer on a death-defying wave—Charlie knows his balance is not to last. And then, like Gollum into the fire, he fell...

> *Charlie is dead! Charlie is dead!*
> *was the pain that shot through heart and head.*
> *But when I catch, I never fail,*
> *by hook or crook, by head or tail.*

In the shards of a shattered second, my right hand involuntarily responded, and with the reflexes of a table tennis champion, I caught Charlie. Or at least had a fist full: two parts scruff, one part ear. But the grip was weak, and to thwart him from becoming a canine pancake, I had to compensate its flaw in the next second or less.

Charlie was down there, and while screeching at this claw-like devise suddenly married to his head, was wriggling with the fury of a hooked salmon. But this was less a time for love than for radical measures, and, left with little choice but to gamble, I threw him into the air.

Charlie was up there, and like the bike and me, he too was travelling at 90 kph. My right hand—composed less of flesh and blood than dread and panic—reached up.

Airborne he went up, and airborne he came down, and having hooked him into the crease of my elbow, I swung him against my chest. But as though that weren't enough, as I dunked him into the pouch, coming head-on was a bus.

Having little choice, I manoeuvred the bike across the face of the oncoming traffic, and with the bus having screamed past my side, we'd made it just. Still, the peril was not at its end, as now caught on the road's gravelly edge, we bumped awkwardly along.

Doing all I could to remain on the bike, we lastly came to a halt, and with the bike stalling as we did, I collapsed my head in my hands. Charlie—his timing for romance questionable—rose from the bag and licked my chin. His heart was racing, my heart had stopped, but like George W. winning Election 2004, he was back in the game despite the mess he'd made.

Shortly after we arrive at the proposed hotel, and like a spinning coin landing on the side of choice, things flip from gloom to fortune. The hotel is glorious! It's four-star at least! 'If I'm about to be killed, at least I'll have freshly-brushed teeth.'

So we—myself and the leading man—stand out the front of this class establishment. With the sound of car doors shutting around us his convoy empty into the car park.

'Surely this is someone's cousin's uncle's hotel?' I think. 'And I'm about to be charged nine times the regular price.'

The henchmen gather around, and together, in some sort of *Reservoir Dogs* re-enactment, we pour into reception.

We arrive at the upstairs desk, and the price is as feared—

extravagant. Surrendered to my predicament, when I reach for my wallet the catch is revealed. The leading man turns to me. 'I want you to meet my daughter.'

'What?' I ask, as a girl about eighteen years of age walks into the lobby.

Probably feeling the closest she had to being in a criminal line-up, she stands opposite with an awkward smile, and I, definitely feeling the closest I had to being in a criminal line-up, return it with the same. I'd heard of these setups before, that although breaking the Hindu circle, Indians try to marry their offspring into the families of westerners.

'So?' he says, pushing for an answer.

'So.' I return, searching for an excuse. And knowing that without a ring on my finger, I cannot profess to be married, I reach for a lower tier. 'I'm studying to be a priest.'

'Really?'

'Really.'

'Very good, Father Dave. Welcome to the family!'

And if ever there's a cue to bring out the party clowns, it's now, as right before my eyes he pulls out a wad of sweaty money and not only prepays for the room, but orders his henchmen to unpack my bike and lug all my gear up the stairs.

The web has lost its stick.

We enter room *101*, and where things are usually dusty and dull, they're sparkling and clean. It's got a telly… white sheets… a door without a hole… and something more treasured than all the gold beneath the Earth—a hot shower! 'A hot shower?' 'That can mean only one thing… I'm about to have a *hot fffuucckkeenn shower!*'

With my bags and guitar in arm, the henchmen file into the room, sealing the occasion by cracking open a bottle of scotch. This is truly a stroke of luck that couldn't have been better timed, and I checkout the next day a rehabilitated man.

The following day rolls on, but with the bike playing up in a major way, I'm sweating on it getting me further than the length of my nose. At every set of lights, every speed hump, it stalls. And despite the fact I've got a bachelors-masters-associate-diploma-on-how-to-distinguish-a-motorbike-from-a-horse certificate, I cannot for the life of me start it.

It's night by the time we get to a town called Songadh. It's dark, freezing, and every time I so much as slow down, the bike cuts out. But worse, so much worse, are the shadow-starers, the men whose lives are so evidently mundane that the slightest display implores them to gather an inch from your face.

Like a concert in the round, I'm so engulfed in a sea of spectators that if handed a mic, I might have launched into *The Power of Love* by Huey Lewis & The News. But mic-less, I do the next most relevant thing, and I kick and kick the kick-starter.

Like the Big Bad Wolf trying to blow the house down, my efforts are futile, and starting on the bike's behalf, my bottom lip begins to quiver. The crowd gathers in tighter, and when 12,583 kicks later the bike roars to life, they erupt into the sort of victorious roar you'd expect if India beat Australia in the World Cup.

With men jumping like popcorn, I click the bike in gear and proceed up the road, but not 100 metres later it stalls again. A new crowd gathers, but unable to better the last performance, I hop off and push us to a not-very-nearby hotel.

I check in. I'm absolutely, tenfold beyond definition, exhausted.

The pending dawn.
The only thing worse than the existence in every moment is knowing there'll always be a tomorrow in which to pack a fresh suffering.

The morning is heavy, and although I wish otherwise, the bike is undeniably not going to start. I know it, Charlie knows it, and every bloke on the street warming up his eyeballs for the next show, knows it. Regardless I prep on.

The beginning of a day's ride is like gearing up for battle—straps, ropes, belts; everything is fastened and locked in. The plight is heavy enough, but it's here that I plonk a sandbag on the scales. 'Before starting the bike, I'll quickly grab some food.'

I sit down in a humble little eatery and begin tucking into a meal. I'm quite happy to be there, but not two minutes in I realise I've eaten peanuts, which give me not a range of nutrients, nice taste, or any form of warm and fuzzy feeling, but a bull's-eye of anaphylactic shock.

My throat begins to swell shut, and I need to induce major vomiting in order to rectify the effect. If I can't do it myself, I'll need to get to a hospital. But when in India, there are few places whose innards I'd rather see less.

I can feel the inner churning begin, as though every internal clockwise system is gearing up for anti-clockwise action. Like a wave of dread that must be ridden, I have to let the reaction simmer before I can vomit. I stick two fingers down my throat, as far as my elbow will allow. I hack like a cat on a fur ball. The result: donuts.

I approach the bike, having decided to pull up and hurl in 20 kilometres or so. 'Please start…' I wince, as I sling myself onboard. My fingers are crossed, my toes are crossed, and like rusted cogs in need of oil, my guts are steadily churning. An ocean of onlookers gather, and, having noticed me fail to start the bike, a man steps forward and offers to lead me to a nearby mechanic. I oblige, concluding there to be no point riding to get stuck between towns. I follow his lead and a crowd of some hundred follow.

We reach the mechanic's, and as though by some ironic symbolism, as I sit there watching him twisting his spanners, my innards grind in replication. A flock of children sit around me, and with sweat pouring off my forehead I try my best to act around my predicament. The spanners are turning and the children are laughing, and I smile the only way I know how—strenuously. One youngster starts dancing on the spot, and when he laughs aloud and jumps into my lap, a microwave bell rings in the epicentre of my guts. The peanut-parcel is ready.

I stand up and try to wander off unnoticed, but noticed entirely; the kids rise to their feet and follow. My wish for discretion has turned into what looks like a victory parade: I'm about to spew and people are waving from their balconies. I'm about to spew and kids are holding my hand. I'm about to spew, I begin to run. I'm about to spew, they begin to run.

Hunched from the pain, I refrain from vomiting and head back to the mechanic's. The bike is thankfully ready. I pay the man, start the bike, and leave the kids in a wake of departure dust. I'm about to spew.

I'm now thumping along the highway, and like towels turning in the wash; my guts are on spin cycle. I'm about to spew. I'm green, I'm yellow, or like a Rainbow Paddle Pop left to die in the sun, I'm the entire spectrum. I need to pull over, but I want to get this over with away from intrusive eyes. I find a place on the roadside. It's quiet, with no one around. I stop the bike, jump off, and it comes...

I am no longer David Kerrigan, I am David Vesuvius, I am Etna, and am erupting out of holes I didn't know I had. I'm on my knees, I look up, there's no one around, Charlie is biting my shoe. I'm now on all fours, convulsing, and like a caterpillar walking on a branch, am giving it that manoeuvre where you thrust from neck to pelvis. Quite sexual in fact, only, I'm feeling about as sexual as a geriatric who cannot for the life of him remember where he left the key to his Viagra cupboard. I look up, there's still no one around, Charlie is licking my ear. I'm now demoted to foetal position, my vision is blurry, my heart is racing, and the throbbing in my temples is like a dull fist mechanically pounding away. I've peaked! I've exploded! I've climaxed in the polar-opposite way to orgasm! This is a trauma-gasm! Charlie is pissing next to my head, I'm lying in a puddle of my own disgust, I look up, there's 40 grinning guys circled around me.

The next day I was eating in another humble little eatery, when, wouldn't you know it.. I ate nuts again. 'May the inventor of the peanut spend eternity burning in the fires of anaphylactic hell.'

I'm hoping the Charlie story ends well, but if I can't find a suitable adopter, I'll sacrifice him into a nut-free hamburger. God knows I need the protein.

To be continued…

16. The Passing of Charlie

Some weeks passed by the time we reached the state of Maharashtra in central India, and where things prior had felt dry and dusty, they now had a cool and forested feel.

After a few hours of riding across the high green planes we rolled into a hill station town by the name of Ellora. I pulled into the driveway of a small hotel, and when I switched off the bike I was sure I heard coming from a telly the phrases *two for twenty-two*, and, *marvellous*.

I walked up the long driveway, where at its farthest end was a bunch of locals watching the cricket. 'Where are you from?' they asked. When I told them they broke into raptures, as right there on the box—being commentated by our very own Richie Benaud—was India playing Australia.

They pulled up an extra chair, and short of having in hand a glass of something chilled, this juncture felt almost like home. Charlie was strapped to my chest, and it wasn't until I pulled him out that anyone even noticed.

'Vhy like dis?' asked the manager.

'Well… because he's me mate, that's why.'

But with his face turning in on itself, I gathered he wasn't too thrilled by the prospect of a four-legged guest.

'Do you have any rooms, please?'

'Will your dog make any noise or mess?'

'Well, if shredding cardboard, pissing, shitting, barking, getting his head stuck between pipes, farting, licking, sniffing, dribbling and whinging are considered unfavourable, then perhaps.' I, for the duration of my hesitance to respond, thought.

'Will your dog make any noise or mess?' he repeated.

'Ahhhr… no.'

He slung us a room key.

'So you've come here to see the Ellora Caves?'

'What caves?

'What do you mean, *what caves*? The Ellora Caves are one of the most sought-after attractions of India!'

'Oh.' I said. (Being a traveller who prides himself in travelling without guidebooks, I probably miss out on the odd attraction, health tip, and do and don't. But I'd like to think I make up for it with the element of surprise when I discover things unexpectedly. Or perhaps I just enjoy the look on people's faces when I point up at monuments like the Taj Mahal and ask for its name.)

Later that day I took Charlie to the caves, which were less than a kilometre from the hotel. And by golly the man was right.

The Ellora Caves, believed to be as old as the 5th century, are an ancient site of 34 temples carved by hand directly out of a cliff face spanning a two-kilometre area. I generally cherish my ignorance, but as I wandered through the labyrinth of rock statues and ornamented pillars, I nearly lost faith.

The highlight of the day, however, was when a family of 30

locals asked if they could have their photo taken with Charlie, all of whom stood in an assembled line while the head of the family nursed the pup in the middle. I wasn't sure why—perhaps they thought he was famous? Or that he brought good luck? But it felt like the official mark of Charlie's graduation to rock stardom— 'little star!'

The day was at its end when we made it back to the room, and as per all predictions, Charlie spent the night shredding cardboard, pissing, shitting, barking, getting his head stuck between pipes, farting, licking, sniffing, dribbling and whinging. In fact, he was such a noisy, petulant, and somebody-please-tell-me-why-I-brought-this-little-wanker-with-me sook, that several times the manager knocked on the door and firmly ordered I shut him up or leave.

I woke the next morning to find him curled up against me. 'Charlie, Charlie, Charlie...' I said, and as his eyes steadily opened, his tail fired up like a wee little rudder. 'Now—' I said, with a tone firmer than usual, 'make sure you be a good little bloke and don't piss on the bed!' to which he rose to his feet, yawned, stretched, and just as he was about to fulfil his morning quota, in walked the manager. 'Make sure he doesn't piss on the bed!' he yelled, to which Charlie farted and pissed all over the bed. 'Ah for farck's sake, Charlie!'

And with the little black dog sitting there, wagging his tail and waiting for me to do whatever came next, the manager did his fruit, veg, and his nut. 'That is it! You barbarians! Fucking get out!'

I swiftly packed our things and we were soon back out on the open road, weaving through the lush landscapes of this evergreen state. Goa-bound we were, for if today we made good time I was hoping to reach Charlie's final destination, find him a taker, and continue south on my own.

The road drew ever on, and with the sensation of riding—and the music in my ears—I drifted into a field of thought deep enough to keep me frightened. Having forgotten almost entirely, when I turned to reach for my bottle my nose registered the most horrific smell. I looked down. 'Ah for farck's sake, Charlie!'

Charlie had shat in the bag, indeed he had and he had indeed. And if this wasn't symbolic of our drawing conclusion, then I didn't know what was. But if I'd hoped for embarrassment to overcome him, then I was gravely denied, as with his head hanging out and tongue flapping in the wind, he just sat there chilling in his shit-soiled pouch—'*not* a little star today!'

The hours on the road rolled forth, and with the smell of Charlie's work haunting my nostrils, I was starting to stretch in patience, willpower, and all of the above. Leagues of asphalt passed our underbellies, and like running from a monster in a bad dream, I wondered if we were getting anywhere at all. But inch-by-inch and mile-by-mile the terrain grew lusher, and by the time the crimson sun was in the latter half of its afternoon shift we crossed the border into the tiny state.

Almost instantly, the tropical promise of Goa granted its pledge—along with the vegetation, the insects seemed to double in size. Butterflies the size of your hand fluttered across the highway, and the buzzing of bugs cut noisily through the roadside forests. The beaches, fringed with palm trees and black lava rock, were strewn with as many westerners as locals. And the emerald green bays, dotted with fishing boats, repeated along the coast.

The coastal road often deviated inland, cutting through rice fields being ploughed by buffalos up to their knees in mud. The Goan houses were a sight as well; as this was the first place in India I'd seen personal residences with tall fences and pebble driveways. Some homes were grandiose dreams—double-storey brick dwellings with classy verandas, set back on acreages of manicured gardens.

The state's former Portuguese rule was evident along the highway; as dotted along were derelict churches crowned with the Catholic cross, and roadside shrines of Jesus and Mary adorned with flowers and candles.

We rode north to south the full length of the state's one-hundred kilometre coastline, and by the time the red sun tucked itself behind the palm-cut horizon, I knocked on the door of a private residence advertising rooms.

A lady answered, but unlike any I'd seen, she stood no taller than about 4 feet. She was one of Goa's native pygmies. 'Are you looking for a room?'

'Yes,' I said, but as her eyes filled with the sight of a grubby pup strapped to my chest, they fell to a puzzled look. 'Vhy like dis?'

'Well, because… I don't really know anymore.'

'Will he shit or piss?'

'Probably.'

'That's ok. I like this little dog. What is his name?'

'Prince Charles. Do you want him?'

She took him in arm and gave him a long heartfelt pat. 'Maybe… maybe he can live with us.'

'Fair dinkum?'

'What?'

'I mean, really?'

'I'll think about it. Talk to me in the morning,' she said, handing me the key and closing the door.

With hope imported, I sat on the bed, and when I kicked my shoes into the corner, Charlie buried himself in them for the night. I laid down, and spending a last few seconds wondering why Superman and Wonder Woman never got it on, I tumbled into an abyss of sleep.

An indefinable amount of time passed.

'Dave, Dave, Dave…'

And waking abruptly to the sound of a Scottish voice, I sat bolt upright from the bed, where, to my absolute bewilderment, standing at its foot end was Ange. I shook my head, wildly, but before I could begin to ask why, when, and what was going on—*bang!*—I awoke and sat bolt upright from the bed. There was no one there.

The Goan sun rose, and regardless of the nice pygmy lady's verdict, I was determined that this be the day I seal an adoption deal. I rose to my feet, yawned, stretched, considered how long it'd been since I'd had bacon and eggs, and went into the yard to find the lady feeding her pigs. 'Did he shit or piss?' she asked.

'Simultaneously, upside down, and probably while rolling a joint,' I thought while yawning impolitely.

She took him in arm for another pat, first wiping a considerable amount of the subject of concern off her hands. It was the longest few seconds of my life, and I felt as anxious as a dealer on the line of bankruptcy. 'So do you want him?'

She looked up at me with her big brown eyes. 'Yes,' she said, and in knowing that my task was done and dusted, my mind couldn't but go for a much-anticipated wander into *Freedom Land*—that thoroughly appealing place where a man can sit back, relax, and free from the judgment of others wipe his hands in his jeans—'

'—But—' she added, causing the retraction of my breath, 'my husband doesn't.'

She handed back the dog, and if ever I could discern increments of growth, he felt at least four times as heavy.

She told me of some nearby villages where I might find an

interested party, and so with little choice, I brushed his hair and straightened his whiskers. Behaviour was an equally key part of his marketability, and when we met prospective takers I could only hope he'd wag his tail and refrain from his favourite pastime of trying to outstare his knackers.

We hit the road.

As the one who loved him most, I didn't want to give him to just anyone, but wanted the heir to the Charlie throne to be someone worthy of my little mate—a devout dog lover, with an open residence, and away from roads.

We made a dot-to-dot trail from one village to the next, but seemed to be getting little interest at all. Better put, the interest we were getting was less than up to par, especially that of one inquiring party who had on his forearm a tattoo of a hanging dog. Although I was keen to keep the motorbiking tour pushing south, I was getting the feeling this undertaking could stretch into a painful process.

Having grown fed up for the day, I figured it was time to hit the water, and so I pulled into Candolim Beach.

With its soft white sands, Candolim was one of the quieter beaches in the area, and was less dotted with tourists than the odd local with a fishing line. There was a rusted shipwreck marooned in the water, and just south, overseeing the panorama, was the Aguada Fort.

The day was hot, and so with my little black dog with his fully built-in white socks in arm, I proceeded into the sea. Perhaps to my subconscious plan, wading in the shallows—wearing a white bikini—was an attractive western girl. She had long blonde hair, and seeming to replicate Ursula Andress in her Bond Girl heyday, kept emerging from the water and flicking her hair onto her back.

Charlie, having no concept of the water being something

he couldn't chew, looked distinctly nervous, though his doggy paddle was down by default. I held him aloft at times, and his legs, like a remote control car with its wheels turning, kept paddling in the air.

The girl drifted closer, smiling at the spectacle. 'My husband has a dog like that in Germany!'

'There falls that apple then.' thought I, smiling politely.

Her name was Siena.

'Where did you get him?'

I told her the full story, in all the nauseating detail I could muster. It was sickening, and if I weren't myself I would have clipped me over the ear. Yet putting her hand to her heart—and making an array of *oo* and *ar* noises—her reaction gave me the business idea of renting puppies to blokes otherwise romantically bankrupt.

'Girls dig this stuff don't they?'

'Very much.'

'Why?'

'Because it shows what a man may be like as a father to your unborn children.'

'I see. So do you want him?'

'No. But I know someone who might,' she said, going on to explain that she was friendly with a local man who ran a nearby beach shack restaurant, who, just the day before, told her he was looking to get a dog.

She agreed to take me.

There were several shacks dotted along the beach, but with the one of reference being at the far end of Candolim, we began the one kilometre trek. She spent it telling me just how in love with her husband she was, and having sprained my face muscles from pretending I cared; I was relieved when we arrived.

The beach shack description proved to be no lie, as set up

on the sand, this restaurant—or better put, western-geared chill bar—was little more than a bamboo gazebo enclosed with dry palm leaves. Fairy lights blinked along the ceiling rafters, and the air was infused with Goan trance music.

We took a seat on some cushions. 'That's Vivash over there,' she said, pointing to the man behind the bar. 'Let me go speak to him.'

'No. Not yet. I just want to scope things out.'

I sat Charlie in my lap. 'So what do you reckon? Do you fancy being a beach mutt?' It certainly looked like a good life for a dog—there were other dogs, no main roads, plenty of folk to dote on him, and it was on the beach for frick's sake. I'd always meant to sort him out, but not to give him a life better than my own. The most important criteria, however, was whether this Vivash-bloke was a fitting soul. Siena called him over.

'Guten tag,' she said as he sat down.

'Namaste.'

'Is this your place, mate?'

'Yes, I've been here for ten years,' he said, his eyes scanning around as though he couldn't fathom a more perfect setting. 'It's a labour of love, and the view makes up for the wages.'

'Half your luck.'

'And you? You look like you've seen more miles than rice.'

'Something like that.'

'And not on your own, I see?'

'This is my four-legged son.'

'What is his name?'

I told him, and when his tail fired up like a wee little rudder when said by Vivash, my confidence in the setup grew.

'I'm looking for a dog myself.'

'I know.'

Siena eyeballed me, but like a surrogate struggling with the handover, I felt suddenly filled with reluctance. I placed Charlie on the sand, and he lay between Vivash and me.

'So where did you get him?'

'Rajasthan.'

'For real?'

'3,500 kilometres ago. Regretted it ever since.'

I looked down at my dog, recollecting the slideshow since our desert highway meeting. He gazed up, as though aware of being the topic of conversation, and he yawned, stretched, and just when I expected his worst he stood up and climbed into Vivash's lap. I couldn't deny that I felt a faint twinge. 'He's like a four-legged pilgrim,' said Vivash, giving him an earnest pat. 'I wonder how many dogs have left the state they were born in?'

'None, I would think. So do you want him?'

'What?'

'Do you want him?'

He leant forward. 'But he's your dog?'

'He is, but I'm not sure of my movements after India, so it's just not practical.'

'Practicality is a disease.'

'You're right, but I know this would be a great place for him.'

Vivash lifted the pup to head height. 'So, Charlie, do you have any thoughts on the matter?'

The pup uttered no sound, but answered by way of relieving his bladder in mid-air.

'Ah for farck's sake, Charlie!'

'I think that's his way of signing the contract. I'll take him.'

Vivash yelled over to his staff, and having obviously given them the adoption news, they, in their own language, broke into rapturous conversation—the only word comprehensible to my ears being *Charlie*. Having always considered him a true blue Australian, it was peculiar seeing him respond to Hindi as much as English.

'The staff sleep here at night,' he said, 'you're welcome to stay a couple of nights so Charlie adjusts before you leave.'

It was a great idea.

I exhaled the deepest I had in a while, but before cracking open a celebratory beer, I needed to make a terribly important phone call.

The phone rang until someone answered. 'Hello?'

'Is that Sir James Boag?'

'What?'

'You probably don't remember me because you were too hammered on the night—'

'—Who is this?'

'The Australian bloke you met a while back.'

'Who?'

'The one who you took pleasure in condescending about bringing my dog to Goa being, as you said, not reality.'

'What do you want?'

'To let you know we made it, and that Charlie now lives on a beach, being fed banana pancakes for breakfast and caviar for dinner. So stick that in your reality-pipe and smo—'

And even more satisfying than the tang of retribution was the fact he hung up on me.

I walked back to the shack and cracked a beer.

It was about 4 p.m., and with Charlie off my hands, I hopped on the Blue Fly and headed into Panaji: the capital of Goa.

Generally, I try to keep my aversions as evenly distributed as possible, but the reason for the city dash was to purchase the one thing I dislike more than anything else—postcards. I hate receiving them, because when I do I'm usually stuck behind a desk, less than happy to have a mate rub in the fact he's on a beach in South America. And—because the last thing I want to do while on a beach in South America myself is sacrifice my time to writing postcards—I hate sending them even more. In fact, I've known people who've come back from holidays in worse shape than when they left, all because they've fallen ill to the expectation of writing postcards.

My feelings towards email are similarly strained, and so I've devised, arrogantly enough, the *Ten Commandments of Email and Social Media:*

1. Thou shall never reply to an email, in which someone has gone to great efforts to tell you all their news with, 'tell me all your news!' They just did.

2. After sending a traveller an email stipulating that home is boring, work is boring, and that you yourself are questioning the point of your existence because you are in fact at home, thou shall never ask free people out travelling, 'when are you coming home?'

3. A tip for us all: thou shall never write 'ha ha!' after a comment considered funny, because if it wasn't the only attainment is having made an unnecessary goose of thyself. For similar reasons, even more socially suicidal is the acronym *lol.*

4. Thou shall ruin their entire life by means other than accidentally pressing *reply all.*

5. Thou shall be mindful of exclamation marks; for overenthusiastic use can suggest a depletion in brain wattage—example: 'today I went to the shops!!!' Ask thyself first if it was really that life changing.

6. Because it's unforgivably rude—so much so that it should merit capital punishment by way of the accused being

subjected to continuous episodes of the *Jerry Springer Show*—thou shall never reply to a personal email with a group email.

7. To bring even the most mundane story to life, thou shall apply colourful language liberally.

8. Thou shall change more than just the recipient's name when copy and pasting the same written material to multiple people.

9. Thou shall never end with PS comments. It's like after serving a seven course meal, asking your dinner guests if they'd like to go for a swim—PS it probably would have worked better beforehand.

10. And speaking of Facebook, thou shall never *like* a post where someone is trying to raise money for charity without also coughing up. It's like giving a homeless person a round of applause.

But ill feelings aside, I figured on this day I best send a few postcards home.

I arrived at the post office in downtown Panaji. 'Hello,' I said to the uninterested-looking lady sitting behind the counter. 'Do you sell postcards?'

'No,' she said, filing her nails.

'Do you sell envelopes?'

'No,' she said, filing and chewing.

'Then I guess an albino Tasmanian tiger is out of the question?'

This lady looked so bored by life that one could fair assume she spent her Sundays thanking the good lord that breathing was involuntary. I'd have gotten better customer service from the dead.

I figured I seek my needs elsewhere, and so down the street I sought. But, safe in the knowledge that around nine out of ten corners was usually someone selling postcards, I figured it'd take a minute or less.

Around and around I wandered, but there wasn't a hawker to be seen. I found the hopelessness even more frustrating than the usual harassment. I wanted to get back; worried that Charlie might have eaten half the sand at Candolim.

After two hours of fruitless hunting, I found a local boy with a tray of miscellanea for sale, thankfully including postcards. I took a packet off his hands.

I quickly headed back to the post office and approached the same lady, who'd upgraded from filing her nails to eating the world's soggiest-looking sandwich.

'Can I have some stamps, please?'

She leant forward, wiped the mayonnaise off her face, and slapped a *closed* sign on the counter. 'It's lunchtime, Come back in an hour.'

'But it's five o'clock in the arvo!'

She tapped the sign. 'In India, everything is possible.'

A muscle in my temple started to twitch, as the rage, like a river of lava, rose north from my feet and into my arse. My lungs, like a combustion chamber, filled with fire, as did my head with noise and steam. I closed my eyes, through fear of a laser beam firing out of them, and in my mind's eye I could see myself standing at a t-intersection of a ghoulish world. At it was a large sign: ◀ left turn *Buddha*—right turn *Hitler* ▶. Singing *Give Peace a Chance*, the figure of baby Jesus floated down, and just as I felt the will to turn left, a crow swooped down and pecked out his eye. I turned right instead.

'Everything is possible, ey?'

'Yes, everything is possible.'

'Is that some slogan you learn at school?'

She tapped the sign.

'All I need is some stamps, like the ones next to your left hand. So if you can kindly reach over all of six inches.'

She leant back and resumed filing her nails. A bitter staring match ensued, but with Indians being, by default, the Muhammad Ali's of staring, I didn't much like my chances. She eventually reached over to her top drawer and slapped a handful of stamps on the counter, and as she leant back and continued filing I saw— in her drawer—not only stamps but a large bundle of postcards.

'And the nominees for the *Most Unhelpful Being in the Universe* are:

1. People who work in *all* national embassies.

2. The slapdash alien who was supposed to check that E.T. was back on the spaceship before they buggered off back to wherever they came from.

3. And the soggy-sandwich-eating nail-filing fiend that works at the post office in Panaji, India. Planet Earth.'

No drumroll required for the winner

It was night by the time I made it back to the beach. I parked the bike, and as I marched towards the shack, a sombre-looking Vivash approached. 'Sorry, David.'

'What?'

'Charlie ran away.'

I took a second to grasp his words. 'What do you mean *he ran away*?'

'He got scared from all the people. He's gone.'

In the hours I'd run my errands, the beach shack had been converted into a Bollywood movie set, as literally, set up in and around it was a crew filming a scene for a movie. Where during the day it was as tranquil as a birdsong, at night it was a flurry of people, cameras and floodlights.

'In India, everything is possible? Too right it is!'

I was furious, and was beginning to get the feeling I'd had more than enough of this excuse for a country.

I wandered the length of the beach, whistling and calling his name, but with no pup coming in return, my calls just died in the dark. I returned to the shack, still calling him, but I was swiftly told to hush, the least of the crew's concerns being some mutt.

'Charlie ran away!' I kept hearing it in my head, making me angrier by the replay. 'Charlie ran away!' I hadn't carried him 3,500 kilometres in a pouch, fed him a hundred times, and patted him a million, to have him banish into being some nameless street dog. 'Charlie ran away!' I considered that perhaps this was my cue to let him go; that it was fate's way of determining his new life. 'Charlie ran away!' But more than this, I was worried he'd made his way back up to the coastal highway, and images of him being hit were flashing through my mind like a strobe light. 'Charlie ran away! Charlie ran away!'

While standing on the set's periphery, I began to notice the actors—buffed-looking dudes in white tees. And some, having taken the advice of Corey Hart pretty seriously, were wearing sunglasses at night.

The lead actress, a stunning Bollywood starlet—with legs as long as her straight dark hair, and a face and body too perfect to be believed—was positioned at the bar for her scene. Wearing a tiger skin outfit, she seemed to have her hair flicking technique down pat, and each time the director yelled *cut* a flock of hair and make-up people swooped upon her.

Two blokes, both wearing caps and staff passes, approached me. 'Sir, we need a westerner for this scene.'

'Have either of you seen a little black dog?'

'No, no dog. Will you be in our movie?'

'He answers to Charlie. He has fully built-in white socks?'

'No, sir, no dog. Will you feature in our scene?'

'He was here during the day, but cleared out when the noise started.'

'You get to kiss that girl.'

'He's only a few months old, and... what? Really?'

'No, but we need you to stand next to her at the bar.'

Although I was too depressed to be excited, I agreed, and the hair and make-up flock swooped without mercy.

After straightening my *this* and powdering my *that*, they instructed me to take my position at the bar. I stood next to Miss Universe, as unsure of myself as distracted by the sensation of wearing lipstick. She looked over and smiled, with the sort of look that says, 'I know how you feel, I'm so fantastic even *I* can't believe it.' And I smiled back, returning it with the sort of look that says, 'I'm not doing anything later, so if you'd like me to—'

'—Quiet on the set!' the director yelled. 'Action!'

My role, quite simply, was to stand next to her and drink a beer, a fairly natural part for an Australian. But the scene was over before it began, and at the time of writing this line, I've never had an acting gig since.

The morning rose, and as my memory kicked in, so did my great sadness that Charlie had done a runner. I sat on the beach, staring into the nothingness—the horizon, the drifting clouds, when I noticed, about 200 metres further up, a scatter of crows on the sand. Jumping, pecking and squawking about, they were behaving as you'd expect, but when I looked closer I noticed that one was moving differently from the rest. I stood up to gain a better view, and could see that it wasn't waddling with the walk of a bird, but flopping. It wasn't a creature with two legs and wings, but four legs and a tail. It was Prodigal Charlie advancing up the beach, as much propelled by his flapping ears as his fat little legs.

I whistled and called his name, and kneeling down to him he crashed into me joyously. He stank of fish, and like a kid dying to tell his dad about his day at the zoo, in his eyes was a look of profuse excitement. I patted him and patted him again, and he licked my chin and chewed my hand—'little star!'

This was to be my last day with him, as finally tomorrow I was to start heading to Pondicherry to see Ange, after not having seen her since she left the ashram in Rishikesh some two and a half months earlier.

With Goa situated on India's southwest coast, and the city of Pondicherry on its southeast, the ride to see her would take at least two full days, and coerce the entire width of southern India—a distance comparable with Melbourne to Sydney, Los Angeles to San Francisco, or greater than London to Edinburgh.

Trying to get him settled into his new life as a beach mutt, I spent the majority of that day just hanging with Charles, who at one point necked a dead fish, gladly eating it *and* all associated grains of sand. It was proving to be a mostly relaxing day, until Siena the German—just so she could tell me how much she loved her husband one last time—started following me around. Tuned entirely out, I took the opportunity to rehearse my twelve times tables, but unable to sense my disinterest, she even offered the details of their sex life. Yet another fine display of German diplomacy.

The day crinkled into night, and by the time the west-descending sun dipped behind the sea horizon, wouldn't you know it.. Charlie ran away again. But figuring he was somewhere in the beach hood, I was this time less concerned.

I sat up until late, but regardless of his return or lack thereof, I was leaving early the next morning. I lay down on the shack's sand-buckled floor; my concluding thought before falling asleep being that it was up to him.

But if I was concerned, then I needn't have been, as somewhere in the wee hours I awoke to find him huddled next to me. After all we'd been through he was no longer just *a* little star, but *my* little star. I lay awake for a while, staring down and consumed with sadness. He was my running mate in the greatest campaign of life to date.

The next morning came, and so did our parting hour. We stood together on the sand, and wagging his tail and waiting for me to do whatever came next, he gazed up with the usual look of morning zest. When for the first time, though, I tied a rope around his collar, and the other end to the beach shack frame, a canine frown appeared. Perhaps I was being overly sentimental, but as though suspecting some end, he began to shudder. I knelt down and kissed him on the head. 'It's up to you now, buddy', were the last words he heard me say, and with a lump in my throat the size of Jupiter, I stood up, turned, and walked away.

Heavy hearted, I kept walking over the scrub-covered sand dunes, but as the distance between us grew, his whimpering grew equally in volume. I turned to look at him a final time, and mired by the rope, his efforts to run towards equalled nothing but jolts at his neck. Causing the lump in my throat to double, he made a final climactic yelp, and with my eyes damp, I backed away, until behind a sand dune he was gone from sight.

I never saw him again.

17. D'ye Knoo Whot?

Things were back to normal—just me, myself and the Blue Fly. Strapped up for the two-day ride, Ange- and Pondicherry-bound we became.

The road twisted and turned, and the leaves of the roadside palms reached from one side of the road to the other, creating a palm leaf canopy. The experience was like riding through a curving tube of tropical growth, and the sun's rays, like the light from a film projector, flickered through the leafy gaps.

Having straightened out, the highway pushed into the open, and with the music of Metallica thumping in my headphones, I forged into a temper of thought too tough to be challenged. I hugged the bike and it the road, and as I came barrelling around an ascending corner—riding at twice the speed limit—I sighted two cops sitting idle on the kerb. Blowing their whistles, frantically they waved me down, but as I began to brake I remembered the words of Mamma Sharvari—

"*The police are particularly corrupt in Goa, targeting tourists on motorbikes, especially young men on their own. They work in pairs, and when they pull you over, one will talk to you from the front, while the other plants drugs in your baggage. If caught, you'll have to pay an amount of money so extortionate you probably wouldn't have it, or, go to jail.*"

My heart changed like the turning tide.

Twisting the throttle back, I tore onward up the highway, and rising to the challenge, I could see in my mirrors the cops swiftly mount their bikes. It was on, and what better music to score a cop chase than Metallica. I turned it up, and as the bike rose to the throttle's command, *Enter Sandman* wholly took me over. 'Say your prayers little one...'

At neither a gain nor loss they were behind some 300 metres, and while keeping our gap maintained I went flying past a road sign: *Karnataka state border 5 km*. The boundary for the chase was set—their jurisdictional line of concession—but I had to reach it fast. 'Tuck you in, warm within...'

Steadily, my speed increased, but it was then—just as the first Kirk Hammett guitar solo introduced the song's second verse— that a fresh concern rose: that surely there were more cops at the border. 'Something's wrong, shut the light...' And turning on their sirens and lights, my enemy to the rear-left began speaking into a radio mouthpiece.

Almost in time to the music, their red and blue lights flickered and flashed, yet despite the intimidation, I held my pace, but so did they. Knowing, too, that the hot water if caught was going to be a whole lot hotter after having tried to get away, the requirement was simple: Don't get caught. 'Dreams of war, dreams of liars...'

The Blue Fly rattled forth, and I held onto it for the dearest of life, but just when my two-wheeled need was at its most dire, it began to splutter and slow down. 'Gripping your pillow tight...'

The cops were gaining, and gaining fast, and as though their tactical intention was to pull up one on either side of me, they split to opposing sides of the road. Panic gripped me.

The bike coughed and coughed again, but it was then—just as James Hetfield's voice ignited the second chorus—that the bike, flaring to life, lunged forward like a whipped horse. 'We're off to never-never land...'

Back in the race, I leaned forward, and as the second guitar solo came burning into the song, I near had to fight the urge to spend its duration playing air-guitar.

With my eyes watering, we were now moving so fast that the bike was close to the point of petroleum orgasm. In my vibrating mirrors the lights of my pursuers grew smaller. 'Now I lay me down to sleep...'

The road rose to meet me, and having reached its summit it straightened into a homestretch where at its far end could be seen the border crossing. 'Pray the lord my soul to keep...'

As feared, my pursuers had rang border control with news of the hunt, for assembled across the width of the road—with their lights flashing—was a roadblock of two police bikes. 'If I die before I wake...'

The water I was in was now so hot there was no point jumping out at all, for having riled half a police precinct; surely I was going to be locked up if caught. And so, with little choice but to get tactical, it was here that things got illegal.

Behind the roadblock was a small red truck halted at the border, waiting to pass into Karnataka. The gate slowly rose in its accordance, and I slowed down: having devised a plan to hang back long enough so before the gate closed behind it I could speed up, maneuver around the roadblock and pass under myself. 'Hush little baby, don't say a word...'

Hanging back, every second was to major detriment, as now growing in my mirrors, my original pursuers were gaining again.

Sweat was beading and pulses were racing, and having realised my intention, it was just as the truck passed under the gate that one of the border cops yelled to the gateman. 'Never mind that noise you heard...'

Speeding up, this was my cue to now or never, and if this wasn't dog eat dog at its most carnivorous then the hairs on the back of my neck must have been on end for some other reason. 'It's just the beasts under your bed...'

The gate was closing. 'Can I make it?' The gate was closing. 'Can I make it?' I was only metres away, and with blatant intent to remove me from the bike, as I swerved around the roadblock one of the cops grabbed me by the arm. His hands gripped but his grip failed, and I clenched for life while breaking through. 'In your closest in your head...'

The gate was closing. 'Can I make it?' The gate was closing. 'Can I make it?' The truck was long passed and the gate near shut. I had a metre's grace and not a metre more, and just as the gate descended to face height I ducked down and flew under. I was in Karnataka, and looking back I could see my pursuers pull up in defeat. 'Ha ha ha...' I relished with the song's devilish outro.

I reached a small town by dusk, and checked into another penitentiary-like motel.

The room was barely worthy of the noun, and as per the end of any day's ride, I was blackened from the road. I hopped under the shower and scrubbed as though it were a way to make love.

I finished up soon after, but with the grime having proven, again, too difficult to remove from around my eyes, my road-induced eyeliner left me looking like an Alice Cooper tribute act, minus the python. I kicked my shoes into the corner, but where Charlie would normally burrow within, Charlie was no more.

*****

Dear Manuel,

I'm sitting on the balcony of a motel room, in some highway town whose name I'm unlikely to commit to memory.

Outside is nothing but darkness and dust: seemingly comprised of the smells of rubbish and smoke, and the unholy sounds of traffic and clanging steel. Inside is a museum where lice reign. The bed sheets are stale and musty, the menu on the bedside table is worryingly sticky, and, to style, there's a clock ticking on the sideboard.

I wish I could tell you that I knew what was next, other than that I'm going to be sleeping on the floor.

*****

My eyes opened at first light. I stood up from the floor, slowly, the solitary force driving me upwards being the knowledge that if today I made good time I'd reach Pondicherry before nightfall.

I hit the road soon after, comforted instantly by the feeling of motion. It occurred to me repeatedly that I was most at peace when on the bike: as though the feeling of movement distanced me from myself just slightly.

With the hypnotic ticking of the engine proving a fabulous pendulum to think to, an hour on the road passed.

By now comfortably over the Tamil Nadu state border, all pieces felt in place, until I felt a large breeze just overhead. I ducked by instinct, and luckily, as when I looked over my shoulder, I realised I'd been swooped by a large hawk. I tried not to take it personally.

The day on the road stretched on, and after stretching on, it stretched on a little more, and with the landscape flattening into a parched bad land, it figured, that, although not pleasing to the eye, it might as well stretch on a little further.

The ride was proving long, very long, and with the day becoming dusk, and the dusk becoming darkness, my goal to reach Pondicherry had fallen way short. I was at least two hours shy, or shier than that, but I pressed on, loathed to split the journey into a third day.

It was madman's rationale, for the roads got only more carnivorous at night. This road—a national highway—was less a thoroughfare of trucks and buses than an unlit wind tunnel of filth and bullets. I could hardly see at all; riding at night left you one of two options—ride with your sunglasses *on*, see nothing, hit a cow and die; or, ride with your sunglasses *off*, endure all the bugs and filth of India hitting you in the eyes and hope like all shit that nothing blinds you for life. Neither of your choices were good. I made one regardless—*sunniesless*, and so I was being hit in the face like a pohm in a Scottish pub.

I was cold, dirty, and far from home, and as I pressed onward I saw—amid the streak of flashing lights—something in the middle of the road. It moved, it moved again, it was a living thing—it was… it was… a puppy. 'Oh fart wee wee fuckety poo!' thought I as my heart closed like a slamming vault. Fuelled by mounting exhaustion, I barrelled past.

I kept riding, trying to maintain my callas, but like the trunk of drunk elephant, grumpy and bitter while trying to find its way home after a night on the turps, my mind swung from ney to frey. 'Should I go back? Shouldn't I? Should I? Shouldn't I?' and as I struggled to know what was best a little-imaginary-devil-with-little-fluttering-wings appeared at my left shoulder—'Forget it, man,' he said in a sleazily relaxed tone. 'You're an arsehole by default. Besides, what's that scabby little mutt ever done for you anyway?' Speaking in response, a little-imaginary-angel-with-little-fluttering-wings appeared at my right shoulder—'Think of that cute, innocent little pup. You can't possibly come to rest knowing harm came to him. Besides, if you step up I'll speak to god personally and see that when you come to heaven you're put up in a room closer to the canteen.'

Fluttering at my shoulders they bashed it out. First having a sword fight, next a sculling comp, and with their attempts at Sumo wrestling proving equally futile, they settled on a best-of-three game of Scissors Paper Rock. The angel won, and summonsed as if by lightning, I braked and turned around.

Like a bullet anxious to leave the gun, I shot down the highway, and my ego, charged with a dazzling sense of purpose, ate like it was Christmas dinner. I wondered if I'd left it too late; if all I'd find would be a mongrel omelette. But amid the trucks and buses—and everything else—when I made it back to the spot, still the pup was strutting his stuff. How he was unscathed was a miracle, and I, having pulled up beside him, rested my foot against him and softly footed him off the road. Startled, he flew with a yelp, and landing in the roadside's grass, he vanished from sight.

I parked the bike on the roadside, leaving its headlight on, and I tried to spot him as I scanned across the grass. It was dark, very dark, and as I stood there straining to see, I wanted to believe he was safe and that my obligation was fulfilled. There were trucks screaming and buses beeping, and just as I mounted my bike, from 100 metres up, a shriek cut the night in two. He'd been hit, and all because of my hesitation.

I ran towards the squeal, my head playing a slideshow of images of what I might find. He came into view; he was lying flat on his side. Dead, half dead or mangled, I scooped him off the road, and with my hands instantly wet with blood, things didn't seem so well. I took us to the roadside, and save for the strobe of passing headlights, there was no means by which I could properly see him. I ran to the bike and held him in front of the headlight, and the mystery-pup came into view.

He was alive, and polar-opposite to Charlie: he was entirely white in colour, except for his feet having fully built-in black socks. He was shaking from the shock of his injuries, and had a long split running from between his eyes to the top of his head.

Much like the way one clocks on for a work shift they're loathed to do, I reached for the Charlie pouch-bag, strapped it to my chest and dunked him in. I'd been riding for two days, and feeling so tired that the word *tired* felt comparatively energetic, adopting another pup was the furthest thing from the plan.

The night was darker and dirtier than before, and with the threat of scaling half the country to rehome him, a threat too real, as we barrelled along, I promised myself I'd remain detached. Proving a very different passenger to Charlie, he made not a sniff, wriggle, or fidget. In fact, he was so lifeless that on occasion I had to pull over to check he hadn't died in the pouch.

45,627 mozzies in my face later, we reached the great southern Indian city of Pondicherry. But rest and relief were a ways off, as we were yet to reach the address at which Ange was actually staying.

Now, when someone gives you an address, it's usually safe to assume that the numbers and letters represent a place on Earth, not a far-flung realm. But that not being the case, the address she'd given me was for a spiritual commune deep in a rural area called Auroville, on the outskirts of Pondicherry. I gradually made my way, but soon learnt that Auroville was not only tucked away in a *Blair Witch* lookalike forest, but within its maze of grimacing woods were countless other spiritual communes equally unmarked. I entered at the forest's edge, and peering down with branches full of personal gripes, the twisting trees loomed overhead.

It was 11 p.m. or so, and having been riding around the snaking dirt tracks for over an hour, I'd seen not another soul. The forest grew deeper and darker, and bluer and colder, and despite a memory of recently being in India, for all I knew I was in Siberia, the Amazon, or Antarctica when it had trees. I was cold, hungry, sexually frustrated, and consumed with wonder when my tax return was going to come through. But above all gruesome, brutal, and inhumane forms of malignant torture was, 'Don't tell my heart… my achy breaky heart…' I was plagued with the music of Billy Ray Cyrus.

It was dark, darker than before, and if I was any more lost then I might have actually found something worth losing again. The stars were the only light, and having failed to locate her address, when I heard another motorbike approaching through the forest, a great relief washed over me. I turned to see, and like the legs of a creeping spider, the light from its headlight stepped through the trees.

Waving my arms like an inflatable tube man, I yelled out to my saviour, and the young Welshman pulled up beside me.

'For the love of Yahweh, Buddha, Shiva and his mates, where the faaarck am I?'

'Nowhere, pal! This ain't the sort of place that comes with a map!'

'I feel like I've ridden into a Michael Jackson film clip!'

'You really shouldn't be out here at night, pal. It's a maze of trees. Where are you trying to get to?'

I told him, and offering to lead me there personally; if not for a ballpoint pen in hand I would have assigned him the sole beneficiary to my imaginary estate. With him in front and me behind, we rode through the forest.

The relief was so real you could bottle it; to be led by something more knowing than my nose seemed in this moment the most top shelf of luxuries. But it was then, just as my smugness began to set in, that my bike began to cough and spit. 'Not now, you utter, utter fuck!' thought I, as the bike—*without compliments*—stopped dead. Panic-stricken, I yelled forward to my guide, but leaving me to die in the woods, he rode into the darkness. A familiar silence descended, and dropping to my knees I looked to the stars. 'Why? Why? Why doth thee smite me with such vengeance?' And like a hallowed fart ascending into heaven, my little canine patient rose from the kangaroo-bag then fell back down.

I lay in foetal position—figuring I could survive in it for nine months or so—and while down there was so returned to primal origin that I wondered if I could exist out here after all. 'Sure I'll have to hunt dirt and coconuts, but at least I won't have to do tax returns.' As the cold reality of logic returned, the fantasy died in its place, and like the infamous monkey who first reached up for a banana, I rose to my hind legs and began pushing the bike along the tracks. 'Please, sir, I want some more?' Fuck. That.

It must have been midnight, and after pushing the bike for a kilometre or so, I reached what appeared to be an old abandoned mansion. I wasn't sure if it was a spiritual commune; with a façade more akin to a haunted house, it looked more cursed than blessed. Its windows, like eyes with ill intent, were smashed and sullen, and its front door swayed in the wind like the mouth of an incurable. A slither of moon hinted in, and with the trees growing vocal in the breeze, I walked around the house's exterior.

As lifeless as it was huge, there was a blatant wickedness to this place: not at all helped by the sound of dry leaves crunching underfoot. 'Think nice thoughts…' I thought, clinging to the pup no less than to my Gonzo teddy when I was wee.

I approached the front door, and having placed a hand lightly upon it, heavily it creaked open. 'Hello, Hello, Hello…' my voice echoed in the dark, and as though magnetised by some deranged curiosity, I stepped inside.

Inside was darker than out, and just when I wished I could rerun memories from *The Wizard of Oz*… *Bambi*… and *Charlotte's Web*… my mind thrashed with those from *The Exorcist*… *Evil Dead*… and *Friday the 13th*. And it was then, as the creaky door slammed behind me, that Jason spoke… 'Can I help you?'

Having jumped through the roof, stratosphere, and all our neighbouring suns, if I was a cat then I was sure I just shed eight and half lives. Standing before me was a local man, wobbling his head as if, although late to the party, he was delighted to have made it.

I knelt down. 'Ah, Mick, you frightened the shit outta me!'

'My name is not Mick. Are you an archaeologist?'

'No.'

'A policeman?'

'No.'

'A clairvoyant?'

'No.'

'I've always wanted to meet such people.'

'Fair enough,' I said, wondering of the many unsettling reasons why this place might be of interest to them. 'Anyway,' I said, edging for the door, 'I best get going.'

'Not joining us?'

'Us?'

'We are having a party.'

'No, mate… I really best be off.'

'And where are you going?'

I told him, and he explained the commune I was looking for was only five houses further down the road. I headed towards, and spotting a worn-out sign with the name of concern, finally I'd made it to the House of Ange.

First I was met by a security guard at the front gate, who, bored lilac by default, looked delighted to have someone to hassle. He flicked his torch to the brightest setting, and shone it in my face. 'You cannot stay here!'

'I understand,' I said, wheeling the bike past him. I looked over my shoulder, and as though worried there'd be no one to bother for another thousand years he slumped to sadness.

Second I was met by an older western man at the main door. I gathered he was the proprietor, and with the disapproval pouring off him so real you could catch it in a cup, I attempted to be friendly. 'Are you French-Canadian?'

'No.'

'Icelandic?'

'No.'

'From Saint Pierre and Miquelon?'

'No. You cannot stay here.'

'I'm sorry to barge in. I got lost in the forest.'

'We don't cater for your…'

'For my, what?'

The bloke looked as though he'd made love to one carrot too many, as though years of spiritual aspiration had knocked every scrap of personality out of him.

'I'd head back to Pondicherry, but I don't think I'd find my way in the dark.'

'Indeed.'

'Is Ange here, please?'

'Yes, she is.'

A long pause ensued.

'Then can I see her?'

'She's asleep.'

I exhaled heavily.

'Then can you please wake her?'

He went off, and I waited in the dark, feeling as welcome as a peanut in my digestive tract.

After a few minutes I heard a Scottish voice. 'Dave!' and a sneeze—*och-choo!*—and in faded Ange from the dark of night. She was smiling from ear to elbow, was wearing all white, and with her blonde hair longer and her blue eyes bluer, she looked rested and relaxed. I, to the contrary, looked like an extra from a horror movie; still she sacrificed her clean pyjamas to an overdue embrace.

We disengaged.

'D'you know what?'

'Whot?'

'Could've you picked a more pain in the arse joint for me to find?'

'Well, I didnae think ye'd tackle tryin' tae find it at night, ya dunderhead!'

'What's a dunderheid?'

'Someone of questionable brainpower.'

'So how is it anyway?'

'Whot?'

'Life at the Shagging Tree? Your man over here isn't exactly the stiffest of drinks.'

'Aye, and I don't think he's too impressed with ye.'

'The lack of black tie?'

'Aye, they're a strange bunch, these commune folk, very closed and precious.'

'I get the feeling he's on the way to a couscous overdose.'

'Och, don't be an erse, he means well.'

'So do people who wear socks with sandals.'

'Well, ye're no' exactly lookin' spiritually kosher, motorbikin' Willy haudin' a blood-soaked dog! Is that Charlie by the way?'

'No, this is Rudolph the Blood-Red Reindeer.'

And as soon as I heard myself say it, Rudolph was his name.

'Well, the pair of ye look like a walkin' windscreen. Come oan.'

'But I don't think Terry Tofu is too keen on me staying?'

'Don't worry aboot him darlen, ah'll sneak ye intae ma room.'

We settled in, and having bandaged Rudolph's head to the best of my inability, I placed him in a cardboard box. Little less shattered than he, I lay down like a heavy cargo. Neither he, she, nor I made a sound all night.

I woke the next morning to find him lying in a puddle of his own saliva. He was motionless, and until he made a long groaning noise when I lifted him up, I thought he'd died through the night.

Ange opened her eyes. 'D'ye knoo whot?'

'What?'

'Let's get ootae this place.'

I couldn't have agreed more.

The goal for the day was to sort the pup, the first step being to find a vet. We soon found one, and clearly amused by my bandaging efforts, a trio of giggling vets gathered round the table. I could have let myself feel stupid, but figuring that a thorough bandaging job should include some secondary discomforts—such as blindfolding, denying him the ability to breathe and cutting off the blood flow to his head—I considered my work to be fine work at that.

His eyes had been shut for about twelve hours, and when the young vet removed the dressing the pup squinted like a vampire in a 7-Eleven. His head was a Monet of blood, and his face was as swollen as a boxer's at an after-match press conference. Thanks to my hack bandaging, the split looked as though it had already begun to knit, and where I assumed the vet would stitch it properly with a needle and a thread, she applied a squirt of powdery glue, something like Polyfilla.

We showered her with questions: What to do with him? Would he live? And most importantly, who might take him? She told us of a Kiwi lady, who, famous in these parts for being the

Good Samaritan of dogs, could be a likely bet for adoption. It sounded ideal, and her name, quite fittingly, was the Dog Lady.

'Do you have her address?'

'No,' said the vet, 'she doesn't have a fixed address. Just go to the Auroville high street and she'll be the one with a pack of dogs following her around.'

It was a mysterious instruction, but feeling that it was our best bet, we hopped on the bike and headed toward. Rudolph was back in the pup-bag, and still seeming less than flash, he groaned as we bumped along.

Ange was on the back. 'D'ye knoo whot?'

'What?'

'I like sayin' "d'ye knoo whot."'

'I've noticed.'

'D'ye knoo whot else?'

'What?'

'I like sayin' "d'ye knoo whot else" as well.'

We made it to the Auroville high street, and instead of the typical hustle of India, the strip was like a ghost town. Tumbleweed blew across the dirt road, and the mysterious Dog Lady was nowhere to be seen. It was still early morning, so we'd pull up a seat.

Playing a few sets of Aussie-Scottish table-tennis-banter, we sat there bashing it out. And as though they themselves were the breeze before the storm, and the Dog Lady the storm itself, after some time dogs seemed to be gathering on the street. Pouring out of the laneways, they were growing increasingly aroused, and as though catching a nearby scent, a group of some ten upped and bolted down the road. They met with another pack, and amid the stir of dust and wagging tails was a figure of form other than canine. Like an old man feeding pigeons at the park, it was immersed in eager partakers, and with the red dust settling to earth, the image of a woman sharpened into view.

I approached. 'Are you the Dog Lady?'

'I am.'

She was in her elder years, had long grey hair, and with her skin deeply tanned for its white type, she looked as though she'd lived in this town for the length of forever. She was significantly lean, and although she was petite in stature, I felt like I was in the presence of a grand soul.

I told her Rudolph the Blood-Red's story, and as though reading my thoughts, she'd often answer my questions before I'd get to ask them.

Wagging their tails in a chorus of joy, some twenty dogs were swarmed around, and although I hoped this was the morning she'd take one more, I couldn't help but wonder how she managed her devotion.

She analysed the cut on the pup's head.

'Thoughts?'

'I think his soul is on the way out.'

'As in, he's going to die?'

'It's nature's justice, as sometimes it's a needle's justice. They can't all be saved.'

'Is there nothing that can be done?'

'I rehome as many as I can, but I often put entire litters to sleep. None of these street dogs are fixed, so they bred like ship rats.'

'So what are my options?'

'I'll take him off your hands, but I get the feeling he'll be meeting the dirt sooner than later.'

Not entirely heartened, but considering my obligation fulfilled, I handed over the little white dog with fully built-in black socks. My time with Charlie spanned several weeks, my time with Rudolph just eighteen hours.

Ange turned to me. 'Soo it's all sorted with Rudolph the Wee Yin?'

'What's a wee yin?'

'It's a term of endearment fur a cute thing.'

'You see, that's what I love about the Scottish. I mean, they'd slap ya purple if you bump 'em in the beer, but they're just the most sentimental race going.'

'Ssshhh… soo is it sorted?'

'It seems to be.'

'Do yoo no' feel a bit cold doing away with him like that?'

'You make it sound like I'm having him taken out by a hitman.'

'Or hitwoman, in her case.'

'I'm a border collie. I just round 'em up. I dunno what more I can do for him, really.'

With our hands free of the kid, we headed into the big city of Pondicherry. It was perhaps due to the wind in our hair, or the relief of being dog-free, but as we thumped along something in our sense of liberty was soaring at its highest. At the top of her exuberance, Ange was singing and throwing her arms, and I, weaving in and out of the traffic, felt in this moment there was truly nowhere else I wanted to be.

I hadn't yet been into the thick of the city, and upon entering its wide-open streets, the former French rule became apparent. Unlike the vague clutter of other Indian cities, Pondicherry— graced with European-style boulevards, and dwellings with garden-spoiled verandas—was a city whose architecture was noticeably different from India's rudimentary consensus. There seemed to this place an air of sophistication, a definite touch from Europe's brush. Manufactured influences aside, though, its most gratifying feature was its rollicking coastline.

Nestled along the southeast coast of India, Pondicherry was lined with beaches competing with the appeal of those in Goa. Just across the seawaters of the Bay of Bengal resided Sri Lanka. I'd originally intended to put the bike and myself on a ferry, to do a side tour of Sri Lanka, but I'd since postponed it for another life.

It had been brought to our attention to visit the Gandhi statue on the foreshore, and having soon arrived, we parked the bike on a nearby kerb. Thousands were in attendance—families out for the day, kids playing cricket on the beach, and young couples strolling ankle-high in the water. Seagulls surfed high on the wind, and with an incessancy of crashing waves; there was a winterish feel to this length of coast that stirred in me a feeling of Melbourne.

With locals approaching just to shake our hands, and kids swarming us at the Gandhi statue, Ange and I were receiving the customary rock star treatment. We spent the majority of the day walking the length of the coast, and with the birds singing, and the ice cream sticky in that feel-good way, it proved to be one of the best days I'd had in my time in India. But all that was about to change.

The time came to move on, so in search of the bike key, I dug into my pocket, but the key wasn't there.

Rummaging through all pockets and orifices, I started to panic, but equalling the trickery of Harry Houdini, it had truly vanished. 'Perhaps I left it in the ignition of the bike?' I thought, running to it, where, to my surprise, standing by the bike's side was a young cop with the key in his hand. 'How did he get that?' thought I, but although surprised, I was more relieved and figured he'd just hand it over and off we'd part to live our lives.

But where hope loomed dark intent rose, for like an addict attaining the hit, in his eyes grew a lustful look. He had scored, and western in its wealth, he knew the stuff was *good*. 'Come see this man,' he said, putting the key in his pocket. And so with little choice, I walked the bike and myself over to 'this man'.

'This man' was an older cop, fatter, greyer-haired and more constipated-looking. A row of subordinate cops gathered, and standing in a coincidental order of shortest to tallest—their assembly not dissimilar to Charles Darwin's *Origin of the Species*—all seemed to be salivating in unison. Perhaps I was being harsh, and my attack, if that, was by no means against creed, but against the notion of authoritative figures drunk on their own power. Knowing that my coming-soon reaming would be carried out not in the interests of the law, but of lining their pockets, my anger was rubbing the sleep out of its eyes.

The older cop, stepping forward from the pack, proceeded to fire a round of questions I couldn't outgun.

'Motorbike licence?'

'Nup.'

'Registration papers?'

'Nup.'

'Insurance papers?'

'Yep! Only joking..'

Becoming the newest key-bearer, he snatched the key from the young cop's hand, and witnessing the loveless juggle of what was rightfully mine, I felt myself fill with a raging Gollum-like lust, 'they stole it from us…' My teeth pressed and my eyes bulged, 'it came to me, my own my love…' I wanted it back whether it cost me my life… by golly I wanted it back, 'mhhy phhreciousss…'

I could feel myself getting hotter by the breath, and like a drunk guy having his bar tab pulled, I began to pace and curse. I got verbal, very verbal, and although it was my intent to disguise my rant in Australianisms that would fall short to the Indian ear, the nature of my performance proved very international.

The older cop muttered something into the ear of the younger, which I guessed to be along the lines of, 'keep an eye on this bastard while I get the gimp,' and still bearing the key in his shirt pocket, he hopped on a small motorbike and took off up the road. The sight brought me to the boil, and I was tempted to chase him on foot. But much like the *Six Million Dollar Man* powered by a ten-metre extension cord, I didn't think I'd make the distance.

There was little to be happy about, for the only thing that could incite me more than having it put over me by a bloke older-than-me in an authoritative position was having it put over me by a bloke younger-than-me in an authoritative position. And standing there with a face as clueless as a teenager taking your order at McDonald's—'would you like fries with your fries, sir?'—this cop couldn't have been older than eighteen.

Wearing a white shirt, navy pants, and a topi-style hat not dissimilar to Mr Cunningham's Leopard Lodge hat on *Happy Days*, he looked as though he'd had his first shave this morning. And there was little about him that gave me faith he knew babies were delivered by means other than the stork.

Assuming this young buck was composed of a more malleable substance than the older one, Ange threw out a blatant line of flirtation. And where other cops, more professional in their conduct, would have seen through her intention, he, like an impressionable salmon, took the hook through the lip and swallowed the sinker.

Batting her eyes, cracking jokes, and lightly touching him on the arm as she laughed, I felt truly ill to watch, for if he was an ice statue then she was the sun. And as he began to melt into a version of himself where he seemed to forget about his duty to keep watch, there was, in his eyes, a definite second where I witnessed his brain switch off.

He was consumed by her, as weak at the knees as glad of the eye, and although her act was to our mutual service, the spectacle was making me age like a sun dried tomato. I tried to look away, or to rerun pleasant childhood memories, but festering as I was, I did something to the contrary.

My right hand, much as it did when it caught Charlie when he fell from the bike, acted involuntarily. But less of the saving-grace kind, it grabbed the cop's hat from his head and threw it into the air. Up it flew, and hoping against all hope it'd be shat on by an army of lactose-intolerant seagulls, I near had to stop myself from making Apache war cry noises. I was the alpha male now! And in at tickertape parade image I could see myself being carried shoulder-high by adoring thousands, until, breaking the haze of my delusion, I made eye contact with Ange. 'You absolute tosser!' her face it read, as did 'you're fair dinkum joking?' did that of the officer. But transcended by great adrenaline, the addition of embarrassment could only set me firmer in my severity.

'Anything could happen now! Anything!' I thought, gaining exquisite pleasure watching him scurry along the street in his hat's retrieval. But with our eyes locking in anger upon his return, something in his boyish nose-picking demeanour had changed.

'Do you understand what you just did, sir? Come with me.'

With a face fraught with concern, Ange looked my way. But still bitter about the hijacking of my key, 'they stole it from us…' as I walked the bike behind him, this young topi-hat wearing cop could compete little with my aggravation. 'Let's get this over with.'

Ange followed.

It was now night, and as we walked along the Pondicherry backstreets, it would have taken the I.Q. of a tadpole to discern that we were being led to the police station—the den, the bat-riddled caves where the players have their way.

We soon arrived, and as the two of us were sat firmly down in the station waiting room, the Blue Fly—rendered hideously unfangable—was compounded and gagged with a large yellow wheel lock.

With Ange exclusively not invited, after a short time I was called into a small backroom, and standing behind its curtain was the older key-bearing cop, wearing a face as though primed for a night of battle. I was half expecting him to be holding a whip, and strewn across his desk an array of bondage instruments, but although not the case the games began.

'Licence!'

'Key!'

'Registration!'

'Key!'

'Insurance!'

'Key!'

'Hat chuck!'

'Pass.'

But as the tiny room filled with cops, it growingly crossed my mind that I could find myself spending the night in an Indian cell. I was deep in the cave, greatly outnumbered, and so I grappled my inner remote and turned myself down. A noisy ceiling fan spun overhead, and the key-bearer, wiping the sweat from his glossy brow, composed himself and sat down. He leant back in his chair and proceeded to read a newspaper. Although mutually declared, the silence felt worse than the arguing, and the fan became insufferably loud.

He eventually leaned forward. 'There's another way this could work,' he said. He knew by the look in my eyes that I knew exactly where he was going, and he set a large jar on the desk. '*Baksheesh.*'

I could almost hear the bubbles starting in my bloodstream. There was a harsh reality to face, a thick pride to swallow—that I was going to have to toe the corruption line or attain the necessary papers. 'We promise to serve the master of the precious...'

It was late. I was tired. And so I walked.

The sun rose. Having settled down, I was starting to think of the logistics involved: motorbike licence, registration and insurance papers. The biggest slice of the quandary pie was that I didn't have a motorbike licence but a car licence only. But it was then that I had a flashback, 'hang on! I'm a graphic designer!'

I made my way to an Internet café, scanned in my car licence, and with the help of my old friend Photoshop changed the word *car* to *motorbike*—all the while the man running the café watching over my shoulder.

Although I had only one of three papers, I knew the licence would be the most crucial, so I printed it out feeling as industrious as MacGyver. Ange, however, felt less optimistic, so it was agreed my return rickshaw ride be a solo one.

Alive with a new day's hustle, by the time I made it to the cop shop the waiting room was filled with fresh victims. I sat in the same chair as the night before. But like a graduate among a company of freshmen, I was seated not ten seconds before I was whisked through to the backroom.

With the curtain drawn, the key-bearer stood behind his desk with a face as contemptuous as the night before. 'Licence! Registration! Hat chuck!' he kept up, fishing as always for the g-spot.

Like a youngster only too proud to present his latest drawing, I placed my fake licence on his desk.

He seized it, and with a face as annoyed as baffled, he kept looking back and forth from me to it.

Suspecting it was fake, he held it up to the light, but unable to prove as such, in a defeated he began moaning about the other papers required… and the thing about chucking the young cop's hat… and concluding his grievance by admitting that, although he'd told his mates otherwise, he'd conquered his Rubik's Cube by peeling off its stickers, I knew his game was lost. He frowned from across the table. I smiled back, and making his defeat official, he opened the top drawer of his desk, where, piled at the top of dozens of others, was my key. My eyes bulged at the sight, and longing to touch it, my hand began to quiver, 'mhhy phhreciousss…'

With his brow damp, he slung it onto the table. I was tempted to lick it all over, like a kid wishing to ensure ownership of his icy pole. One of the subordinates led me to the compound area and, having removed the bike's yellow handcuffs, I jumped onboard, fired it up, and thumped up the road.

'Ah... freedom at the flick of the wrist!' I sighed, as the briefly forgotten feeling flowed through my veins like a renounced drug welcome once again. I belted it express to Auroville, to give Ange the update, only just resisting singing Frank Sinatra's *My Way*.

Soon after, I arrived at the Auroville high street, and I figured I'd sit, have a cup of chai, and spend time some smoking the victory.

The main drag, like the ghost town I'd come to know, was all but dead. But as though appearing from behind the doors of its vacant shops, dogs seemed to be gathering. With some of them barking and others howling, a canine mardi gras ensued. And before I could doubt my suspicion, standing beside me was the Dog Lady. 'David,' she said in a grave tone. 'I have something to tell you.'

'Rudolph has died?'

Leading me up the street at a large pace, she took me into a gruesome building and down a flight of stairs. 'I want you to see something,' she said, switching on a light switch. Rudolph was alive, very alive, and with his tail wagging and his eyes smiling, he came flopping over. In his tenure with me he'd been like an old toy with dull batteries, but with the creases of his once sad mouth turned into a canine smile, he was dusted off and loaded with Duracell Maxi-Mutts. Sad little Rudolph was Charlie-like.

She went on to explain that she'd found him a home on a farm, and that with no pay, perks, or anything other than the satisfaction it gave her to see their tails wag, she'd been doing her work in this grubby little town for over 25 years.

But the admiration, it seemed, ran both ways—with kind eyes she expressed that it was thanks to the efforts of other devotees of the four-legged that she felt encouraged to continue. Although humbled, I left some room for pride, and, appearing at my shoulder, the little-imaginary-angel-with-little-fluttering-wings spoke into my ear—'That request for a room closer to the canteen has been approved by god. I hear the t-bone and mash is particularly good.'

A week or so passed, and still in Pondicherry with Ange, my proceeding plan was to ride to the southwest state of Kerala to attempt a ten-day Vipassana meditation retreat. Remembering it was Ange's birthday in only a couple of days, however, I grew torn. Including the two-day ride, if I was to leave Pondicherry in time to make the retreat, I'd need to depart the day before her birthday. Bearing in mind she'd specifically stayed in Rishikesh for mine up there, I felt particularly guilty at the prospect of missing hers.

It was lunchtime.

'D'ye knoo whot?'

'What?'

'Ah'm Hank Marvin?'

'What's Hank Marvin?'

'Starvin'!'

'Why don't we get some tahli then?'

'D'ye hink?'

'Hink? Who's he? Hank's brother?'

The day was hot, so after putting away a lunch of tahli, curd, and chapattis, we decided to hit the Pondy foreshore.

We sat ourselves on the sand, and Ange, gazing at the crashing waves of the Bay of Bengal, turned to me with a youthful air. 'D'ye knoo whot else?'

'What?'

'It's ma birthday in a couple of days.'

'I know,' I answered, swallowing.

'I cannae believe ye're gonnae be here fur ma birthday!'

'Darlen?'

'Aye?'

'I don't think I've ever felt so shite in my life, but I'm not going to be here.'

'Why no'?'

With the greatest of difficulty I told her I was attending the retreat. Unable to hide it, her blue eyes fell to a look of disappointment. But as difficult as the decision had been, in some strange roll of the dice, it might have been the very thing that saved our lives, as five days after I left, the Pondicherry seaboard—which we'd frequented most days in our time there—was wiped out by the Boxing Day Tsunami of 2004.

By first light the next morning the Blue Fly was packed for Kerala. Standing on the dirt road out the front of the Shagging Tree, we found ourselves in farewell position once again. A breeze blew around us, but more encompassing was the tangible air of awkwardness.

'I feel like a right arse.'

'As long as ye feel bad ah'll consider that compensation enough.'

'But it's not, and to put things right I'm wanna sing you a birthday verse I dreamt up.'

Her face fell to a look as though her inner leaf turned brown.

I inhaled.

'Dave?'

'Yeah?'

'How aboot ye refrain from being a claw baw and we consider that ma birthday present?'

'What's a claw baw?'

'Someone who spends too much time with their hands doon their pants.'

'Could make for tricky riding?'

'Aye. Soo when ye get the end of this road, are ye turning left or right?'

Her question split me in two, literally and metaphorically.

'Left. I think.'

'Och well, I guess that's me away then.'

'As in you're leaving?'

'Aye.'

We were unsure when we might see each other again, and as I clicked the bike in gear, I felt consumed with sadness. 'Ange?'

'Aye?'

'Why exactly did you set out on this trip?'

'To broaden ma horizons. And you?'

I paused at length, my mind drifting back to the dorm room in Dublin. 'It's a long story.'

'Och well, ah'm sure our paths will intertwine someday.'

'I hope so.' I said, feeling at a terrible loss for words as she turned and faded up the road.

I sat for a minute, watching her, until I clicked the bike in gear and turned the throttle.

18. The Vipassana Meditation Retreat—
Ten days of silence. Three days until the tsunami.

Day One—December 23rd, 2004

After a blissful two-day ride across India's south, cutting through the hilly labyrinth of Kerala's emerald tea plantations and its snow-capped mountainous terrain, I made it to the Vipassana meeting place, close to India's southernmost tip.

The retreat was being held in an old mansion on one of the many diminutive islands of the Kerala Backwaters. (The Kerala Backwaters are a vast network of rivers, canals, lakes and inlets that meet with the parallel waters of the Arabian Sea.)

Having loitered on the mainland pier, myself and the group of nameless aspirants were loaded onto a small boat. With its engine ticking like an old watch, it moved slowly across the lily-covered water. Birds migrated between the palm-covered islands, and dotted on the briny water were boats casting fishing nets this way and that.

The boat soon moored at the destination island. But this waterlogged tuft of land being so small that it was only a couple of kilometres wide at its broadest—and, much of its middle residing below sea level—the title of *island* could barely be granted. Less than tidal wave-proof, some of its locals lived on soggy strips of land as narrow as a few metres. Still their spirits were bright, and as we were escorted by minivan to the mansion, a host of delighted kids ran alongside.

Having soon arrived, the mansion presented itself. It was a huge double-storied dwelling with a high-pointed ginger-coloured roof, and its pale yellow exterior, flaked from countless years under the sun, was made of brittle concrete. An oak balcony, deeply-set, circumnavigated the full diameter of its second storey, and from out of the large windows that ran its length, blue curtains billowed in the breeze.

Full of coconut-rich palms and nature left to mingle in its own will it had two large yards—front and back. With full communication still intact, one of the retreat organisers offered some details of its history.

It had been built in 1788, the same year as European settlement in Australia, and to this day was owned by the same family of Indian nobles who'd built it back then. The interior was equally dramatic, with long dark meditation hallways and cedar floorboards; this giant mansion was both kept and unkept, loved and left to be, untouched just enough so as to preserve its story in its walls.

'Ten hours of meditation for ten days of silence?'

Wanting to be as devoid as possible of the self-consciousness that might have come with telling family and friends, the solitary person I'd told I was attending was Ange. In fact, having sold to Mum and Dad the fabricated story that, because I was going to be in a remote zone, I wouldn't be ringing home on Christmas Day,

I'd already made the pre-Christmas phone calls. Bearing in mind I'd be spending the day sitting idle with nothing but the company of my thoughts, the *remote zone* description wasn't entirely untrue.

Why I was doing it was another matter. I think more than anything I was open to it. I hadn't come to India to just ride around on a motorbike, but to get involved in new things. I'd had several friends in Nepal, who after having done a Vipassana recommended it as the highest form of self-psychotherapy possible. Feeling fully equipped with the emotional creases that duly come with being human, I felt I could do with the ironing.

It was twilight on day one, and still in the general hustle of settling in, we were yet to fall to silence.

With men in one sleeping quarter and women in another, and men on one side of the mansion and women on the other, and men to inhabit the backyard during break times and women to inhabit the front, as we were led to our rooms the sexes were officially segregated. Including myself as one of three westerners present—the other two a Slovenian married couple challenging themselves to celibacy and no eye contact for ten days—the group came to a total of 30.

As a cue to make our way downstairs to be briefed by the meditation teacher, a bell was rung at 7 p.m., and while standing in his vicinity I couldn't help but notice the quality of the teacher's eyes. They were menacingly dark in colour, so much so that the pupil could barely be discerned from the iris. And yet with the pupil's rim lined with a ring of flaming blue, he was left with an ethereal and devilish demeanour. 'All men gather to me!' he said in a booming voice, 'all men gather to me!'

With the idea of this retreat becoming the reality, everyone swallowed and gathered in.

'So what is Vipassana?' he asked, rhetorically. 'Vipassana is a simple Buddhist practice to accomplish peace of mind and lead a happy and useful life. The word *Vipassana* means, "to see things as they really are". It's a logical process of mental purification through deep self-observation.

'We all experience agitation, frustration and disharmony in our lives, and when we suffer we don't keep our misery limited only to ourselves, but distribute it onto others. The practice of concentrated self-observation leads us step-by-step to full liberation from all mental defilements. It's by eliminating the three causes of all unhappiness—*aversion, craving* and *ignorance*—that the deep-seated causes of suffering are eradicated and true liberation achieved.

'Its purpose is never to simply cure a physical symptom,' he said, filling my mind with the default headline: *Man, Peeved Beyond Description, Still Struggles To Breathe,* 'for the physical symptom is just a by-product of the mind which will be eliminated with successful practice. The student can only arrive at his own realisations by his own efforts—no one can do it for him, just as he can do it for no one else,' he said in a tone neighbouring anger, to which everyone, like troops before entering the battlefield, stirred in their places.

'You'll be out of bed at 4 a.m. each day, and we'll be meditating for ten hours a day until the tenth day being January the 1st. You're required to practice *noble silence,* which means refraining from all speech, eye contact, reading or writing materials, and any form of physical communication whatsoever, be it gestures, written notes, sign language, or even a watch that beeps on the hour, for that in itself is a communication.

'We'll have zero contact with the affairs of the outside world, and you're required to have full abstinence from killing, stealing, sexual activities, telling lies, and from all intoxicants, including those by prescription. And any man who feels he cannot conform to this code is asked to leave right now.'

And like a classroom of school kids wondering *who did it*, everyone's eyes scanned the room.

It was then that a rather dumpy local man came and stood beside the teacher. 'This is Mr Mitesh. He is the senior retreat coordinator. He'll be handling all cooking, bell calls for wake ups, break times and so on.

'Good luck gentlemen. By day ten you'll checkout a new man. We'll go to silence in a minute before retiring to our rooms. But first, does anyone wish to say anything? If so speak now or hold your peace.'

And as we broke eye contact and our gazes fell to the ground, ten days of silence officially began.

Day Two—*December 24th, 2004*

The 4 a.m. bell soon came around, and Mr Mitesh, making a theatre of shadow puppets dance on the walls, came shuffling into our sleeping quarters, shining an oil lamp and jingling a bell.

I flicked back my mosquito net and sat upright, and although I wished to swear and grumble, I knew I had to shut it. It occurred to me plainly that this could be the very definition of a waste of ten days, and the part of me that wished to yawn loudly, scratch freely, and knock up a cup of tea, truly believed it.

With our gazes kept to the ground, we walked downstairs to the bathrooms, and although required to practice noble silence, this didn't seem to exclude the local lads from hocking, spitting, and blowing their noses into their hands. There was nothing about this situation that was remotely inspiring.

Like prisoners on the chain gang, we were next led to the meditation hall—a long room with pine-panelled walls and large windows that let the breeze through. A long straw mat covered the entire floor, and set up as our meditation thrones were individual cushions arranged in rows. I yawned lengthily, gambling that its sound was confined to the inside of my head.

At the front of the room was a raised platform, where the teacher would be perched for his ten days, and as his right- and left-hand men, sitting either side was Mr Mitesh and another coordinator.

With men on the left side of the room and women on the right—and all facing the teacher—we were led to our designated places. Knowing, too well, that I was going to be sitting in this spot for the next ten days, I knew that I'd better get comfortable.

It was 4:30 a.m., and still dark outside.

In my time in India I'd learnt that it was the belief of meditation enthusiasts that dawn and dusk—being neither day nor night, light nor dark—were considered the best times to meditate.

Having settled into his place, the teacher addressed the class. 'We will now meditate until the sun has fully risen. You are encouraged not to move in your places, and if you get any physical discomfort, to move the focus of your attention into the soreness and further concentrate on your breathing. As you advance in your practice, the pain will ease.'

This was some truly terrifying shit, for the cessation of his voice acting as our cue, it was with eyes closed, legs crossed, and hands resting in the palms of each other, that the meditation began.

Ten seconds passed. 'This isn't so hard?'

Eleven seconds passed. 'This isn't so hard… I think?'

Twelve seconds passed. 'This isn't so hard… I wish?'

And bubbling in me was a feeling of horrible anticipation—like in my head I was in a dark cinema waiting for some unknown movie of thought to start screening.

My back was starting to bother me.

'Fuck this f#&k'n fuck of a cushion!'

'Must you swear so much?'

'Yes. It's necessary for effect. But hang on, who are you?'

'I'm *you* dickhead!'

'Don't call me dickhead! Cockhead!'

'Well, don't call me cockhead! Dickhead!'

'But I can't remember that recipe for Mum's banana cake!'

'Good! Because I swear it was that girl with the coke bottle glasses that knicked me Batman showbag in kindergarten!'

'God, are you there?'

'Yes my son…'

'I never did admit that it was me who put that porno in Sister Mary's top drawer in grade five.'

And it was then, as though from a place of great significance, that into my head faded the theme music from *Entertainment Tonight*.

'Oh, I don't know why she's leaving, or where she's gonna go…' *Living Next Door To Alice* came in. 'You got to know when to hold 'em…' Kenny Rogers followed. But in all its brutal, vile, malicious horror and gore, irrefutably worst was, 'Agadoo-doo-doo, push pineapple, shake the tree…'

'Shut up! I hate that song!'

'Shut up! I hate you!'

'Shut up the pair of you! And besides, who are all you wankers if not me anyway? Just as you, you, and *you* the most… the one who thinks because Kermit the Frog does it, it's ok to stand there not wearing any pants.'

And it was then, after years of needless suffering, that it occurred to me that to avoid irritable bowel syndrome it might be best to peel my bananas before eating them.

Anything brave I'd previously faced was dwarfed in comparison to taking on my head's army unarmed from distractions. I started breathing heavily, contrary to the plan. I was so desperate, in fact, that if someone slung me a copy of

Ok! Magazine, I would have leapt at it with interest, willing myself to give even the faintest of fucks that Jennifer Aniston stubbed her toe on a turtle in Tahiti.

But magazine-less I was, and while sitting there sweating—feeling sad upon realising that, unless she'd lived well into her fifties, Lassie the dog would be, by now, probably dead—Mr Mitesh rang the bell for break time.

'Oh thank farck for that!'

The room rose to its feet, all of them hopefully as miserable as me, and with all keeping our gazes to the ground, we walked into the eating area where a vegetarian breakfast was being served.

Desperate for any form of pleasure, it was only shy of bringing my imaginary Ute around the back that I loaded my plate to capacity. And having disappeared into a far corner of the grassy yard, I sat silently to myself. I thought about Pramesh, and wondered if he was sitting on the balcony in Rishikesh, and if this morning Mamma Sharvari was making her coconut chili chutney.

Moreover, I sat there feeling heavy and hopeless. If I could discern one feeling above all, it was sadness. Sad to realise how futile was the material on my inner movie reel. Sad that I felt I needed to be here at all. Or perhaps just sad that I still had eight days to go.

Day Three—*December 25ᵗʰ, 2004*

The 4 a.m. bell again came around, and Mr Mitesh, making mouse-sized objects cast bear-sized shadows, came sauntering into our sleeping quarters, shining his lamp and jingling his bell.

I flicked back my mosquito net and sat upright, still in shock that any sound from the outer world had found its way into the centre of my head at this hour. I shook my head, hoping to drown out the jingling and the gathering storm of thoughts protesting against it.

'We will now meditate for two hours until the sun has fully risen,' the teacher began as we lowered ourselves onto our cushions. 'Today you are encouraged to focus your full attention on the area between your upper lip and your nostrils—to observe the breath as in it comes and out it goes. As for any aspirants of the Christian faith, try to refrain from thoughts of Christmas, family, and all other attachments to this event.'

And having thus been prompted, my mind couldn't but go for a little imaginary wander into *Australian Christmas Land*—that great-southerly place where Christmases aren't laced with snow, but sun, where Santa, in all his nobility, isn't bestowed a smoked ham after his duties, but is dacked and chucked in the pool. Where in Norway, little wee Norwegians gather around with candles singing *Hark the Herald Angels Sing*, in Australia, cousins sneak a tinny out on the service road while blaring Midnight Oil out of their panel vans. Where in Germany, wee children click their wooden shoes in time to juggling fancily wrapped chocolates, in Australia, aunties hearten the kiddies to run along and busily injure themselves on their newly-acquired slip and slides. And where in Switzerland, stoic men chop firewood in some gallant display, in Australia—sufficiently pissed come five o'clock in the arvo—your terry towelling short-wearing uncles reckon it's a top idea to have a smack of cricket in the vacant block of a few doors up. Indeed, Christmases in Australia are uniquely our own, and with all this stuff going on with my very own family, I couldn't but feel nostalgic.

But with eyes closed, legs crossed, and hands resting in the palms of each other, here I sat thousands of miles away.

Second-by-second, minute-by-minute, hour-by-hour, thought-by-thought, the day folded into night. For those whose backs were made of plasticine, I couldn't speak, but for those of the flesh and blood variety, there were few positions more physically challenging than sitting stationary for this long.

The aspirants sitting up the front, known as *old students*, were those that had completed previous courses. Informally they were known as *the rocks,* in that some were spiritually realised to the extent they were above the notion of physical pain. But sitting there, as I was, made not of rock but a personal collection of knots and tension, I could scarcely feel further from their rank. And less than confident I was going to finish this course, I was unconvinced I'd ever become one.

Day Four—*December 26th, 2004*
(The day of the Boxing Day Tsunami)

We were led to the meditation hall at the usual time, and having lowered ourselves down cross-legged, the teacher addressed us as always. 'Today you are again encouraged to focus your attention on the area between your upper lip and nostrils, to observe the breath as in it comes and out it goes...' And as we sat paying attention, little did we know—neither did the 200,000 people who were about to lose their lives—that in three and half hours southern India would be struck by the tidal wave.

For some reason I remember this day more vividly than any, for feeling happy to be nowhere near a telly that could show the highly-minded individuals tripping over themselves in the annual *9 a.m. I-need-that-six-pack-of-boxer-shorts-so-much-more-than-you Myer Door Dash,* I remember thinking about all the Boxing Day hype back home. I remember also thinking about what I'd be doing if there—probably packing the car and heading down the beach, or up the Murray River for the Christmas break.

But home I wasn't, and as I sat there focusing on the area

between my upper lip and nostrils, trying my hardest to observe the breath, as in it came and out it went, as in it came and out it went… time drew on. And as it did, somewhere around then—just off the coast of Indonesia—the Earth cracked open under the sea. Some time later the wave hit Sri Lanka, and southern India after that. And if not for a thin strip of land acting as an impact breaker between the Kerala backwaters and the offending ocean, we would have surely been claimed, for as little as 50 kilometres south of us, the tsunami had torn away the lives of countless thousands.

But with eyes closed, legs crossed, and hands resting in the palms of each other—and with no one but Ange privy of my whereabouts—I sat there oblivious to Mother Nature's wrath.

My family's panic had just begun.

Day Five—*December 27ᵗʰ, 2004*

As though the layers of an emotional onion were being slowly peeled away, perhaps this Vipassana thing was working, for my general feeling of sadness was seemingly converting into purée anger.

But although I hoped this would be an empowering shift, it proved also to be an increase in vulnerability—for while sitting there I became especially agitated by a peculiar chewing noise coming from just next to me. I kept my eyes closed, trying to battle against its grating power. But as my dam of patience began to crack, I was rendered little choice but to open them.

Sitting to my left, seeming to have discovered some sort of nice taste that the rest of humanity failed to detect, was a skinny local man just casually chewing the atmosphere. Perhaps he was deep in meditation, and had since become a camel or cow, an ailment I wished to correct by feeding him a gentlemanly fistful of grass. But attempts to understand aside, I was itchier with frustration than a twelve knackered dog in handcuffs.

Now conscious of the fact, the chewing could only grow louder, and as I sat there barely containing the waters of my nuisance, a different guy, a huge local man sitting directly behind me, started joining in on the quest to abolish me by swallowing air and burping into the back of my head. *Chew burp, chew burp, chew chew, burp burp…*

'Dear me…' I sighed; they seemed to be in some sort of coincidental rhythm. And so agitated I was that just as my eczema began to relapse—*ring ring!*—Mr Mitesh rang the bell for break time.

It was mid-afternoon, and with men in the backyard and women in the front, we were allocated a fifteen-minute break to walk around.

Interlocking our hands behind our backs, we meandered in extensive laps. I wondered how the others were coping in their silence, all of us as alone in the cage of our own souls as each other.

We walked around, refraining from eye contact, when a large white dog came into the yard and sat in the middle of our circuit. We kept walking our laps, but they gradually shrank until we were standing in a circle around it.

Wagging its tail and doing the rounds, the dog, like newlyweds making their exit, walked from one man for a pat before moving onto the next. I knelt down to it when my turn came, and when I stood up, another man and I made accidental eye contact. Never had I had zero eye contact with another person for almost a week, and it was only after this period of abstinence could I appreciate its magnetism. As though all other focal possibilities were rendered powerless compared to the strength of meeting eyes, it was like being hit by a laser beam, or, in cornier terms, as though our souls had brushed across each other's path.

But this was just a taste of the power of Vipassana—of its ability to reenergise the essence of all things. (I later learnt of a woman, who, after having done a course for two years, became so overawed by a simple road sign that she stood on the roadside studying it for an entire day.)

After the break we settled back into our places, and with the only difference between one neighbouring minute to the next being the diminishing light, day turned to dusk, and dusk to darkness. From outside could be heard countless insects buzzing in the grass, and I tried, with marginal improvement, to use the noise as a focal point to get out of my head and into my senses.

There was no question that I found the day's final hour the longest, like the last futile kilometres in a marathon. I'd developed the habit of looking very forward to the evening's discourse: an hour-long recording of Goenka—the godfather of Vipassana—talking all things just that.

The discourse began with chanting, which acted as a cue that we were allowed to sit any way we wished. It was difficult to know if it was from his baritone timbre, or that it marked the day's end, but I was as comforted by his voice as when our grade three teacher would commence reading *Green Eggs and Ham*.

'This discourse is not for your intellectual entertainment,' Goenka would insist at the start of each night's instalment, cueing my brain to gear down, relax and consider it precisely that.

I tried to refrain from getting carried away with his stories—which he told with lush detail and rollicking humour—but to invest, instead, in his message about dharma: the regulatory order of the universe, to which we are all equally subject. 'By day ten you will checkout a new person!' he kept reiterating. I hoped he was right, for although we were halfway through, I felt a lot less than half new.

Day Six—*December 28th, 2004*

The 4 a.m. bell faded into my head, and Mr Mitesh, looking somewhat tubbier than usual, came waddling into our sleeping quarters jingling his bell.

It was still dark outside, and a warm breeze flowed through the meditation hall. The teacher spoke. 'By now you should have made some progress with your ability to focus on one part of the body. Today you're encouraged to slowly scan your attention from head to toe—to *flush* yourself with consciousness. We'll spend the entire day doing this exercise. Try to refrain from giving licence to unconstructive thoughts and distractions.'

Beginning the scan at the top of my head, I sat with eyes closed and legs crossed, yet by the time I'd lowered my attention to my eyebrows, I was sure I heard a blowfly buzzing overhead. I opened my eyes, but proving to be static on my inner movie reel, there was no insect to be seen.

The skinny chewing guy started chewing to my left.

Having recommenced the scan, I closed my eyes again, yet by the time I'd lowered my attention to the tip of my nose, Madonna's *Like a Virgin* faded in.

'Dear me…' I sighed, 'of all the laxatives.'

I could hear everything; the bodgy bass intro, the *shiny and new* bit, and even the bit where she squeaks—*hey!*—in the chorus.

In time to the music, I started swaying in my seat, and as though equally in time the big burping guy started belting his greatest hits into the back of my head.

'You're so fine… *chew burp*, coz you're mine… *burp chew*, I'll be yours… *chew chew*, 'til the end of… *burp!*'

High noon, dubbed *Unhappy Hour*, was always contentious: as though the sun was at its most determined to get you onto your feet and into your day. I always found the heat unbearable at this time. But whether it was from the sun, or from the fires of frustration—in that I wished to be doing anything but sacrificing my day—I couldn't say. I think it was both, and I think each fed the other.

Regardless, with the heat came increased irritability, and with increased irritability came thinning skin, and with thinning skin came decreased resistance to the most ancient of all cravings: sexual cravings.

Somewhere in my body was a little uniformed commander-in-chief, yelling through a megaphone the international mantra worshipped by all the world's men: 'when the going gets tough, have a wank! Treat yourself, have a wank! Fed up with rising car insurance? Have a—'

Sitting there as I was, it was impossible to be anything but riddled with blue images real and imaginary—images from the dawn of my lust, awoken by Olivia Newton John music videos and Kmart underwear catalogues, all the way up to my most recent experience. The battle was genuine, and when one's reproductive organs were threatening divorce, the voice of the commander-in-chief was even more influential. With difficulty, I upheld insubordination.

Day Seven—*December 29th, 2004*

Midday came around, and so did *rest hour*, in which we were allowed one of two choices—walk laps in the yard or sleep. But truly sick of both, I went upstairs, sat on my bed, and taking pen to paper I officially broke the code of conduct.

Streaming with words like a tide given voice, my pen was near burning a hole in the page, and I was writing and filling pages and writing and filling more, when, ever so faintly, I heard footsteps from behind.

Flicking the pen under my pillow, I sat still, pretending to be idle, when Mr Mitesh peered over my shoulder. I turned to look up at him, and seeing the guilt on my face he began to scan the area. 'Come with me, young man,' he said.

Be it from embarrassment or shame, I was near on fire with exasperation. This entire Vipassana endeavour had proven to be the very definition of a waste of ten days, and sick of this noble silence drivel, I wanted to pack my bags, pack the bike, and get off this Robinson Caruso island.

I was swiftly led to the meditation hall, which, except for the teacher sitting on his raised platform, was empty. Mr Mitesh, after instructing me to sit at the teacher's feet, began speaking in a language foreign to me, and the teacher, listening carefully, studied me with his devilish eyes.

A tense silence ensued.

'These 2,500-year-old teachings are for your own benefit,' the teacher said, 'and it was your choice to come here.' He paused at length, during which even if I were allowed to speak, I wouldn't have. 'I'm sorry, young man, but I'm afraid I'm going to have to ask you leave.'

My heart plummeted into my stomach, feeling as though I'd been invited to someone's house for dinner and had shown my appreciation by knocking granny's ashes off the mantelpiece.

'But,' he said reticently, 'because you're a westerner and are less familiar with the teachings, I'll pardon you this once. Unless, of course, you wish to leave of your own accord?'

I thought about all the time I was losing, and of the many things I could be doing with it. I questioned my progress also. Nevertheless, with a faint shake of the head I passed on his offer and I was led back to my seating place, where with eyes closed, legs crossed, and hands resting in the palms of each other, I sat.

Time: the continuous train track stretching out into the future and backing off into the past, on which I'm told I was born, I travel daily, and I'm being personally escorted towards my death, ticked on.

My back was getting slightly more used to the challenge of sitting idle. Still I questioned—if not for sitting in such a position for so unnaturally long, would there be any physical pain on which to focus?

By my own admission, I'd so far spent a lot more time surfing wave after wave of thought than I'd made a genuine attempt to run the physical sensation scan. I checked in with my brain, our verdict being that some time apart might be good for the marriage.

The start of the scan line was truly daunting, and it was, at first, impossible to get from head to toe without thinking about shortbread biscuits or the marvellously flexible knees of a baby giraffe. My brain, almost always, would take the opportunity to let itself in for a cup of tea. But slowly I realised that the more I managed to flush my body with consciousness, or, steer the tingling, the more the physical discomfort would dissipate. And with less physical discomfort came more capacity for stillness.

Throwing me back into my head, however, I thought I heard someone crying, and losing the battle with my curiosity, I opened my eyes. Up the front, interestingly, one of *the rocks* was sitting there sobbing as quietly as he could. Aside from the ambling of feet, and the light tingling of cutlery, it was the most human sound I'd heard in days. I wondered whether it was a sign or regression or progression.

'This discourse is not for your intellectual entertainment,' Goenka repeated later that night. An hour later the teacher dismissed us for the evening. In our chain gang, all us men made our way to the bathrooms, creating a scene not dissimilar to weary soldiers returning to the barracks.

Although out of eyeshot of higher-ups, none of us engaged in eye contact or making noises other than hocking, spitting, blowing noses, brushing teeth, coughing, shaving, splashing and scratching. I looked in the mirror; unsure whether eye contact with myself was illegal.

I lay on my bed for the best part of an hour, encased in my mosquito net. But due to the sounds of men snoring, turning, and tossing—for lack of a better word—in their beds, I was unable to sleep. The night was hot, unbearably hot, and with the heat came, typically, the little uniformed commander-in-chief. His message rang loud and clear, perhaps louder and clearer than ever. I did my best, though, to wrestle the megaphone from his hands and uphold insubordination.

Day Eight—*December 30th, 2004*

I have no memory of this day.

Day Nine—*December 31st, 2004*

The morning stars lost their faces in the light, and as the sun slowly rose, we sat cross-legged as always.

The silence was like an essence in itself, like a veil in which all form was wrapped—immeasurable, infinite, and inexhaustible, until some bloke farted and it mutated into a jaded sepia tone.

I sat as the morning drew forth, and finding few things as tiring as sitting so idle, I grew at war with my eyelids.

Burp! the big bloke behind me fired up.

Chew! the skinny bloke to the left joined in.

Burp!

Chew!

Burp!

Chew!

Trying to source the hidden pleasure, I started chewing the air myself, but acquiring zilch, I was quick to give up.

Regardless, the *Bodily Function Brothers* kept tap-dancing their flatulent favourites. *Burp chew, chew burp...*

'Dear me...' I sighed, 'does anyone here have a f#&k'n harpoon?'

The chewing guy faded out his work, but there was no stopping the burping guy as in he swallowed and out he belted.

It was officially too much. Having put up with his shit for nine long days, I clenched, turned around, and punched him in the face...

...His nose exploded, and as he fell face first into a puddle of blood, everyone in the room reached for their guns and—*bang!*—suddenly I woke up. I'd been asleep on the spot. Mostly relieved, I relaxed back into myself, when—*burp!*—just for old time's sake, he belted one into the back of my head.

'Fair dinkum, mate, only your mother could love ya.'

The day spanned its full length, until dusk gradated in, pilfering the light an inch at a time.

Neither day nor night, light nor dark, Meditation Happy Hour was upon us. Sitting as I had for many hours, it was then—after nine days of rollercoaster-like restlessness—that my mind went totally quiet. It went so quiet, in fact, that much like the way the buzzing of a fridge is noticed only after it cuts out, it was only after the layers of thoughts had ceased to haunt that I realised how much had been going on in there.

Perhaps this was the end of my inner movie reel? Like the last slack inches that slap against the projector, after the film producers have thanked the Tajikistani government for their cooperation during filming.

But as though behind all this mental activity was a feeling of purity in simply existing, I felt a greater connection to everything around me—the ground I was sitting on, the air I was breathing. It seemed, in this moment, that the parameters of my *self*—or my body, my soul's prison that had all my life kept me separate from all other form—were largely diminished. The wall, the floor, intrigued me, and where the light, like a coating in which I'd been doused, had always felt like an essence outside me, it felt now as though we were part of the same fundamental nature.

With this realisation came a greater understanding of what *I* really am—that never was I actually born, and that even after the death of my body—it being nothing more than a perishable entity living through the infinitely imperishable—never could I in fact *not* exist.

Causing me to sink into a state of bliss that far surpassed anything I'd experienced chemically, with this recognition came a profound feeling of warmth and safety—a sense of total belonging beyond any quality or quantity I'd ever experienced. And all my usual urgencies—the external endeavours that for longer than I could remember had driven me outward to seek feelings of self-worth—were rendered comparatively redundant.

But my ego wasn't vanquished entirely; as on top of this euphoria was a fear that I'd lose it. But, per the Vipassana laws of eliminating aversion and craving, I tried to not push either way, to not desire or dislike, but to experience it impartially. And the less I managed to give licence to my mind's desire to control, the deeper into the warmth I journeyed.

With eyes closed, legs crossed, and hands resting in the palms of each other, I sat there for what might have been a couple of hours of the greatest high of my adult life, until, at 9:30 p.m., the teacher spoke. 'You may now retire to your rooms.'

Having been subjected to another evening bathroom performance of hocking, spitting, blowing noses, brushing teeth, coughing, shaving, splashing and scratching, I lay on my bed for not two minutes before making a firm decision. 'It's New Year's Eve. I'm ready to leave.' I sat upright on the bed, and stood up next.

But my verdict was less along the lines of packing the Blue Fly and heading on out than it was to go for a walk outside. I didn't care if it was disallowed, and I cared even less if I got caught.

I wandered around the backyard, retracing the steps of our usual lap circuit, all the while doing my best to be feline in my footwork. The silence was so exquisite I wished I could bottle it, and the solitude was even more so.

But dreaming of more, I approached the gate to the neighbouring field. It was old and busted, and leading me to believe that no aspirant of the past had dared to push it open, it was overgrown with vines at the base. I assumed leaving the premises would be illegal, and as I clasped the gate's handle I couldn't but think of Jim Carrey in the closing scene of *The Truman Show*.

With countless palms and shoulder-high grass, the neighbouring field was as dense as it was wild. I stood amongst it as a free man, the excitement naturally transpiring into needing the toilet.

There was a thin path leading to a large clearing in the middle of the field, too idyllic not to follow. I toed forth until the canopy of stars above rendered me unable but to lie down. There was a shooting star directly overhead, seemingly moving in slow motion. I wondered where it came from, and where it was going, and although I wondered the same for myself, I felt, even for a second, that there was nothing more I needed and nowhere else I needed to be. Perhaps this Vipassana thing had been worthwhile.

Day Ten—*January 1ˢᵗ, 2005*

The 4 a.m. bell rang for what was to be the last time, and Mr Mitesh, making pint-sized objects cast keg-sized shadows, came moonwalking into our sleeping quarters, shining his lamp and jingling his bell.

I flicked back my mosquito net and stood up, and where I'd usually wish to swear and grumble, I felt notably straight and steady. We made our way downstairs for what was to be our final meditation, for as soon as the sun was fully risen the silence would be broken.

We settled onto our cushions, and while scanning the room with his devilish eyes the teacher spoke. 'Today is the last day of the ten-day program. We will now meditate for two hours before breaking the silence with *Om* chanting led by Mr Mitesh. Congratulations on your achievement. We encourage you to continue your practice independently.'

The room fell quiet, and of all the topics that had run through my mind over the days of silence, on this day I recalled the final conversation I'd had with my Irish nana before she passed away. I'd tried to recall it in the past, but only after having cleared some mental rubble could I reach it underneath. It was hauntingly detailed, like I was present in the room of memory, with its temperature, sound, and the dialogue playing back as though being performed from a script.

In full sight, the sun was streaming through the windows of the pine-panelled hall. And as we sat in agonising anticipation of when the clock would strike freedom, Mr Mitesh commenced the *Om* chanting.

All joined in, and with the soprano voices of the women harmonising monophonically over the baritone voices of the men, the sonic result was truly haunting. Singers or not, the impromptu choir seemed to produce no offending frequencies. Our performance lasted some ten minutes, until, signalling the official release; Mr Mitesh rang his bell for the last time.

Stretching our arms and legs, all stood up, and in an exchange of smiles, eye contact shot across the room like happy crossfire. Turning my head here and there, I tried to keep up, but if I was hoping to return gently to the world of communication, then I was gravely denied, as the locals, typically curious of a westerner, bombarded me with questions.

Looking to shake my hand, the big burping guy came mincing over. And it was only when standing with him face-to-face that I could gauge his height—close to seven foot. Having never heard his voice but only his burp, I was surprised to hear him speak with a voice as high-pitched as Pee-wee Herman. It was here, too, that my aversion of him was neutralised. Where during the silence I was convinced he'd been sent from hell to destroy me death-by-burping, now, unable to urge me enough to stay with his family up north, he revealed a heart that matched his height.

This was the official release, and with people hugging and exchanging contact info, there was a tangible air of union among the group. The Slovenian man, who'd attended with his wife, came limping over, looking stressed and sweaty. 'My friend,' he said, clasping my arm, 'why are women are so complicated?'

'What's happened?'

'My wife is angry that I never spoke to her for the ten days.'

'But that was the point?'

'Exactly, but she's been sitting there festering about it for ten fucking days!'

Finding the only thing scarier than the sound of a jet plane flying low overhead being the sound of an entire fleet *in* my head, the retreat had been one of the most intense challenges of my life. Aside from feeling like a frog wanting to jump from his lily, though, I definitely got several previews of the higher meaning of meditation, where all things wonky straightened into a clear road where you catch yourself *as yourself*, not as the series of reactions that run you. If I learnt only one thing, it's that there's an immeasurable difference between the way *things are* and the way *you think things are*. And undoing the ceaseless compulsion to be *doing* and allowing yourself to realign with the state of *being*—as nature intends—is, I guess, the ultimate goal of Vipassana.

The silence had been lifted, and our isolation from the outside world, too. I packed my things and said my goodbyes, but as I slung myself onto the Blue Fly, the Slovenian approached with a newspaper in hand. 'There's been an earthquake in Indonesia.'

He handed me the paper, but printed in the local language of Malayalam, I couldn't read a word.

There was a picture on the front cover—a small photo of what appeared to be a flattened house. It by no means portrayed even a teaspoon of what had happened, let alone that the earthquake had resulted in a massive tidal wave that had reached as far as our vicinity in Kerala.

And so with my bubble of ignorance maintained, it was here that my involvement ended, for now.

I fired up the bike, and it too, sounding rested from the time off, idled like a purring animal.

'Where are you going?' asked the Slovenian.

'South to Varkala. If you're down that way we can meet up?'

'Sure! If my wife forgives me.'

I smiled and took off up the road.

'Ah… freedom at the flick of the wrist!' I sighed, as the ten-day forgotten feeling flowed through my veins like a reformed stoner reunited with the bong. The feeling of motion, and the wind on your face. It seemed to me in this moment that no amount of cross-legged meditation could ever replicate this high.

It was New Year's Day 2005.

The day was hot, very hot, and as I cruised along the coastal highway, the waves of the Arabian Sea crashed hard against the shore. Yelling 'Happy New Year!' and giving me the thumbs-up, locals were riding alongside, and the traffic was moving along nicely until it ground to a sudden halt.

I edged my way to the front, where, lying on the road, heedlessly covered by a potato sack, was the mangled body of a man.

It lay in a vast pool of blood, and sticking out from under the potato sack was a foot twisted 180°. I was rather taken aback, but, reinforcing the Hindu belief that death is just a gateway to a new life, hordes of local men stood around joking as though this was nothing more than the play of cards on any given day.

I continued along, until after hundred kilometres or so, the heat inspired the need for a roadside coconut. I spotted a place and pulled over. Without even needing to ask, when I sat under its palm leaf shelter, the merchant approached with a coconut in hand. 'Two lakh dead,' he said.

'Sorry?'

'Two lakh dead.'

But as I had no knowledge of the word *lakh* (which I later learnt, like a *grand* is for 1,000, *lakh* is a Hindi term for 100,000), his point eluded me entirely. I paid him his money, hopped on the bike and continued up the highway.

Later that afternoon, I made it to the small coastal town of Varkala. After taking my sweet time to settle into a hotel, my thoughts turned Oz-bound. 'It's New Year's Day. I better ring Mum and Dad.'

19. A Wave from Home

I first dialled Dad's number—*ring ring! ring ring!*—'Hi, you've called John. I'm not here at the moment...' I got his answering machine, on which I left a knockabout message. 'G'day, Dad, it's David. I'm still in India. You might have heard something about an earthquake in Indonesia, probably not. I'm nowhere near it so don't worry. I'll try you later.'

Phone hangs up.

An English guy about my age approached, looking to use the phone. 'I've got to make another call here, mate,' I said, 'I won't be too long.'

He didn't seem fazed.

I dialled Mum's number—*ring ring! ring ring!*—*clink* 'Hello?' she answered in a voice feebler than normal.

'Mum?'

'Stephen?' she said, mistaking me as my older brother.

'Nah, it's—'

'—David?'

'Yeah, it's David.'

And never in my life had three words that came out of my mouth had such a volcanic effect.

'DDDaaavvviiiddd!   DDDaaavvviiiiiiiidddddddddddd!' she   screamed,   'DDDaaavvviiiiiiiiidddddddddddd! DDDaaavvviiiiiiiiiiiidddddddddddddd!'

I had absolutely no idea *why* the frenzied response, and I was initially quite irritated by what I thought was a massive overreaction, as the Maltese, in their big-heartedness, are not without the tendency to be hyperemotional.

'Calm down, Mum!'

'We thought you were dead, darling!'

'Dead?'

'Haven't you heard, David?'

'About what?'

'The earthquake!'

'In Indonesia? I'm in India!'

'It caused an enormous tidal wave that hit Thailand and India, and over 200,000 people have been killed!'

And it was then, after an entire week of no knowledge that reality dawned.

Amid the emotion of her relief, she explained that my family had commenced an independent investigation, registering me on the missing persons list in Australia, and that she and Dad had been lighting candles at Melbourne Cathedral. She also explained that when they'd attempted to track me through my ATM withdrawal statements, they learnt the last place I withdrew money was in Pondicherry, and that Pondicherry had been the worst hit city in India. But if anything overwhelmed me most, it was when she told me my brother Stephen had got his passport organised, and was due to fly to India any day to scale through the unidentified western bodies in the Pondicherry area.

'How bad was Pondicherry hit?' I asked, my mind turning

immediately to Ange.

'When the wave hit on Boxing Day morning 7,000 people were killed on the spot. When we tracked your last ATM withdrawal to have been made there, we pretty much lost all hope.'

It would be no lie to say that hearing Mum quote words like *Pondicherry, missing person* and *candles at church* was all very unexpected. Having merely rang to say Happy New Year, I stood in this tiny phone booth feeling vague and disjointed. I was so overwhelmed, in fact, that if I was emotional I couldn't feel it, but becoming emotional for me, the English guy stood outside with watery eyes.

'How could have you not heard about it, David?' asked Mum.

'I was in a silent retreat and we were only released this morning. I'm sorry!'

'It's ok, darling, you weren't to know. This is the best New Year's Day ever!' she said, her words striking in me a feeling like I was a little boy.

We wound up the conversation, and keen to tell everyone I'd made contact, she pledged to do the ring around.

I hung up the phone as the English guy tapped on the glass. 'Bloody hell, mate, how d'you not know? You been living in a bubble?'

'Yes, mate.'

Next I tried to ring my brother Stephen. But with his phone engaged, I opted to check my email, where I discovered 117 emails from concerned family and friends. At least ten were from Stephen, in which he still referred to me by my kid nickname of *Snake*.

Dec 26th—

'Snake, there's been an earthquake up your way. You better call home.'

Dec 28th—

'Where are you, Snake? Urgently contact home. They're all worried sick about you.'

Dec 30th—

'Snake, I've got my passport organised. I'm coming to find you.'

I quickly emailed him back, in a message subjected 'I'm fine', to which within a few minutes he replied:

Jan 1st—

'You just gave us the best news of our life. I'm crying as I write this, you little shit! I fair dinkum thought you were dead. I got my passport yesterday, and was dreading coming to look for you. We're so lucky, and I feel for all those poor people.

I tell you, Snake, if you ever had a great mate, Keasy is a legend—if I were fighting in the trenches I'd want him beside me. He was so helpful with information and phone calls. We couldn't have done it without him. He even got on the phone to India to try and piece things together. Mum was great too, she checked out all sorts of stuff.

We figured out you'd bought your plane ticket through Eddy the travel agent. He was really helpful also, and even went into his work on his day off to check the system to see if you'd flown out of India before the wave hit. We learnt you were scheduled to fly out of Mumbai, but were alarmed to discover you hadn't left the country.

We also learnt through Keasy that you've been getting around on a motorbike, and after we found out you'd been in Pondicherry I tracked an approximate overland course from Pondicherry to Mumbai, emailing any youth hostels with an ID picture and a message. What I was hoping for was that you were somewhere on your bike cross-country to Mumbai. But if you were alive no one could figure out why you hadn't contacted home. The slither of hope grew thinner by the day, and come New Year's Eve we'd pretty much given up. It was real tense.

Snake, I've been checking my email all through the night, every night, and to finally get an email from you is unreal. I broke open the scotch after the good news. I tell you what, if I didn't know anything about India before, now I'm an expert. How long are you going to be there? I'm still thinking of coming up to see ya. Give us a call at home tonight.

Talk to you then.'

*****

Understandably, I was pretty blown away by the efforts everyone had gone to back at home, especially those of Stephen. My brother Stephen is a dramatic activist; he's in the business of getting things done and he hops to his feet no matter how epic the task. But my other brother Shaun, the oldest of the three, works differently. He'll say less, but pacing and dragging his cigarette with that bit more intensity, he's more of a silent strategist. He'd also been in on the case, and with the help of his Indian neighbour in Byron Bay, had researched much of the geography of southern India.

Next I rang Dad again. And where an hour before I'd left the most blasé of messages, this time things were different. He answered the phone, and with the exhaustion in his voice apparent, he told his own account. 'It was real bad. Initially I had a father's intuition that you were all right. But when Keasy rang and told us you'd been in Pondicherry, well… it was the worst New Year's Eve of my life.'

'I fair dinkum had no idea about any of it.'

'Don't worry about it, as long as you're all right. But when

Keasy rang that day it fair dinkum gave me such a shock I stalled the truck.'

And let it be said that lesser things have made front-page headlines than my old man stalling his truck.

'But you're full of surprises, aren't ya?'

'What?'

'Matty and Mick tell us you're on a motorbike?'

'Well, yeah,' I returned, thinking he ain't going to be too happy to hear it.

'And that you had some dog called Charlie?'

'Yeah.'

'And that you rode the bike, with the dog, north to south across the length of the country?'

'Yep.'

A paused ensued.

'Ya know… I wouldn't mind doing something like that.'

I was quietly gratified, for what might have been the first time in our lives, there felt a certain role reversal, like I was the man and he the boy looking up. Even Mum, who by maternal default, I expected to be horrified by the idea, had been quite unruffled. 'So Matty and Julian tell us you've got a motorbike, darling? Oh, and what colour is it?' she asked, attempting to sound impartial. Never in my life did I think she had it in her to be interested in the colour of a motorbike. But so exceptional was this case that it wouldn't have mattered if I'd been moonwalking across India naked while juggling a pair of oranges. As long as I was alive.

There'd been many contributing factors that had built their case for concern—my failure to contact home, the constant media feed of images and statistics, and time drawing out to a full week with no word. But the final nail in their coffin of dread was when they'd learnt I'd been in Pondicherry—the most severely hit city of India. And standing now in the quietness of Varkala, this was the fact that hit me hardest.

I quickly rang Ange, who having luckily been inland at Auroville on the morning of the wave, was still in Pondicherry. We also had a mutual Kiwi mate in Sri Lanka, who was, by chance, up in the mountains the day it hit.

I even wondered about Charlie. But I later learnt that the water at the beaches in Goa, literally at the tsunami's northern periphery, had gone out for an extended period of time before returning without a ripple.

It was perhaps sickeningly ironic that where the Vipassana retreat was cause for so much grief for everyone back home, it might have been the very thing that saved mine and Ange's lives. If I'd opted to stay in Pondicherry for her birthday, there would have been a likely chance we'd have been hanging out on the very beach where, on the morning of the tsunami, 7,000 people lost their lives.

Placing the image of the wave's horror against the times we'd walked along the beach—with kids playing cricket on the sand and young couples strolling ankle-high through the water—it seemed such a cruelly idealistic setting to be so unjustly smashed apart. I even thought about the cops on the foreshore with whom I'd had the run-in, wondering if they themselves had been claimed. Be it fate, luck, or providence, we were just so lucky not to have been there.

But whereas I was in some form of bewilderment on January 1st, my unease was barely comparable to what my family and friends had been through. It had been the longest week of their lives, with every silent day like walking one more step toward a door you don't want to open. It was strangely coincidental, too, that during the time I was considered missing, Stephen's wife found out she was pregnant with a boy, as though in replacement of one lost.

Although I was the subject of concern, I'd been the most

emotionally removed of all: when they were in an anxious tangle of phone calls and growing doubt, I was sitting idle with eyes closed, legs crossed, and hands resting in the palms of each other. In fact, looking back at the retreat, I felt sick to think that we didn't know. That a group of 30 people—considering ourselves universally mindful and energetically sensitive—sat only 50 kilometres away from the rim of the disaster. Feeling no guilt, pain, or penitence.

For its many sickly connotations, I struggle to even say the word *love*, let alone write it. But if I learnt anything through the incident, it's what actually defines it.

Unlike the sort of *obligated love* that Christmas, Valentine's Day, and other commercial monsters need for their survival, *real love* is not chosen, forced or elected. Instead, it's an all-dimensional entity kindled by truth and presence. A force unable but to be expressed, real love is when a mother collapses with relief at the sound of her live son's voice coming through the phone. Real love is when an older brother chokes on his words upon learning that his younger brother isn't dead. Real love is when a best mate is so mortified by the thought of losing you that he's unable to get off the couch to go to work. Real love is when an uncle who lives a hundred kilometres away gets in his old beaten up van and drives for two hours to come see his brother whose son is missing. Real love is when your network of mates back home are so worried they sit around at their New Year's Eve party failing to drink. And real love is when they find out you're ok they go to the pub to especially mark the occasion. Like an injection too big for any vein to handle, the outpour was so overwhelming it was difficult to absorb. Surprise aside, never had I felt so valued, regarded, and worthy of the space I occupy. In fact, like having had the chance to sit quietly in the back row of my own funeral, it was something I'll never forget.

I wasn't alone in my astonishment, however, as friends and family had also gained some sort of rebirthing and dose of perspective. To quote the conclusive words of my good mate Keasy, 'All that matters in life is your mates, your family, and your dog. The rest is bullshit.'

20. O' Brother, Where Art Thou?

Dear Manuel,

Stephen was so braced to come to India that he's coming anyway. We're going to hire a second bike and buzz around the south. I just hope his culture-shock suit is cleared at customs.

*****

My task was set.

Stephen was to be here by the Tuesday, giving me only two days to ride the 800 kilometres north to Dabolim Airport in Goa.

It was a jetsetter of a ride, one in which I have little memory other than the highway grinding to a banked up halt on the second day.

I sat amid a sea of exhaust pipes, being as baked by the sun as garrotted by the fumes. I eventually weaved forward, capitalising on *pushing in* being totally inoffensive in India.

Surprisingly, there was a human roadblock of several thousand people lying on the road, and adding to the drama was a multitude of police lights and flashing cameras. I edged toward the picket line, and causing the photographers to turn to me like the paparazzi, the people lying down stood up and cleared me a path.

Aside from a beard and a walking cane, I felt like Moses parting the Red Sea—as soon as I passed through, the crowd immediately laid back down, blocking any vehicles intending to make a dash through my immaculately conceived opening.

I was gratified at the least, and if I had have been Moses— after first having a shave—the first commandment I would have instated would be: *Thou Shall Not Turn Lies Into Religions.* I mean do you honestly expect us to believe that Mary fell pregnant to a cloud? And isn't a young girl defaulting to 'naaah…' when asked by her father if she's had prepubescent sex, the most probable answer anyway? Nevertheless, there came the immaculate conception of Christianity. Three cheers for Mary!

Two days later I made it to the airport. Sitting in the arrivals lounge, after months of being Kerrigan-less, I struggled to believe my brother was going to stroll through the gate any minute. I wondered what I was going to say to him, and if unlike the time we met up at Philadelphia airport when I was seventeen, he was going to say something other than how much my nose had grown.

He came strolling through. 'Shit, Snake, ya looked like a bronzed version of Mr Bean.'

'Thanks,' I said, wondering if he was referring to my weight loss, tan, or both.

'So what now?'

'Dunno, d'you want some chewy?'

'Nah, but let's get something to eat. They were only serving rice and tahli on the plane.'

'Well, you've come to the wrong joint if you're expecting something else.'

'Maybe I should have some chewy then?'

We loaded his baggage onto the Blue Fly and rode along the Goa coastal highway.

'Snake, look at this bloke with the dead pigs on his motorbike.'

'What?'

'Look at the bloke—'

'—Yeah, I heard you the first time.'

'Then why would you ask me to repeat myself?'

'To be annoying.'

'Well, it worked.'

We overtook the guy with the dead pigs, and I could almost hear in Stephen's voice the culture shock setting in. 'Is this India's food transportation at its most hygienic?'

'S'pose. Most deliveries come with an air-blown guarantee.'

With me at the handlebars and him at the back, this seating arrangement was a perfect flip of our childhood, back when I'd be clinging to him like a koala as we tore through the Australian bush on a dirt bike. Stephen, being skinny enough that I could reach around his waist to clutch my hands together, was my preferred choice of pilot. Shaun being slightly older and thicker set came in a close second. Dad took the bronze by a long shot.

We pulled up out the front of a small highway eatery.

'Nup,' he said stopping in its doorway.

'See that tumbleweed? There ain't no Red Rooster in these parts.'

We went inside and sat on two crates, accompanied by a plank of wood posing as a table. The sound of flies seemed to increase, and several street dogs gathered at the door. Our food arrived shortly after, making the sound of the flies increase.

'What d'you call this stuff?' he asked, his face having turned to a look as though a camel had shat on his plate.

'Brains.'

'Well, I'm not eating—'

'—I'm only joking! What d'you think this is—*Raiders of the Lost Arc?*'

'Well, you wouldn't exactly call it rissoles, would ya?'

'Yeah you would, ralph rissoles.'

I walked to the communal washbasin when I'd finished eating. Washing my face and blowing my nose into my hand, my performance was at least as audible as the locals by my side. Stephen, still at the table, looked over with a face of pure repulsion. I walked back to my crate-seat, wiping my hands into my jeans.

'Good one, Snake.'

'What?'

'Blow you nose in a restaurant a bit louder next time.'

'I'd say a thousand apologies, but I'm saving 'em for greater wrongdoings.'

'Unbelievable.'

'It's the way of things around here, using your hand as a hanky, and Dad taught me to do it that loud. He calls it Irish yodelling.'

The bill came, and I slapped my hand on it.

'So what's the damage?'

'Three dollars Oz.'

'Fair dinkum?'

'The food mightn't look like art, but your wallet won't even know you were here.'

'My shout next time then.'

The next day rose. Without even needing to discuss it, we set out to hire a second bike and recommence the tour as biking allies. Having spent much of the morning scaling the length of Palolem Beach, we sighted a man hiring bikes. Noticing us notice him, he approached. 'Hello, sirs, where are you from?'

'Keilor.'

'Oh! I have a brother from there.'

'No, you don't, but we do—his name's Shaun. So how much for the blue Pulsar?' I asked, and seeing not one but two westerners present, he quoted not double but four times the price.

'I'll triple it if we divide it by ten.'

'Ok!' he said, 'but even if the sky turns black and the mountain crumbles into the sea, you must not, under any circumstance, take this bike out of Goa.'

'Fair enough,' I said, taking the bike off his hands with absolute intention of taking it out of Goa.

Two brothers and two blue bikes. We strapped them up and sat idle. But I noticed Stephen was looking like a yellower version of his usual self.

'Jeez, if you were auditioning to play a sunflower, I reckon you'd get the part.'

'I think that Red Rooster from yesterday mustn't have been properly plucked. Anyway, you're the bloke with the map. What d'you reckon?'

'I reckon we head to Hampi in Karnataka.'

It was decided, and so with black jeans, black vests, and Stephen's Essendon beanie—

('Is that the same beanie you've had since 1981?'

'Probably.'

'Whatever happened to being cool?'

'These days I don't have time.')

—we were off.

The day was shaping up to be as hot as expected, and although invalidating to the concept of being an island, the toughness of riding wheel-to-wheel definitely outweighed the heroism of riding solo.

'Cool?'

'Cool.'

In essence, this was the first time in our lives where I was the more experienced one. And with monkeys scurrying across the road and bats swooping overhead, in Stephen's eyes was the look of a young'un seeing unfamiliar animals at a zoo.

'Snake, what's with the cows eating cardboard on the roadside?'

'Dunno, d'you want some chewy?'

'Look at the pot guts on 'em. That's gotta make 'em fat.'

'The cardboard or the chewy?'

'The cardboard!'

With the sun belting down with its usual devotion, we soon crossed over the Goa/Karnataka state border, and, three-quarters parched, we pulled over for a breather.

Sitting out in the open, there was no way two resting westerners would remain unseen, and we were soon swarmed by a sea of enthused kids who stirred up the dust as they hurtled towards us.

We hopped off our bikes, obligingly, and as the children tugged at Stephen's hands, I could see on his face a look of bemused endearment.

'Wunpin! Wunpin!' they urged 'Wunpin! Wunpin!'

'What are they saying, Snake?'

'One pen, the kids here are fascinated by pens. Getting one off a westerner is like the ultimate score.'

But pen-less as we were, we had little choice but to disappoint, and I could see Stephen, the father of his own kids, grow stirred by the poverty.

It had been a big day on the road, and we rolled into the ancient town of Hampi just as the orange sun met with the horizon.

'If dreams were made out of stone, it would be Hampi,' I'd heard it said. The fable of the stone city was proven true as we rode through the outskirt area of temple ruins, pillars and giant boulders. Monkeys scurried throughout and birds flew across the face of the dust-laced horizon.

As we rode along the high street, known as the Hampi Bazaar, a young local boy came running alongside. 'Hello, mister! What is your name?' he asked. Stephen replied and I accelerated out of there.

We rode into the twisting laneways of the old town. There were more hotels than you could count, and all had rooftop terraces designed to take in the 360° templescape views. We chose one and checked in, and when the landlady led us to our rooftop room, sitting on the terrace was an older western man playing guitar.

Our room was simple but clean, and when I stood in front of the mirror, I was quietly pleased to see Stephen as blackened as I from the many rides before.

I finished the humanisation shower soon after, but with the grime having proven, to style, too difficult to remove from around my eyes; I was left with the usual road-induced eyeliner.

'Snake, you look like a skinny version of Boy George.'

'Well, you look like a less skinny version!'

'So what now?'

'Dunno, d'you want some chewy?'

'Nah, let's sit on the roof.'

We went outside, where the same man was still playing guitar. He had a head of grey hair and was wearing thick-rimmed glasses. We sat at his table, and when he stood up, stubbed his toe and elected the word 'feck!' I could fair guess his nationality.

'Irish?'

'Right you are,' he said, with a glint of the green hills in his eyes.

He sat back down and the three of us exchanged names, his being—as though it'd be unpatriotic otherwise—Jimmy.

'What sort of name is Kerrigan anyway?' he barked.

'Well, it's an Irish—'

'—I know that! But what's being Irish got to do with actually being Irish?' His voice, so throaty that the only thing that could save it would be a lifetime subscription to Strepsils, seemed to have an incomprehensibly grumpy quality. And hard to know if you were being spoken to or yelled at, as he continued laying down his riddles, its volume increased. 'Being Irish is about being lyrical and poetic, and so upside down that you're the right way up again. D'you follow me, young Kerrigan?'

'Ahhhr I—'

'—It's like when asking an Irishman asks for directions and he'll sing it to you as clear as mud, "go you down the road as straight as you can, but if when you get to the cliff you drive off it, it means you've gone too far."'

In under a minute it was proven that this man was so Irish that when he washed his face he likely left on the cloth a holy impression of two potatoes in a punch up. His poetic value was without end, and we sat on the roof until the night took charge of the sky.

The sun hopped to its feet, and having hopped to ours we sat at a table of a nearby rooftop brekky bar.

'So what colour are you planning on turning today?' I asked.

'Green.'

'Well, if you're auditioning to play a beanpole at least you'd get the part.'

'Yeah, you can talk.'

'What?'

'You better eat some meat, Snake. You've gone from looking like a python to an earthworm.'

'Cheers,' I said, for if the truth was like cordial drink, then you can always bank on your brothers to serve it undiluted.

'So have you had any troubles with anyone on the bike tour?' he asked, to which I told him the story of the blokes that hassled me out in the Rajasthan desert. And another story that failed to make the pages of this book, where, resulting in a gang of ten guys physically restraining me until I paid the applicable money, I accidentally snapped the number plate off a car by clipping it with my bike. And another story that, if this book should become a bestseller, will likely be the basis for the sequel, where a local man threatened to punch me because he was convinced I was trying to arrange a marriage for his daughter with myself.

'Have you thought about writing a book, Snake?'

'I've got a fair old collection of emails to a mate back home, but I'm not quite sure it's book-worthy.'

'Just remember what ol' George used to say, if you can make 'em laugh, they'll want more of you.'

The sun broke through the trees, resulting in a cease-fire in the banter. Our table, white in colour, became blindingly bright, and Stephen's face turned to a look more serious than I was used to. 'Don't you get a bit lonely out here, Snake?'

'Sometimes, I s'pose, but there's a big difference between being lonely and being alone.'

'What about the hassle factor? The food? The language barrier?'

'It's a major hassle, and sometimes I lay on a bed of some hotel, staring at the ceiling and wondering what I'm doing. But I need it, and somehow I know what I'm doing.'

'To get lost in the hope of finding yourself?'

'Something like that. You know when your computer is playing up, and you press control-alt-delete to clear it? Well, that's what this trip is about. An overall reboot.'

We finished up, and figuring we'd spend the day wandering the temples, we made our way to the Hampi Bazaar. As just two of countless westerners present we walked along. Where ancient Hampi was famous for being the former capital of a fallen empire, modern Hampi was laden with jean shops, Internet cafés, and all such things aimed at the tourist pocket.

'Hello, Steve!' said a voice from behind. We turned to it to find, standing there, the local boy who'd run alongside us the night before. 'Is this your brother?'

'Yes. Which one do you think is older?'

'He's got more hair than you, but you've got more muscles than him. So I think you are older.'

He had a tray of bananas for sale, but smarter than your average street-business-hopeful, he seemed to understand that pushiness was bad for business. Putting to rest the usual drill, he meandered calmly alongside, talking facts and figures and rattling off his knowledge of capital cities. His name was Raju.

Resultantly charmed, or fraught with a hankering for bananas, Stephen bought a bunch. 'Can you tell us the name of that temple at the end of the street?'

'It is the Virupaksha Temple, the main Hindu temple of Hampi. It's still an active place of worship.'

'So you're allowed inside?'

'Oh yes! It's the highlight of the town, and there's a grand elephant who blesses all the visitors.'

'What do you mean, *blesses all the visitors*?'

'Go in and see!'

'Ok, see ya buddy.'

'Will you be back?'

'Not sure.'

'Then you're not my buddy,' he said, putting the banana money into the hands of his little sister.

Like a pyramid stretched from its top point up, the temple's entrance was a 120-foot tower of stepped stone. As we strolled into the temple grounds, a red Bandar monkey began to hobble our way.

'Chuck you bananas.'

'What?'

'Chuck you bananas!'

'Why?'

The monkey began to charge.

'Turf ya f#&k'n bananas!'

He threw them to the heavens, and just as the monkey was at his feet, it snatched the bananas and peeled them in a way we were glad wasn't our faces.

Raju was right about the in-house elephant. Standing before it, in single file, was a long row of people waiting to be blessed. It was a curious sight, as with its trunk it touched them first on the shoulders and second on the head.

'You going to give it a go, Snake?'

'Not without a Stackhat.'

'Why not?'

'Coz I'd rather it not reef me head off like the top off a stubbie!'

But despite my protest he kept up: pushing his point with a tone of family-group pressure reminiscent of when I was five years old and he and Shaun forced me to sit on the frighteningly high knee of the Humpty Dumpty statue in Mildura. An era where the strongest words of defence a minor could muster was 'shuuud up!' proving, of course, to be as effective as throwing a marshmallow at King Kong.

This day was no exception, and with Stephen still at it, and the elephant looking somewhere between routinely depressed and vaguely curious, I stood milling on the idea. 'Come on, Snake!

Don't be a fairy! A wimp! A skinny little nut allergy-having ponce! A pin—'

'—All right!' I said, walking up to the great beast frown-to-frown. 'G'day. How's it hanging?'

'Did you know that if you take the lateral prediction of when Nostradamus proposes the coming of Armageddon, and divide it by the rate in which the hole in the ozone layer is growing, you get the square root recipe for shortbread biscuits?' said the elephant back.

'Jeez,' I thought.

Hoping he wouldn't have a sudden surge of creativity and with his trunk pick me up and use me as a q-tip, I stood with it face-to-face. I closed my eyes. But with all other senses at work, I could feel him touch me with his trunk—first on the left shoulder, then on the right, and lastly, making a strong python-like curl, around the top of my head. Quite a clever trick really. But not as clever as when he first took the required money out of my hand and gave it to his master standing to the side. Just another occasion where, like Harry met Sally, religion met money.

We made it back to the hotel, and standing over the washbasin, I figured blowing my nose into my hand was as good a way to pass the time as any.

'Good one, Snake, you've really taken your Irish yodelling to the next level.'

'Irish yodelling?' objected a voice, 'the Irish don't yodel, they bellow from their toes!' It was Jimmy, sitting out on the rooftop. 'It's like the time when my father came home from work with a steering wheel down his jocks, and I asks, "Da, what's with the steering wheel?" and he says "dunno, but it's driving me nuts."'

We sat outside, and as the dusk fell to the darkness of a starlit night, he played a tune to match.

'D'you sing, Kerrigan?'

'Which one?'

'The skinny one.'

'Only when I'm washing.'

'Now I'm starting to smell your heritage. What about you old Kerrigan?'

'Harmonica for me.'

'Well, none of us are getting any younger. This song is called *Dancing Around Corners*,' he said. 'It's about when you get home drunk and are unable to get your shoes off.'

He commenced his song, and where old Jim was crusty on the outside he had a singing voice that could calm a wild sea. With Stephen glossing over with the harmonica, I followed with a few songs next, and a small crowd of on-listeners gathered on the roof. Candles flickered in the wind as the music rolled into the night.

The next morning it was time to leave Hampi. Having strapped up the bikes early doors, we sat idle.

'Well, you're the bloke with the map, Snake. What d'you reckon?'

I told tell him about Sai Baba, a famous Indian spiritual leader who I'd read a book on some years back.

'His ashram is in the next state, Andhra Pradesh. If we leave now we might make it before dark.'

It was decided, and so with black jeans, black vests, and enough sunscreen to make us look like a pair of geisha girls—

('Fair dinkum, Snake, wipe that crap in properly!'

'Well, at least I'm not the bloke with me t-shirt tucked into me shorts!)

—we were off.

We stopped on the Hampi Bazaar high street to get some

supplies before hitting the highway.

'Hello, Dave!' said a voice as I dismounted the Blue Fly. It was our mate Raju. 'Leaving I see?'

'Yes, mate.'

'Are these your motorbikes?'

'This one is mine. But Stephen's is hired.'

'Yours is a four-stroke of English design, and his is a two-stroke of Japanese design.'

'How do you know all these things?'

'I read.'

He then went on to explain that through his years of dealings with tourists he'd taught himself Spanish, Hebrew, and even Japanese. And as it was mainly his job to earn the family's wages, he was the man of the house at the ripe old age of eight. This kid was so smart that if he had the political solutions to the world's problems sitting in his back pocket, I wouldn't have been surprised. Surely someday he'd become mayor of Hampi.

'So have you ever been on a motorbike?' Stephen asked.

'No,' he said, with a grin as though suspecting the offer, to which Stephen lifted him up and sat him up front.

'You be on handlebars, and I'll be on footwork,' he said, as off they went for a ride around the main drag. By the time the boy hopped back to the ground, he had buzzing in his eyes the light of a thousand stars.

'Farewell!' he yelled, running behind us as we rolled outbound.

Two brothers and two blue bikes. We rode along the highway wheel-to-wheel.

'I tell you, Snake, cruising along with you is a far better feeling than when we thought you were missing,' he said, proceeding to speak about the week post-tsunami. 'Mum was the first to raise the alarm, but for the first couple of days Shaun and me were giving it the he'll-be-right vibe. Every day grew bleaker, and the day before you rang I was swimming in our pool, and when I accidentally swallowed some water I almost started crying thinking about you drowning in some faraway place. When we found out you were ok, we even had a news crew knocking on our door.'

'I didn't know that! I fair dinkum had no idea about any of it. About an hour before I rang home I'd pulled over to have a roadside coconut, and the guy at the stand was saying something about "two lakh dead", which means "two hundred thousand dead". But I had no idea at the time.'

We continued riding, and with both of us having fallen silent, I thought about the host of stories I'd learnt in the aftermath of the tsunami. Stories of communities brought together. Of people of opposing faiths flocking indiscriminately to temples, mosques, and churches for shelter. Of Buddhists looking after homeless Hindus, and Christians taking in orphaned Muslims. Yet for each of the positive stories was a negative equivalent. Of the scavengers arriving in trucks to raid the scattered stock of flattened jewellery shops. And of people foraging through the wallets of the dead lying next to what had been a passenger train tipped over like a die-cast toy.

With the afternoon sun belting down without bias, we soon crossed over the Karnataka/Andhra Pradesh state border, and, four-quarters parched, we pulled over for a roadside chai.

The merchant tottered over with two hot glasses in hand. Stephen recoiled at his debut sip. 'Sorry,' he said to the man, 'can I have one without sugar?'

The man looked at him blankly.

'Again, you've come to the wrong joint if you think you'll get one without sugar. They're pretty keen on it in these parts.'

'Keen? Don't they like any tea with it?'

Sitting out in the open, there was no way we'd remain unseen, and by the time we took our second sip, a sea of enthused kids had surrounded us again. 'Wunpin! Wunpin!' they urged 'Wunpin! Wunpin!'

Tugging at his hands, the children surrounded Stephen, and while scanning their expectant faces with a familiar look of bemused endearment, he reached into his daypack and fished out a packet of coloured pens.

'Where d'you get them?'

'Raju. Like *Red* from *Shawshank*, he's known to locate certain items.'

Becoming the Santa of Pens, he handed them out, and the kids broke into raptures—some furiously scribbling on their hands, and others, probably to show their parents, running off into the distance.

Back onboard the Blue Fly and Stephen's bike—which could be logically referred to as the Bro Fly—we pressed along the highways of Andhra Pradesh.

'So who is it we're going to see again, Snake?'

'Sai Baba. He's an ultra-famous spiritual leader.'

(Sathyou Sai Baba was born in 1926 in the remote village of Puttaparti in southern India, and claims to be the reincarnation of *Shirdi Sai Baba*, a Muslim saint who lived in a small village in the state of Maharashtra.

It's said that he left his family at age thirteen, claiming that his devotees were waiting for him and that he'd leave his current body at age 96 to reincarnate eight years later in the third and final manifestation as *Prema Sai Baba* in a village in Kerala. Interestingly, *Sathyou Sai Baba* died in 2011 at the age of 84. In his own words—'Yes I incarnate from age-to-age, and time-to-time. Whenever strife, discord and disharmony overwhelm the world, god incarnates in human form to show mankind the way to love, harmony and peace.'

He openly describes himself as an avatar, an incarnation of god with all his powers, and having defined himself as superior to Jesus, Muhammad, and Buddha, he, in one of his discourses, is quoted to say that Jesus, in reality, was not an avatar but just a man who became aware of his own divinity.

Many argue that his actions—feats that defy the laws of science, like multiplying food to feed the masses, materialising jewels from his mouth, curing the sick by the touch of his hand, and even resuscitating the dead—are mere tricks. However, with thousands of devotees flocking from all over the world, the one fact that can't be argued is his popularity.

First from the people of India, and then onto those of the west—many now living with him at his ashram in Puttaparti—from the dawn of his mission, his number of devotees has continually grown, and with thousands of centres all over the world, their numbers now reach into the millions.

Many sceptics write that Sai Baba is no more than a master of deception. Aware of such stances, he responds, 'Since I move about with you, eat like you, and talk with you, you are deluded into the belief that this is but an instance of common humanity. Be warned against this mistake. I am also deluding you by my singing with you, talking with you, and engaging myself in activities with you. But, any moment, my divinity may be revealed to you; you have to be ready, prepared for that moment. Since divinity is enveloped by humanness, you must endeavour to overcome the *mayou* (delusion) that hides it from your eyes.')

By the latter half of that afternoon we made it to his ashram in Puttaparti. Once a humble village, Puttaparti's high street was a modern thoroughfare strewn with topical paraphernalia—Sai shoes, Sai posters, Sai books, Sai Internet, and a wide range of other capitalisations all shunned by Sai Baba himself.

Rising out of the ground as one of the most elaborate expressions of wealth I'd ever seen, his ashram was a sight to behold—blue, pink, and white in colour, it looked like a giant wedding cake. Adding to its sterility and mystique, at its glittering entrances gates were gatemen dressed in white. I wondered how it was funded, but later learnt that this building, housing up to 50,000 people, stood thanks to the donations of certain billionaire devotees, perhaps including those of Isaac Tigrett, the founder of the Hard Rock Cafe chain.

My first impression was that it seemed unashamedly materialistic; inspiring the same repulsion I felt when I saw the Vatican. But despite the ease of jumping to such conclusions, I was open to more than just pedestrian thoughts. Having removed our road-induced eyeliner, we checked into a hotel, and along with the crowd of thousands, entered the ashram's grounds for a closer look.

Like a modern university, inside was an assembly of marked buildings, ornate and colourfully landscaped gardens, and a range of eating halls also, some serving to the palette of westerners and others to the spicier preference of locals.

Matching the multitude you'd expect to see after a major international concert, there were tens of thousands of people pouring through the grounds, as many westerners as locals. Having met, in the following days, people from New Zealand, Australia, Russia, America, Latvia, Lithuania, Iceland, South Africa, England, Spain, the Netherlands, China, Switzerland, Canada, Malaysia and more, I doubted it possible to find a more international melting pot on Earth.

Present throughout the grounds, too, were hundreds of stray dogs, and as I got a closer look I couldn't help but notice that the entire external part of their ears were cut flush with the skull.

I turned to Stephen. 'Are you seeing this?'

'What?'

'The dogs' ears?'

'Yeah, it's pretty rough. I was speaking to an American bloke before who was saying they do it because they reckon they'll rip their ears off in dog fights anyway.'

'Which is about as logical as having your nuts lopped at birth in case someday you catch 'em jumping a barbed wire fence!'

'Sai Rum!' greeted a man as he walked past.

'What'd he say?'

'Dunno, something about rum.'

A bell rang throughout the grounds.

'It must be time for darshan.'

'What's that?'

'When Sai Baba makes his daily appearance.'

We made our way over to the main pavilion, and sat amongst the crowd of thousands sitting cross-legged and singing bhajans (religious chants).

At the front was an elaborate altar, boasting gold, crushed velvet, and strewn with a generous blanketing of flowers. To its left was an ensemble of musicians, sitting idle as though waiting for a cue.

On the pavilion's far right-hand side was a set of large gates, and as the gates began to open the musicians broke into a drum-heavy, almost tribal-sounding music.

(When he was younger, Sai Baba used to walk out amongst the crowd, giving offerings of *Vibhuti*—a fine powdery ash that he produces in the palm of his hands, claiming he has access to an ever-burning light. But being now in his late seventies, his entrances had become somewhat scaled down.)

With the collective efforts of the singers and drummers creating the fiery-sounding music, the gates kept gradually opening, and after a minute or less, out drove what looked like a small golf buggy.

From the distance we were sitting, it was difficult to see. But as it advanced, the figure of a petite man came into view. There he was, Sai Baba, wearing an all-orange robe, and sporting his famous Afro hair.

Inch-by-inch the buggy edged through the crowd, and with many people breaking into tears at the sight of him, and others desperately trying to hand him letters, all—in a tide-like motion—bowed as he passed.

He himself appeared humble and composed, and he spent the short journey gazing vacuously across the crowd, commanding the attention of an entire side of the pavilion with the mere turn of his head.

With the buggy having reached the altar, he got out with assistance and stood at the gold handrail at its front. He appeared frail, but it was hard to know if it was from age or other—as it was rumoured, of late, that he'd voluntarily broken his legs to take on the suffering of one of his devotees. The music intensified his presence, and he stood in clear view as thousands continued their fanatical bowing.

I was mostly unsure about my own beliefs, and I admit that I felt very little on the day. But sympathetic to the notion that there are surely universal laws and forces that work on a much broader scale than can be grasped by the human mind, I also felt that barefaced objection was too easy a conclusion to draw. It had been said to me by one particular devotee that Sai Baba was just a man, who, through his own mind, had trained himself to manipulate the higher powers of energy, an ability that each of us has if only we'd allow ourselves to realise it.

Be it truth or illusion, I'd measure his authenticity through what I gauged was his intention, which seemed good-willed. Through his life's work he's built a universal community, a support network for thousands, even millions, where all races and religions are made equally welcome. Some argue that too many dollars have been tumbled his way. But when their expenditure lies in aid programs to destitute villages, building a modern hospital where the most advanced operations are entirely free, and starting schools where children are taught honesty over dishonesty—the intention, again, appears sound. As well, when he conveys the likes of the following—words that promote universal truth, open-mindedness, and exploration of the self—it's my feeling he's an asset to humanity.

> *'There is only one religion, the religion of Love;*
> *there is only one language, the language of the Heart;*
> *there is only one caste, the caste of Humanity;*
> *there is only one law, the law of Karma.*

Having ridden through cities as large as Bangalore, and towns as small as Londa—constituted of little more than a desolate train platform, a coke machine, and a man sitting on a stool smoking a bidi cigarette—after a couple of weeks of buzzing around the south we made it back to Goa. We returned Stephen's bike; reassuring its owner we never so much as considered taking it out of Goa. And the following day we stood outside Dabolim Airport, at a fair old loss for words.

'So what now, Snake?'

'Dunno, d'you want some—'

'—No I don't want some chewy! So what's your next step?'

'Well, I've been here for at least three times longer than intended, so now that you're off, tomorrow I'm going to head to Anjuna Market and sell the bike. When that's done I'll get a bus to Mumbai.'

An awkward silence rose as his face turned to that same

serious look. 'Well, I guess I'm glad to be leaving you here alive than bringing you back dead,' he said, my gaze shooting to the ground as a result. 'I'm not here to guilt you, Snake, but this adventure you're on has put all of us to the test. No one really knows what you're up to.'

He paused, as though waiting for the admission from the condemned before the floor drops. But my voice box, somewhere within my constricted chest, seemed barely able to muster a response. 'Neither am I.'

His flight was boarding. He extended his hand to mine. 'Well, I guess I'll see ya around, Snake.'

'Yep. I'll see ya around.'

'Go forth and conquer, just don't forget us back in Oz,' he said, picking up his bags and walking towards the silver doors. I was sad to see him go, not that I was going to admit it, and although I had plenty of experience with being on my own, I felt suddenly weighed down by the prospect.

'Hey Snake?' he called from yonder, 'how d'you keep a bastard in suspense?'

'How?'

'I'll tell you next time.'

21. The Red Car

My breathing was at a record tight as the doors closed behind Stephen, but I was determined to press onwards nonetheless. I took a puff of my inhaler, just for luck. But it didn't work.

I walked out into the car park, and slung myself onto the bluey bike. Without Stephen and his bags, it felt unfamiliarly light. I started it up, and revved for all its worth. But seeming unable to click it in gear I caught myself in a fixed gaze. I continued to rev, focused on nothing in particular, and rev and rev some more. I clicked it in gear, finally, and my eyes focused forward. But before letting go of the clutch, I hit the kill switch and all fell quiet. 'I should be on that plane.'

I quickly hopped off the bike and headed for the airport's main door. But as the automatic doors opened I was caught by something to their left—a phone. There was one voice above all others that I wanted to hear. I rang the number.

'Hullo?' it said.

'Ange, it's Dave.'

'Oh! How are ye, ma Aussie darlen?' she was still at the spiritual commune in Auroville. 'Where are ye?'

'I'm in Goa.'

'With yer brother?'

'He just left. I'm at the airport. He's inside the terminal.'

'Whot's wrong?'

I exhaled at length.

'You know how you've sometimes asked me why I set out on this trip?'

'Aye?'

'Well, I often have this recurring dream. Where I'm travelling in a red car, on a dead straight road, like a bridge over water, and there are no exits, and I'm desperately looking for one as I want to get off.'

'Whot are ye talkin' aboot?'

'And I can see the car from above—and the top of my head through the sunroof—and the camera goes up and up, for miles and miles. Until it goes so high that I can see the ends of the road in front and behind.'

'Dave?'

'But the road is growing at a faster rate than I can drive. So I drive faster and faster, and faster and faster. But the faster *I go* the faster *it grows*. So it can mean only one thing Ange.'

'Whot?'

'That I'm never going to get off this road and that I'm always going to be running. Yet the only thing that scares me more is the thought of standing still.'

'But that doesnae exactly answer the question.'

'What question?'

'*Why* ye set oot oan this trip? What are ye running *from*?'

'The same thing as you.'

'Which is?'

'Drudgery.'

'Aye, but I sense there's somethin' more tae it fur ye..'

'It's a long story, a very long story, one that I'm not sure I want to bore you with.'

'There wis a time when I'd appreciate ye no' borin' me. But do I sound like ah've got anywhere tae be?'

'It's hard for me to explain.'

'Try.'

I paused at length.

'I have this inexplicable breathing condition.. where I feel kind of permanently unable to catch my breath.'

'How long huv ye had it fur?'

'About five years. It's the bane of my life. For some reason it's worse when I'm in Australia and better when I'm away. Particularly when a few years back I had a major breakthrough from something that happened in Dublin.'

'Whot wis that?'

I proceeded to tell her the story of the Indian doctor in the dorm room, leaving out not a dot of detail.

'Soo has it lifted since ye left Oz this time?'

'No, it seems everywhere I go, there I am. It included.'

'D'ye no' think it's like an emotional thing?'

'No. It's just a physical problem, like my chest is locked for some reason. And when it loosens, on occasions, the difference is night and day.'

'Darlen, I knoo ye're a bit more sceptical of the spiritually-minded than me..'

'Not these days, really.'

'But I see things, Dave.'

'Like what?'

'I see yoo and me.'

'What do you mean?'

'That we're like a pair of swans—calm on the surface, but beneath the water our feet are gaun a million miles an hour.'

'Maybe you're right.'

'I am right. But more than this, I see you, Dave. I see who yoo really are. I see ye as a little boy. I see ye as a young man. And I see that fur some reason ye've got a giant padlock oan yer heart.'

Like a hairline fraction appearing in a rock face, I felt myself starting to give way emotionally. But I was determined not to cry, particularly not into the phone. It had been over five years since I'd shed a tear, not a single drop had I allowed myself, not in a movie, not in a moving passage in a book, not in the grips of crippling anxiety, and not even through several funerals.

'I see yoo right now, Dave.'

'What do you see?'

The fracture began to gain momentum.

'I see that ye're aboot tae explode.'

'Ange?' My voice started to follow.

'Allow yerself, Dave.'

'The road never stops.'

'Yoo need tae let yerself cry fur two weeks darlen!'

'I'm still in the red car and I can't get out.'

'Allow yerself.'

'Ange?'

'Aye?'

'I'll ring you back.'

With my mind running a slideshow of horrors of the past, and fears of the future, I walked back towards the bike. 'Allow yerself, Dave.' I could still hear Ange's voice in my head. 'We thought you were dead, darling!' Mum's as well. My chest was so sore I considered that perhaps I was having a heart attack. But still I was determined to contain myself. 'I accidentally swallowed some water and I almost started crying thinking about you drowning in some faraway place.' I could hear Stephen's words after the tsunami. 'Allow yerself, Dave.' My whole body was shaking as I approached the bike, and the fracture in the rock face was growing only wider. 'It was the worst New Year's Eve of my life.' Dad's voice came in. I reached for the bike keys. 'Allow yerself, Dave.' And then the rock face gave way.

Hiding behind the bike's back wheel, after five long years without a drop, I let forth the very tide of emotion that I didn't realise I'd been too scared to face. As though a dam had given way, I sat there for the next two hours, sobbing to the extent that my entire body, even hair, was utterly saturated.

Although I was out of view of intruding eyes, there was, by perhaps male default, a part of me that was consumed with embarrassment. But far outweighing this concern, the more I cried the more I realised something else—I could breathe! I could breathe! My god, I could breathe!

I eventually stood up, wiping away the tears and snot, and feeling propelled into the same state of natural ecstasy as I had been that day in Dublin.

Relishing each full inhalation like a smoker does with a cigarette, again, where there was once great heaviness, there was now a tingling lightness. As though a veil, or constriction, had been removed from my senses, I could see, hear, smell, and most of all *feel* with a heightened awareness that instantly reinstated my self-worth and the notion that I am both loved and I matter.

Consumed with disbelief, I looked skywards; this was, in effect, the second time I'd been released from the curse of restricted breathing. But whereas last time the miracle was inexplicable, it was this time more understandable.

Like a valve for the very purpose of reprieve, the crying had released the pressure in my chest. Perhaps this was, ultimately, the very heart chakra release I'd been told I so desperately required? If so, then I was far less sceptical of the theory than when it happened in the dorm room in Dublin.

From that day forth I've had a better understanding that my

breathing condition was nothing less than massive emotional suppression resulting in a physical constriction. Be it my founding grievances were in relation to past hurts or future anxieties, the effect of compounded emotions made me less able to feel the impact of things separately, as opposed to being overwhelmed by them collectively.

What I learnt also is what facilitates authentic healing. Emotions are stubborn energy charges that can no more be defeated by alcohol or drugs—which only facilitate their permanency—than they can be masked by distractions such as television, workaholism, or material wealth. Emotions, like committed friends, are signposts that never yield until they are faced or released, and only on the other side of this is genuine salvation.

I straightened myself up and walked back to the phone.

'Ange?'

'Aye?'

'You were right about the padlock.'

'Are ye ok darlen?'

'Very ok. It just broke,' I said, turning around, and just for luck, throwing my inhaler into the neighbouring field.

22. Escape from Planet India

'Hello, Mr Sir! There is something in your ear.'

'Excuse me?'

'There is something in your ear.'

I leant down to the motorbike's mirror, trying to achieve the angle to see this *something*, when the man handed me a business card. *Ranjit Puneet—Ear Cleaner.*

'Please, Mr Sir, let me help you!' he said, reaching for my ear like a cat burglar to the diamond.

'Mate, your finger and my ear ain't ever gunna be mates.'

'Why?'

'Because your nostrils would get jealous.'

'But they shared intimate relations just a minute back?'

Word on the street was these guys told you that you had something in your ear, and with a premeditated dab of yellowy matter on their fingernail, tricked people into believing it came from their brain.

'Besides, I wouldn't stick my own finger in there through fear of what might be found.'

'No, Mr Sir! In the unlikely event that we'll be doing business, I'll be sticking not only my finger,' he said, unrolling a leather kitbag full of what looked less like ear cleaning instruments than remnants from the Frankenstein Museum of Dental Catastrophes.

'Hunting for the Holy Grail?'

'Yes, Mr Sir! The deeper the dig, the more interesting the find!'

'Mate, I don't care if you're the second *and* third coming of Jesus, or an accountant with a knack for vaporising money, but the chances of you scrubbing my brain with your rusty toothbrushes are as slight as Walt Disney being successfully thawed from his cryogenic freezing,' I, for the duration of my hesitance to respond, thought.

And as he rolled up his kitbag and walked away, I couldn't help but get the feeling he was immune to having his heart broken.

With ear waxologists, handicrafts, elephant rides, fake sadhus, painted cows, not painted cows, and… motorbikes, there were as many westerners at the Anjuna Flea Market as locals.

The time for us to part having come, I stood in the bike selling area with a *for sale* sign on the Blue Fly. There was an array of other bikes for sale, and all of us hawkers lingered around, sweating on buyers and pretending we liked each other.

The afternoon sun was high and hot, and as fed up as a fisherman not getting a bite, I walked away after a couple of hours.

I forgot my water bottle, and when I turned around I could see from the distance a swarm of cops descend on the bike area.

With a whole lot of shrugging of shoulders and paperwork being produced, one of the lads handed over some baksheesh, which ever so greasily slipped into the pocket of his interrogator. A couple of cops circled my bike, tweaking its mirrors and playing with its throttle, when a prospective buyer approached it.

Unable to approach in return, this was another case when I wished I'd had a water pistol handy. If I was fretting, though, I needn't have, as like a pair of wise guys, we made shrewd eye contact.

He approached me in the shadows.

'Jesus?'

'What?'

'Nothing. It's just…'

This bloke looked so much like Jesus that if he chewed water and ralphed wine I wouldn't have been surprised. He was Israeli, of course, and he was so sinewy he could have framed Iggy Pop for an Arnie lookalike.

'Is the blue bike yours?'

'Yes,' I said, 'but we can't go over while the cops are there.'

'I see…' he said in a tone as though enjoying the notion of misconduct.

'So what's your plan, mate?'

'I want to ride a motorbike across India.'

'You've got some experience with riding?'

'No, I've never ridden before.'

'India's a pretty mad place to learn.'

'I know, but I'm Israeli, so I surely can't go home without fulfilling my national obligation.'

'Fair enough,' I said, banking the gravity of his interest.

'So does she purr or complain?'

'She makes the fat lady sing.'

'What fat lady?'

'That fat lady,' I said, as a particularly stout woman walked past and waved from the distance.

The cops cleared out and we approached the blue beast. 'So,' my newest friend paused, taking a brooding drag from his cigarette, 'how much?'

'Six hundred.' I said, wanting five.

His face openly contorted, but the fact he was talking money, before giving it a test ride, revealed he was the sort of bloke that fills a cup with ice and then adds boiling water. 'I'll give you four-twenty,' he said.

'Five-fifty, plus a set of steak knives.'

'Four-fifty.'

'Five-twenty, steak knives and a free tank of air.'

'Four-eighty.'

'Why don't we meet at five?'

He put his hand firm into mine. 'Fuck, man!' he said, 'I can't believe I'm going to ride a motorbike across India!'

'It's the best thing you'll ever do. So do you want to have a ride now?'

'Like I said, I've never ridden.'

That being the case, I agreed to dink him the 30 kilometres to where he was staying before handing it over.

I started it up and he jumped on behind, and just as I clicked it in gear, the same cops as earlier appeared from around the corner.

'Hey!' my passenger yelled back to them, 'fuuuck yooouuu!' he said, closing his sentiment with a generous extension of his middle finger. 'My friend?' he asked, turning back as we barrelled along the dusty market road, 'do you think I'll be ok on this motorbiking venture?'

'Somehow, mate, I think you'll be fine.'

We soon made it to his place of residence, and when I handed him the key and he handed me five scrunched up hundred dollar bills I felt overwhelmingly sad to swap my beautiful machine for what might as well have been five bits of toilet paper. 'I can't believe it's not mine anymore.'

'I'm glad to be taking a bike that's been loved, brother,' he said. And although I failed to tell him that the brakes were nearing the end of their life, I graciously accepted the sentiment.

He hopped on and gripped its handlebars, and watching him ride shakily around the corner, the Blue Fly was forever gone.

*****

Hello Mr Kerrigan, the Australopithecus, (*southern ape*)

After a few hectic months in the big smoke of Delhi, I'm back at the ashram in Rishikesh. I'm once again perched on our infamous balcony, but your neighbourly company has since been replaced by a somewhat dull Canadian, whose abilities to converse seem to struggle getting past *hello*.

Enough of my platitudes. I felt I should write to inform you that somewhere around the turn of the New Year, Mamma Sharvari passed away here at the ashram. As you know, she was very old and certainly comfortable with the notion of her own death. Oddly, a week later, Mr Teen Tang joined in her passing.

In context of this news, and in that of our own departures, there's a lovely Persian phrase I once read... meaning *life goes on*. So, my old friend, until, if, or when, our paths should ever cross—*zendagi migzara*.

Love to you,
Professor Pramesh

*****

Still digesting the news, I left the Internet café. And while walking along the bustling streets of Panaji, much to my delight, a familiar face came wandering around the corner. 'סולש חא' I yelled its way. It was Lior my Israeli mate from Pushkar.

'Shalom to you too, brother! You remembered it!' he sang, holding his shoulders in mid-shrug. 'And where is your bike?'

'I just sold it today. To another Israeli.'

'Of course you did!' he said, relaxing his shoulders.

'Mate, what a spinout bumping into you!'

'I know, and look at you, Aussie brother—skinny and tanned. I think the Enfield experience turned you into a virtual-Israeli.'

'Thanks, I think. So did you ever come off the bike?'

'Four times! You?'

'I almost hit a bus on a freeway near Delhi. I still shed a life just thinking about it.'

'What about the police, any trouble?'

'Almost, but my successor might have some explaining to do if he gets misidentified. I'm quite worried about him. I once had a schoolteacher who stood before the class telling us in a lathery rant when Jesus returns he'd be getting around on a motorbike. I think I just served the fable.'

'I guess he can pay for your traffic sins.'

'I guess,' I said, wondering if I should change my middle name to Judas.

'So anyway, mate, are you going to relieve me of the suspense you've had me in all these months?'

'What?'

'Have you ever remembered the question you were going to ask me that night in the restaurant in Pushkar?'

'Oh yes! What I was going to ask you was… what does—' but when an attractive girl walked past, his mind, typically, blew a testicle-linked fuse. 'Ah, man! Did you see her?'

'Yes, mate, I did, but you're not getting out of it this time.'

'Ok, ok. What I was going to ask was… is it true in Australia you can get eaten by an animal just walking down the street?'

'What, like Godzilla?'

'No, like snakes and things with furry legs?'

'Mate, if being a wanker could make you money.'

'I'd be loaded?'

'Just saying.'

'No, what I was going to ask you was... what does it mean, this "she's a Bette Midler" that Aussies say?'

'Fair dinkum?'

'Fair dinkum.'

'My country's slang pollutants must have become airborne, we should head indoors. It's a term indicating that *from a distance* someone is nice-looking, but up close..'

'Oh, I see. So the fact that from a distance you looks like an Israeli makes you a Bette Midler yourself?'

'Mate, I unsheathe the sword, if you've become so sharp you can frame me for being an *Israeli* Bette Midler, then I knight thee a virtual-Australian.'

'Cool, you want a cigarette?'

'Absolutely. I've been meaning to start again.'

'And so, Aussie brother, what ever happened with you and Kayley back in Pushkar?'

And having been prompted, my mind couldn't but go for a little imaginary wander into *Being-Fucked-Around-Land*—that all too familiar place where lovers ignore each other's needs like the plague. Where promises are made and broken as though found by the dozen in cornflake packets. And where urgent long-distance matters are resolved by one simply pressing *block sender* on the other's email address—

'—Ahem?' he coughed, 'so, Aussie brother, what ever happened with—'

'—Ahhhr... nothing.'

Where I'd originally guesstimated I'd be in India for six weeks, it had consumed me for over five months. Ready for new things, the next day I put myself on a bus to Mumbai airport, from where I was flying out to London.

I sat gazing out the bus window, more than happy to be a passenger and no longer a rider. Yet amid the nostalgic images of India streaking past, I was dismayed by the reflection. I'd lost 13 kgs (28 lbs) since arriving in Nepal. Where such a thing might have appealed to others, the sight of thinned arms and extenuated cheekbones was to me less than pleasing. I rightly put it down to the stop in beef, beer and conformity, and looking to the silver lining I knew if later in life I became rotund, India was the very tonic.

The bus journeyed north through the night, and by the time the pink dawn crept over the rubble-strewn horizon, we were somewhere on the outskirts of Mumbai. The city's fringes were host to some typically deplorable slums—people living at the foot of huge billboards, sheltered by nothing more than raggedy pieces of tarp tied up as loose roofing. But although such abhorrent conditions—settlements often adjacent to blackened pools of stagnant water—would, in the west, be considered a misery to inhabit, even in the slums of this country could be seen the overwhelming happiness that swept through its people.

Whereas I once might have been baffled by this attitude and utterly unable to imagine how one couldn't but feel repressed by such lowliness, on the other side of my time here I felt I'd learnt why. Somehow their unshakable happiness stemmed from an overall less-hindered sense of freedom—freedom of expression, freedom from status, freedom from deadlines marked to the minute, freedom from socially-imposed restraints, and freedom from fearing death.

Living at a far lower material standard than our average, Indians are a race that the west is quick to regard as poor and underprivileged. But where the west is largely blinded by its material objective and is as a result missing so much of the natural and social riches that nature intends, Indians—far less affected by such spiritual disorientations—are infinity richer for it.

Humans ourselves are pack animals. Yet in the west, due to predefined social restraints, we seem to largely store ourselves away from each other. It was Mother Teresa, beatified *Blessed Teresa of Calcutta*, who said, 'loneliness is the epidemic of the west'.

But having not lost their sense of community, this is where Indians are denied not. Less separated by fences and locked doors—and spending the majority of the day's hours together— families work to survive as a unit rather than a series of individuals.

A consideration of their freedom too was the less hindered nature of their general behaviour. Indians seem lesser bound by decorum and etiquette, and speaking in truth, never was I remotely bothered by the spitting and nose blowing. As for the groups of men walking around with arms slung over each other— often even holding hands—although foreign, I could appreciate it was as natural as the way a litter of pups pile on top of each other to achieve a feeling of security.

Freedom of expression was a particular point too. Where in the west we consider it civilised behaviour, Indians, less inclined to bottle things up for the sake of appearances, seem freer to express their emotions from the heart up. Without a sniff of self-consciousness, whether they're standing on the street belly laughing, or, a dissatisfied customer expressing his disapproval by ranting until the anger is expended from his system, laughing or punching you'll always know how an Indian truly feels.

Some of the happiest Indians I saw were in fact the homeless. Free to come and go as they please, they were more often than not a picture of children laughing and playing, and families happy to be habitually bound in each other's company.

In blatant contrast—and only further endorsing the values of freedom—some of the most sombre Indians were those I saw in the business districts of the big cities: corporate men in expensive suits, full of checklists and hypnotic routine. Ultimately bound, hence ultimately less free. It's surely for this reason, too, that you can sit on a crowded work-bound train in the big cities of the west—in a setting where souls are squeezed together, yet are unavailable to each other by default as eye contact is considered intrusive—and see an expanse of dull-eyed people, children included, looking as though they wished each day was over before it even began. Surely there's more horror in this than in a league of socially buoyant bright-eyed spitting Indians?

I'd always felt there to be an overt pretentiousness in the all-too popular remark that 'India changes you'. But having been its subject, I now felt I had to agree.

For the endless reasons it challenges you—the staring, the extortion, and the business-as-usual dishonesty, I would, in the beginning, become incurably frustrated. But having learnt that the best way to bruise less was to less resist its bumps, after a few months of practiced surrender I relaxed into a greater patience.

Perhaps, too, I'd grown incrementally calmer thanks to the discovery of yoga, or from the confidence gained through the biking quest. But realising that no amount of fire was going to burn or change its ways, I'd consequently made room to more fully embrace the positives—that Indians, the country over, have limitless time for you, are infinity fun-loving, and regardless of who you are they seem to love by default.

I was also quietly proud to have never got sick. Sure, I once or twice nearly inverted, thanks to an anaphylactic backflip courtesy of my friend the peanut. But never did I get sick in that anticipated way that many fear so inevitable with travelling in this country. Perhaps my prevention was purely psychological, that the fact I believed I'd be fine dictated that I was.

Not to suggest total lack of precaution, and bearing health and social precautions in mind, I've devised, primarily for my own entertainment, the *Ten What-I-Reckon Rules of India:*

Reckon No. 1. When dining at an Indian restaurant, never look in the kitchen. Really, you don't want to know. In fact, I've known health inspectors that have quit and become priests, claiming that the shock blinded and drew them closer to god.

Reckon No. 2. Be it by foot, motorbike, or jumping into the ocean, execute whatever means necessary to escape from the police. Their interest in the law is a hobby, and their interest in your money a profession.

Reckon No. 3. For the fact that even if you weren't interested in the first place, the merchant was going to be difficult to deter—unless you're in the business of encouraging stains to be even harder to remove—never show interest in buying something you aren't 197,000 percent sure you want to buy.

Reckon No. 4. Because, in terms of your health, it might be the difference between make or break, wash your hands at least 12,000 times a day. India is a nation that handles bodily imports with the right hand, and bodily exports with the left. So hands touching money, money being passed on, little kids clutching at your hands on the streets, anonymous blokes introducing themselves by shaking your hand, and rickshaw drivers sneezing into their hands before giving you your change, are all occurrences involving the first frontier of hygienic liability—*hands*.

Reckon No. 5. For the fact that within the first ten seconds you'll be so overwhelmed by people, options, and marriage proposals that you'll no longer be able to read your own handwriting let alone honour your own plans, try to refrain from going to India with much of a plan.

Reckon No. 6. Never underestimate the true communicative power of the head wobble. In my time it served as the most useful tool of communication. But a note of observation: white man can't jump, white man can't dance, and generally speaking white man can't head wobble. (For a good wobble, remember to pivot from the tip of the nose.)

Reckon No. 7. Blow your nose really really loud. Indians dig it.

Reckon No. 8. Unless you're under a general anaesthetic, equipped with a spacesuit and an oxy torch—or, pronounced dead—never subject yourself to an Indian public toilet.

Reckon No. 9. If the staring bothers you completely, the one, singular, and solitary remedy employable is to get on a plane and leave.

Reckon No. 10. Even if the police do catch you, handcuff you, and tie you up in a mouldy potato sack—keep running.

We drove bit by bit through the choked streets towards the airport, and with more black cabs, red double-decker buses, and Victorian architecture than my eyes could digest, the rumour of Mumbai being the London of India was proven true. Ironic to its British feel also, it was the only place in the country I saw an overcast sky. Perhaps this was in preparation for the parent city of the great north.

The bus stopped at the terminal, and though I struggled to believe this was the end, the end it was nonetheless. I hopped onto the footpath, slung my bags and guitar over my shoulder, and, breathing deeper than I had in years, turned to take in the glistening palette of India one last time. 'We came, we saw.'

IN THE AIR

23. Mumbai to London

Another world I barrel towards,
no one to have to bow.
A clean slate, an open floor,
no when, or where, or how.

We were high in the air when a flight attendant came walking up the aisle. 'Excuse me, sir, tea or coffee?'

'No thanks, I'll just have a tomato juice.'

I leant back in my seat, pondering, by default, the joyous combination of tomato juice and altitude.

'Excuse me, sir, would you like the lamb?' she asked, reaching for the most peanut-covered item I'd seen this side of my own death.

'Ahhhr... what's that exactly, please?'

'It's a peanut-cashew-almond-pistachio-walnut-macadamia-satay, soaked and marinated in peanut oil, with a hint of Nutella and a generous sprinkling of pine nuts!'

'Does it have any nuts?'

'I'm not sure, I'll have to check with the senior attendant.'

'Ahhhr… no thanks,' I said, causing the Grim Reaper at her shoulder to sag in disappointment.

*****

Dear Manuel,

My pen is getting dry as I sit on this plane, finally barrelling away.

As you know I was considered missing during the tsunami, and Stephen came here as a result. Hanging out with him in a foreign setting made me understand we're more alike than I realised, and that my attempts at humour, however faint, stem from a Kerrigan code we inherited along the way. All us brothers vary in front-end words, but in a world where 1 + 1 doesn't equal 2, but half of 4, I think how it works from the code-end is that *he who sows the greatest metaphorical tangle* wins. I don't know what they win, and it certainly isn't the cessation of their childhood nickname (mine being *Snake* from having a lisp when my front teeth fell out and I *hissed*). It was good to see him regardless, and I think he got to see that his little brother ain't so little no more.

I then sold the motorbike. North to south I rode over 7,000 kilometres on that bike—approximately Melbourne to Perth and back, London to Mumbai, or Los Angeles to New York return. After buying, selling, and all running costs, the whole venture cost me under five hundred dollars. I can't deny I've since fallen into a mild case of pride, for if ever I've done something worth doing that might have been it. I'm also quietly relieved I never came off—that I'm on the other side without a nick, scratch, nor my wig out of place. I may do something similar someday, and film it next time.

So I think about the closing curtain as I fly away from Planet India. I think about Charlie, I think about the Blue Fly, and I think about that I am, without question, well and truly more story-rich. I think about the vast land of India undulating from desert to rainforest, from plains to mountains, from its silent temples to its frenzied cities. I think about the one billion people dreaming under its stars, and that like all of us, none know what tomorrow will bring. I think about the 160 days I was here, and how each stains me like a tattoo. I think about having felt well and truly ready to leave, yet I think about the ache now that I have.

I also think about my kids, all unborn at this point, and that although I'll encourage them to invest in the authentic education that travel most certainly is, that I'll hearten them to never forget where they came from.

Snake Kerrigan
January 21st, 2005
Somewhere over India

AFTERWORD

As though in karmic retribution of having narrowly missed the tsunami, a few months after I settled in London I was a passenger on a commuter train that was bombed in the London Bombings July 7th, 2005 (full story on *www.davidkerriganblog.wordpress.com*).

Trapped for an hour in the dark bowels of London's underground—with the charred carcasses of the dead lying nearby—by the time we were evacuated from the tunnel I'd gained the last inch of belief that my story, independent of the bombing, was indeed book-worthy. Gazing skyward—with eyes as close to tears as the grey sky above—the experience had given me an aggressive dose of perspective: that there's a definite end to life, and if I'm going to expire then it best be after I get done the things I should. I left London one week later, unable to put myself on subsequent commuter trains.

I took on a work-to-live job at a hostel in Switzerland, which gave me both the time and stimulus to write. Poetically, I sat on the same balcony I wrote my first ever songs back in 1999. Perched with an enviable view of the Alps, I went over the body of emails written to Manuel, sifting through and writing much of the in-between detail and events that hadn't made it to the page. It was a task that proved incredibly cathartic, and resulted, eventually, into this book.

My writing journey subsequently bounced me onto Crete, London (take two), Australia, London (take three), and most recently to Austin, Texas, where I sit as I write this epilogue. Regardless of sticking a stick in the ground or setting sail, the journey, it seems, goes ever on.

Over the next eight years, I would submit the manuscript to various publishers in Australia and the UK. The feedback, unable but to be subjective, included comments such as 'We love your book.

It's really funny! If only you were famous and anyone cared.' And, 'The problem with your book is it's too funny. I can't read it.' And the remark that will go to my grave: 'I never laughed once, young man.' (I still ponder the brand of bitterness that drove her pen to write, *young man.*)

So it seemed the literary world was far from exempt from the old artistic pickle of *white not being black enough*, and *black not being white enough*. I admit I was discouraged at the time, but thanks to the confidence recouped from starting a blog, I decided to take the self-publishing reins and ride like the wind.

In the time it took to finish the book, do subsequent drafts, walk the house and paint the dog, I also recorded the album's worth of songs I'd written on the ashram balcony. Somewhere within the realisations of both, it occurred to me too, that— having a certain symbiotic lean on each other where the book told the story of the songs, and the songs the story of the book— the book/album was in fact a conjoined project. I was delighted with the result.

Sincere thanks to you the reader! Amazon reviews and online word spreading genuinely appreciated. To obtain the album, photos from the journey, and information on other ventures please visit ♪:

www.davidkerrigan.com

David Kerrigan
March 22nd, 2017
Austin, Texas

AUSTRALIAN GLOSSARY OF SLANG, TERMS, AND THINGS

abso-bloody-lutely *adv* : an expression of agreement beyond all doubt.

AC/DC *n* : a famous Australian rock band that as far as this author is concerned put the rock into Rock n' Roll.

AFL *n* : Australian Football League.

ages *adj* : a period of time considered long in context.

any tick of the clock *adj phrase* : an expression signifying that an occurrence is about to happen.

arse *n* : ass.

arsed *v* : to be bothered—'I can't be *arsed*!' or *vt* : to be dismissed or rejected—'he got *arsed* from the squad.'

arvo *n* : abbreviation of *afternoon*.

Aussie *n* : a person from Australia.

Australia's Funniest Home Videos *n* : the truly unfunniest show ever to air Down Under^.

Ayers Rock *n* : a large sandstone rock formation in Australia's red centre. Also known by its Aboriginal name *Uluru*.

bar fridge *n* : small refrigerator, commonly used for stocking alcohol.

belter, *a* **belter** *n* : an occasion or action of greatness.

bloke *n* : a guy, a man, the male of the human, or *any* species for that matter.

bluey *n* : affectionate abbreviation of *The Blue Fly*.

bodgy *adj* : something of poor quality.

bogan *n* : a generally unconscious organism with limited intellect, usually wearing a flannelette shirt, tight jeans, and sporting a mullet haircut, who commonly displays indiscriminate disrespect towards his/her fellow man/woman. The bogan habitually lacks any semblance of sophistication, and is often passionate about heavy metal, cars and/or motorbikes. Oddly, a bogan doesn't necessarily know that he/she is a bogan.

boot *n* : trunk of a car.

bottle shop *n* : a licenced alcohol vendor.

box, idiot box *n* : see telly^.

breather *n* : a short period of respite.

brekky *n* : abbreviation of *breakfast*.

bronzed *adj* : the tanned skin colour achieved by exposure to the sun.

budgie *n* : abbreviation of *budgerigar*—a small broad-tailed parrot native to Australia. In some Aboriginal languages the word translates as *good eating*.

cactus *adj* : tired or worn out.

caned, *to* **cane** *v* : to move fast or achieve something with ease.

canteen *n* : a private cafeteria.

carrying-on, *to* **carry-on** *v* : acting overly emotional.

chewy *n* : abbreviation of *chewing gum*.

chips *n* : thinly sliced deep-fried potato snack food. Known in the UK as *crisps*.

Chisel *n* : see Cold Chisel^.

chuck *v* : to throw.

chunder *n* : vomit—the word originally derived from the First Fleet, in which cabin mates in the upper bunks would, as they vomited, warn their cabin mates below to 'watch out under!'

cockhead *n* : see dickhead^.

Cold Chisel *n* : a legendary Australian band popular for their heartfelt brand of working class ballads.

comp *n* : abbreviation of *competition*.

Coober Pedy *n* : a desert town in South Australia famous for its residents living underground. The town's Aboriginal name *kupa-piti* means 'white man's hole'.

cop *vt* : tolerate or *n* : police officer.

cop shop *n* : police station.

cordial *n* : a flavoured drink that is diluted with water. Known in the UK as *juice* or *squash*.

coz *conj* : abbreviation of *because*.

crack it, to crack it *adj phrase* : an expression describing when someone, having tried to withhold their frustration, loses control.

croak *v* : die.

cut and run *adj phrase* : to retreat—the expression originally describes when a sailing ship in danger would cut the anchor and run with the wind.

dack *n* : to have one's pants removed by another much against their will.

deck *v* : see snot^.

dial *n* : face.

dickhead *n* : someone who through their lack of intelligence, or tendency to embarrass themselves, appears to the eye of the beholder as a giant dick.

dill *n* : a person not overly blessed with intelligence.

dim sim *n* : a Chinese-inspired meat dumpling, consisting of pork or other meat, cabbage, flavourings, and usually served with soy sauce, popular as a snack food in Australia. The dim sim, or, known colloquially as the *dimmy*, was first developed in

Melbourne by Chinese chef William Wing Young.

dink *v* : to have a passenger on the back of your motorbike or bike, i.e. the rider being the *dinker*, the passenger being the *dinkee*. Known in the UK as *doubling* or *pillion* and in America as *riding bitch*.

do his nut, *to* **do his nut** *adj* : see crack it^.

dodgy *adj* : something considered suspicious.

donuts *n* : a sum total of naught. Or to create circular motorbike tracks by applying the front brake while accelerating.

Down Under *n* : colloquialism of *Australia*.

dunno *n* : slang substitute or common intonation of *don't know*— 'quantum physics fascinates me too, Brian, but when it comes to changing car oil, I *dunno*.'

dunny *n* : a toilet or shithouse^.

durry *n* : see smokes^.

early doors *adj* : at a time before expected.

'em *pron* : slang substitute or common intonation of *them*.

empties *n* : empty beer cans or stubbies^.

Essendon *n* : a northern suburb of Melbourne, and a football team in the AFL^.

fair old *adj phrase* : an expression signifying a large quantity.

fairy floss *n* : cotton candy.

farck *vt, vi, n, adj* : slightly gentler version of *fuck*.

flake *n* : shark meat, grilled or battered.

flat out *adj phrase* : an expression signifying busyness—'I went down the post office to send off that stuff of yours, George, but the buggers were *flat out*.'

footy *n* : abbreviation of *football*.

galah *n* : a large pink-breasted parrot with a grey back and wings. The most common cockatoo in Australia. It's also a backhanded word for a person whose judgement is generally in question.

garbo *n* : abbreviation of *garbologist*. Known in America as *trash collector* and in the UK as *dustman*.

g'arvo, good'arvo *interj n* : informal abbreviation of *good afternoon*.

g'day *interj n* : informal abbreviation of *good day*.

g'morn *interj n* : informal abbreviation of *good morning*.

gig *n* : a show of music or other entertainment performed in front of a live audience.

glad-eye *n* : a term describing the approving look from one's eyes transmitted consciously or unconsciously to another they're interested in romantically or sexually.

g.o. *n* : acronym/extension of *go*. Used to acknowledge the status of a person or thing. 'Look at the wig on this bloke^! What's the *g.o.* with that?'

gob *n* : mouth.

good on ya *adj* : slang substitute or common intonation of *good on you*. Used both sincerely and sarcastically.

gotta *vi* : slang substitute or common intonation of *got to*—'I really enjoy studying the non-materialistic ways of Buddhism, but I *gotta* get me an orange robe to match.'

g-spot *n* : a faraway imaginary place where Santa Claus, the Easter Bunny, and the Tooth Fairy spend their days singing *Ring Around the Rosie*.

guesstimate *n* : marriage of *guess* and *estimate*.

gunna *contr* : slang substitute or common intonation of *going to*—'yes, I'll go to church in the morning, but afterwards I'm *gunna* go to the races.'

hack, *a* hack *n* : a person attempting a task in which he or she has no certified knowledge.

half-empties *n* : a half-empty beer can or stubbie⊠.

hammered *adj* : see pissed^.

hanky *n* : abbreviation of *handkerchief*.

Head's up, *the* **head's up** *v* : to inform.

high street *n* : see main drag^.

icy pole *n* : a frozen dessert on a stick, made from flavoured liquid. Known in the UK as *ice-lollies*. (wankers!)

info *n* : abbreviation of *information*.

Jack *n* : a generic male name which can be used as a friendly substitute for someone's actual name, or as a temporary surrogate for someone whose name you are not yet informed of.

James Boag *n* : a popular Australian beer brewed in Launceston, Tasmania.

JB Hi-Fi *n* : a music shop, originally specialising in hi-fi equipment and vinyl records, established in the Melbourne suburb of East Keilor by John Barbuto in 1974.

jocks n : see undies^.

joey *n* : a baby kangaroo.

joint, *a* **joint** *n* : any defined area, location, or place in which a person or thing can reside, i.e. city, house, tent—'this pantry is a terrible *joint* for ripening these tomatoes!' or 'Greece is a top^ *joint* for getting bronzed^!'

jumper *n* : sweater or pullover.

Kiwi *n* : a person from New Zealand.

kookaburra *n* : a native Australian bird known for its call sounding like human laughter.

knackered *adj* : exhausted. Or *vt* : to have suffered an injury to the knackers^.

knackers *n* : testicles.

knick *v* : steal.

knick off *adj phrase* : to depart, or to be given orders by someone to do so.

knockabout *adj* : blasé.

laughing gear *n* : see gob^.

local *n* : affectionate abbreviation of your *local pub*.

lollies *n* : sweets and candy.

lotto ticket *n* : abbreviation of *lottery ticket*.

Mad Max *n* : a 1979 Australian apocalyptic action thriller starring the then-unknown Mel Gibson.

main drag *n* : a chief street where a town's main stores are located. Known in the UK as a *high street*.

me *adj* : slang substitute of *my*—'I sometimes hate life, but I always love *me* dog!'

Melbourne Bitter *n* : a popular Australian beer brewed by

Carlton & United Breweries.

mic *n* : abbreviation of *microphone*.

Midnight Oil *n* : a legendary Australian band popular not only for its powerhouse anthemic rock but for its lyrical content being focused on environmental and political issues.

Mildura *n* : a river town in northwest Victoria, Australia. It's on the Victorian side of the Murray River. The bar at the Mildura Working Man's Club is noted in the *Guinness Book of Records* as the longest bar in the world.

milk bar *n* : a small convenience store usually located on a street corner.

mincing *v* : a style of walk that employs a noticeable degree of arrogance.

Mondee *n* : colloquialism of *Monday*.

mozzie *n* : abbreviation of *mosquito*.

Murray River *n* : Australia's longest river, over 2,500 kilometres. It forms much of the state border between Victoria and New South Wales.

Myer *n* : a department store chain founded in 1900 in Bendigo, Victoria, Australia.

nappy *n* : diaper.

neck, *to* neck *vti* : to drink or eat quickly.

newsagent *n* : news agency.

not much chop *adj phrase* : an expression signifying that something is of poor quality.

nup, nah *interj* : slang substitute or common intonation of *no*—'I'll think about it, Gary, I really will.. actually, *nah* I'm not interested.'

nut *n* : see scone^.

nuts *n* : see knackers^.

off its chops *adj phrase* : an expression signifying that something is crazy.

old boy *n* : father.

old girl *n* : mother.

olds *n* : parents.

outta *prep* : slang substitute or common intonation of *out of*— 'Henry, there's no air freshener in the bathroom, we gotta^ get *outta* here!'

Oz *n* : see Down Under^.

panel van *n* : a motor vehicle without rear side windows, in which promiscuous activities commonly occur.

petrol bowser *n* : gas pump.

pickle, *a* **pickle** *v* : bind or spot of bother.

ping *v* : to make a romantic or sexual advance.

pissed *adj* : intoxicated.

plonk *v* : to place something down without restraint.

pohm *n* : a person from England. Acronym for Prisoner Of Her Majesty.

preaching to the choir *adj phrase* : an expression describing when someone, presuming to be informative, is stating a view already shared or understood by their peers.

pushy *n* : abbreviation of *pushbike.*

ralph *n* : see technicolour yawn^.

reckon *v* : to think, conclude, or consider.

reef, *to* **reef** *v* : to pull with force.

relos *n* : abbreviation of *relatives.*

Richie Benaud *n* : an extremely respected former Australian cricketer and famous cricket commentator.

Ricky Ponting *n* : captain of the Australian cricket team between 2002 and 2011.

righto *adj* : elongation of *right.*

ripper, *a* ripper *adj* : a term expressing disbelief, whether approving or disapproving, towards a person or thing.

rissoles *n* : fried meatballs made of minced meat and onions, great condiments for a bowl of tomato sauce^.

rooted *adj* : exhausted. Or *n* : sexual intercourse.

run-in *n* : argument.

scone *n* : head.

service road *n* : a personal access road parallel to a main road.

shat *n* : past tense of shit—'you're *shitting* me today, Fred, and to be frank, you rather *shat* me yesterday.'

shite *n* : slightly gentler version of *shit*.

shithouse *adj* : a word signifying that something or someone's competence in a particular task or skill is beneath the satisfactory standard—'these apples are *shithouse*!' or 'look at the *shithouse* job Harold did on his lawns!' or *n* : an outdoor toilet.

shit-yeah *adj* : an expression of high endorsement.

shonky, shonk *adj* : untrustworthy, unsafe.

shoot through *v* : depart.

showbag *n* : a themed bag of merchandise sold at carnivals.

Skippy the Bush Kangaroo *n* : a popular Australian children's television show about the adventures of an eastern grey kangaroo.

smokes *n* : cigarettes.

smoko *n* : a short morning break accommodating the time required to smoke a cigarette or drink a cup of coffee. Usually taking place around 10:30 a.m.

snot *v* : hit.

sook, *to* **sook** *vi* : to complain in a whiny manner. Or *n* : somebody who has a tendency to do so.

sport *n* : see Jack^.

s'pose *v* : abbreviation of *suppose*.

squiz *v* : look.

Stackhat *n* : a sturdy bright orange bicycle helmet made from plastic. Extremely popular in Australia in the 1980s.

star, *a* **star,** *little* **star** *n* : affectionate nickname directed towards a person or living thing.

stubbie *n* : a 375 ml bottle of beer.

sunnies *n* : abbreviation of *sunglasses*.

sunniesless *adj* : without sunglasses.

taking the piss *adj phrase* : an expression meaning to make fun at the expense of others, or to be excessive or irrational.

tanked *adj* : a word by which one's capacity for alcohol is measured, i.e. their *tank* is full.

technicolour yawn *n* : vomit.

telly *n* : abbreviation of *television*.

terry towelling *n* : a fabric with loops that can absorb large amounts of water, that, although unfashionable in the rest of the universe, has in Australia remained popular for barbeque and poolside attire: such as hats, shorts, headbands and wristbands.

that's it *adj* : see shit-yeah^.

tinny *n* : a 375 ml can of beer.

tomato sauce *n* : ketchup.

tops, top *adj* : a descriptor for the highest quality. Or *n* : any article of clothing worn on the trunk.

tosser *n* : see wanker^.

true blue *adj* : patriotically Australian.

turf, *to* turf *vt* : to throw.

turps *n* : traditionally, an abbreviation of *turpentine*, but more commonly used as an informal word for alcohol.

two-bob *n* : two shillings or a 20 cent coin.

undies *n* : abbreviation of *underwear*.

unfangable *adj* : a word signifying that a vehicle is unable to be driven.

unreal *adj* : weird or unbelievably good.

Vegemite *n* : a dark savoury yeast extract that's eaten as a spread. It's considered a rite-of-passage to Australians, and you'll sooner find a white peacock than a non-Aussie that doesn't grimace at the taste.

Victa *n* : a popular Australian lawn mower invented in 1952 in Sydney by Mervyn Victor Richardson.

Wagon Wheel *n* : a circular-shaped biscuit with a marshmallow centre and chocolate coating.

wanker *n* : someone whose opinion of themselves far outweighs their aptitude—'look at this *wanker* mincing^ over to tell us about his latest accolade!' Or someone who performs the act of making self-love.

wanna *vt* : slang substitute or common intonation of *want to*—'I would, I truly would, Ted, but come to think of it, I don't *wanna*.'

whinging *v* : the act of incessantly complaining while failing to do anything to change one's circumstance.

wombat *n* : Australia's fattest marsupial.

ya *pron* : slang substitute or common intonation of *you*—'what a great party! Harry is here! Larry is here! Ah, Barry! How are *ya*?'

yeah-nah *adv* : an expression unconsciously employed to buy a second's time while searching for a suitable answer or response to something or someone.

young and old, *on* **for young and old** *adj phrase* : an expression signifying that a situation is chaotic.

youse *pron* : slang plural of *you*.

THANKS

Andrew McUtchen (alias *Manuel*) for fierce intuition, loyalty, and for helping the seed of this book spring. Katie Williams for thoughtfulness, sensitivity, and for encouraging the dreamer within. Christopher Michael Keogh for big-heartedness, for means/spews, for efforts during the tsunami, and for helping me differentiate *effect* and *affect*. Mick Spillane for effortless charisma, pragmatism, and for backing me from the soul up. Angela Clocherty for commitment to truth, for clan banter, and for whose boundless understanding is surpassed only by her generosity. Mum and Dad Kerrigan for guidance, character, and for whose love never budges regardless of the miles. Brothers Shaun and Stephen for mentorship, for efforts during the tsunami, and for instead of telling me my childhood rabbit Snowy was found at the bottom of the pool, telling me he knicked off to work for the Easter Bunny. Tricia Maddock Kerrigan for banter and generosity in Mullim and over the years. *Little Nana* Frances Agius for warmth, enthusiasm, and for eggplant, tomato paste, and żebbuġ sandwiches. *Little Granddad* Hannibal Lawrence Agius for wisdom, storytelling, and for having been the most eloquent man I ever knew. *Big Nana* Madge Kerrigan for strength, rapport, and rationality. *Big Granddad* David *George* Kerrigan for whose love-motivated walk across a religious aisle ensured our family tree, and for despite having reached 80 never losing his inner child. Nieces Jessica, Brooke, Olivia, and Nephew Tomas Kerrigan for being commendable heirs to the throne. Tammy the dog for tail wagging no matter what. Misty Catalano and Bart Bauer for welcoming me like family from day one. Maggie for occasional obedience. Newman for perpetual enthusiasm. Brother Matty Ryan for innate wisdom, natural rhythm, and for having encouraged me down the treble clef road. Brother Julian Senserrick for boundless emotional intelligence, wittiness, and for understanding before any of us that the stars are surrounded not by nothing but something. Donnie Dureau for grassroots solidarity, for having written more good songs than is fair, and for being the only man I'd buy a guitar with when eating a steak and kidney pie. Jason *Felts* Felton for smarts, for top mateship despite the miles, for etiquette and dance tuition, and for lasting commitment to earl grey. Paul *Hairy* Speight for lethal wit, for best man training, and for overall strength and honour since open mic No.1. Andy Page for impersonations, industriousness, and for not so much as dreaming of missing a vocal note. The Leaning Tower of Edward Kift for astuteness, running willpower, and the notion of a cup of tea with a drop of cold water. Patrick Whelan for wisdom, mentorship, and commitment to keeping the banter sword sharp. Catherine Reddaway for limitless energy, effortless intelligence, and keeping the group in check. Nadine Tree Spillanester for cleverness, fierce wit, and graduating with honours in Chicology. Chico the dog who despite professional training just wouldn't roll. *This Sister* Angela Senserrick for warmth, maternality, and for our gold medal performance in the 100-metre Jurassic dash. *That Sister* Carmen Senserrick for sincerity, contagious laughter, and for hfna-rinsing at Percy's Bar. Margaret, Anthony, and Pat Senserrick for taking me under their wing since day dot. *Little Sister* Jane Senserrick for cleverness. Claudia Senserrick for Dabi-ism. Mick Ryan for youthful wit and daily commutes. Irish aunties Maureen Burgoine and Wendy Gallagher for wisdom and for keeping a loving matriarchal eye on all. Irish uncles Dave Kerrigan, Billy Kerrigan, and Jack Kerrigan for story stylisation and banter coaching. Cousin Paul Kerrigan for wit and celebrity. Cousin Donna Devine for sincerity and blog encouragements. Cousin Marnie Bignell for quarter-life crisis dialogue and for sharing the opinion of quality over quantity. Cousin Peter *Santa* Burgoine for big-heartedness and for his commitment to generating a laugh. Cousin Adrian

Burgoine for raillery, and motorbike and fitness tuition. Cousin
Victoria Stanway for radiance and for being the closest thing to a
sister. Cousin Diedrie Kerrigan-Zech and Herbert down in the
valley for understanding, schnapps, and George cat eye
impersonations. Cousin Samantha Kerrigan for fortitude and
mullet discouragement. Cousin Robert Kerrigan for keenness
and expatriate understanding. Cousins Megan Hutchins, Nathan
Gallagher, and Lauren Gallagher for sharing in the plight of being
the youngest. Aunties Sindy Kerrigan, Jan Kerrigan, and Lyn
Kerrigan for maternality and exuberance. Aunty Moira Gallagher
for high-spiritedness and pavlova. Uncle Peter Gallagher for
humour and running camaraderie. Uncle John Gallagher for
earnestness. Uncle John Burgoine for Taekwondo and motorbike
riding. Maltese aunties Anne Elbourne, Cettina Jurgelait, Miriam
Nathanael and Patricia Agius for sincerity, and Cett for biscuits.
Uncles Garry Jurgelait and Doug Nathaneal for joviality and
fitness. Uncle Bill Elbourne for billiards. Cousin Philip Elbourne
for reading me *Charlie Brown*. Cousin Peter Agius for big-
heartedness. Cousins Donna Rutherford and Dean Jurgelait for
taking me under their wing. Cousins Simon and Matthew
Nathaneal for also sharing in the plight of being the youngest.
Maltese uncles Vin Agius and Guido Agius for merriment and
storytelling. Monica Wilson, Billy and the girls, John Gallen,
Marion, Brenda, Caroline, Aiden and Theresa in Castlederg—
and John Gallen, Dianne, Todd, Gerry and Raymond in
Pennsylvania—and Aunty Kitty, Galena, Edgar Ruggier and
Lilian in Malta for welcoming me like family. Cousin Tony Valla
for joviality and for being the 4th brother. Cheryl Diggins, Charlie
Dispenzeri, Michael and Rose Mineo for Dad camaraderie. Rosa,
Bruce, Judy and Brian from Cornwall for Mum camaraderie. Paul
Delboy Kristian for perceptiveness, tea, bundy, and for living on
the poetic side. Victoria Charlotte Claney for salt of the earth
realism, and for whose friendship and understanding is

impervious to the miles journeyed and the years passed. Rachel Perry for sophistication, curls, and for truly appreciating the travel itch. Xave McMahon for musical fellowship and for having a voice surpassed by none. Jade Ghezzi for shopping guidance and for being a virtual sister. Kylie *formally-Smith* Ryan for sincerity and for keeping Matty upright. Elise *formally-Nunan* Senserrick for bravado and fashion direction independent of whether it's wanted. Fi *formally-Erskine* McUtchen for fervent opinions and for allowing Andrew to put down the frame. Andrea *formally-Jonhammar* Kift for fierce intelligence and for crying during Mick Spillane's best man speech. Lauren Whitmore for radiance. Nick Reddaway for equanimity. Tania Rivett for sharpness. Carrie Kania in London for taking me under her literary wing. Babette Kulik, Robert Pereno and The Society Club for introducing me to Carrie. Sabrina Leroe and Steve Boggan for grammatical overview. Suzanne Proctor for mutual Icehouse and guitar obsession. Chris *OzPohm* Brady for whose written word is so sharp it could cut your finger. Anastasia Foster for her charmingly estranged fang. Warwick and Cheryl Thomas for making the experience of recording an album a joy beyond measure. Glen *TNT* Crawforth and Zoe for genius, industry jeer and early writing encouragements. Charly Richardson for legendary fifths, brotherly nurture, and a right cracking time in Austin. Martyn Potter for humour, licks, and a keen interest in all things lewd. Pavan Sawhney for wisdom, wheels and supervision. Amber Lee Martin and Sarah Limerick for being the indisputable Texan dream team since Vietnam, and for leading me to Katie. Linda Martin for always casting a maternal eye. Fleurette Vincent in New York for intuition and life-saving Skype parley. Takis Nahatis in Dallas for singing from the same hymn sheet, and the partly endearing fact he asked for this book to be dedicated to himself. Hayley Van Emmenis for elegance and bus approachability. Rebecca Culpin in Spain for braininess and her devotion to the four-legged. John *Dennis* Molesworth for composure, for mutual admiration of stand-up comedy, and for his ability to excel *over all our heads* at whatever he chooses. Teja *Denise* Kocjancic and Kobi Molejancic for fellow love of dogs and *The Castle*. Claire Fiander for being the indisputable London Aunty. Elena Eliseeva for wholesomeness and truly appreciating Aussie humour. Gina Geoghegan for charm since day one and her exquisite use of swear words. Michèle Haddon for humour and sensitivity. Andy *Two Easy Brother* Smyth in Galway for being a political party unto himself, and for electric spoon playing. Jim and Eileen Clocherty, Linda Robertson and Bonnie Foster in Glasgow for welcoming me as their own. Laurent Nguyen-Van for buoyancy and optimism. Big Rob Pullen for his wandering spirit. Sudhi for informing that the coming ice age is 10,000 years late. Petra and Walter Brunner (and Nicole and Michelle) for allowing free reign at their mountain hostel in Switzerland. Johnny *Ameri-Brother* Garofalo for unparalleled musicality and his nonchalant yet powerful use of the word *dude*. Dana *Valley Girl* Gerrard for wit, granny pants choreography, and for enduring the ongoing devastations of Swiss dairy products. Allison *Swiss Sister* Corsi for introspection, for life-saving mountain walks, and for getting a bandage for my hand. Marc Jones and Dianne for their Vegemite delivery service to Gimmelwald. Amy Davies for eye contact. Veronika for her flat up in Mürren. Katie Skillen. Edward Carrette and Devon Bench for AU understanding. Glenn Kewley and Kinzy Ann Kewley for UK understanding. Zoë Butcher-McGunnigle for NZ understanding. Justin Combs and Crysta for USA understanding and for neighbourly camaraderie. Carl Callaway and Mary Koniavitis for all things artist, and Vegemite. Virginia Avalos for repartee and senior counsel. Christina Riedy and Cathy Price for high volume Keilor coffee. Sir Jopee Pipher for life and literary musings. Yenni for welcome. Kacey Gorringe for fireball, ambition and acumen. Chris *Creeping Moses* Moran for being 'round the outside'. Jessica Jones for social direction. Meg Ordoyne for power hugs. Rich Bickford for o.p's. Marc Schwarz for political deliberations. Julie Ball Schwarz for teaching encouragements. Marcus Alan Hodges for hands and theoretical musings. Heather Burt for thoughtfulness. American relos John John and Josie Catalano, Sarah Williams and Chris Havins, Jodi Bauer Loup and Matt, Agnes D'Angela O'Reilly and Lance, Tim Mccune, Kristen Jennifer L, Ashley Sercovich, Betsy Williams Cadle, Ricky Cadle, Todd Blanchard, Patty Blanchard, Jacquie Williams Gillman, Matt Bodie, Lucie Fitch, Chase Catalano, Karon Bravender, Keith Bravender, George Preis, Diane Middour Preis, Brandy Chandler, Malachi Chandler, Janette Cariker Cassano, Wayne Cassano, Grandma Ruth and Holly Graham for welcoming me like family from day one. Richard Hemmings and Emma Curran and all the literal wickedness of Bristol. Matt Harris and Chris Handsley for UK music scene comradeship and capo ingeniousness. Treana Morris for writing the song *So Wrong*. Panama Dave Parrett for fingerpicking. Ciara Chinniah for rhythm. Allan Cuevas for AU understanding in the UK. Darren Banks for universal musings. Clarky for sound. Adrian Harper for solid banter. Meg Cavanaugh McCullough for theatrics. Wayne Brennan for stairway fireworks. Jessie Pie for work ethic. Carl Chamberlain for unyielding devotion. Carol McLeod for a voice as large as her heart. Cam Ringel for chic, Tanya Marshall for poetry, Mardi Williams for instrumentation, and all the RAW crew for collective fireworks. Prim Burger for skills and wisdom. *Sister* Freya Defoe for razor wit, perceptiveness, and for writing encouragements. Jonathan *Jay* Brodie for banter, critical thinking, and for mutual love of leather jackets. Jess Joy Harvey, Basile Cuvelier, Rahul Ramanuj, Meghan Hagerty, Ross Fordham, Miranda Bolter, Sam Lachlan, The Disler, Mike Paisley, Tracy Richmond, Danielle Kirjalainen, Keith Hancox, Matthew Hill,

Tom Leach, Kevin Lan, Camille Gatin, Greg Baxter, Amy Baxter, Carrie Bryan, Helen Jones, Brinley Clark, Zannya Castillo, Tony Phillips, Christian Horsfall, Suzanne Neal, Tiffany Hultgren, Elspeth Ross, Amy McHenry, Matt *Nev* Morgan, Uri Baruchin, Berengere Cortade, Jim Prior, Nick Eagleton, Andrew Webster, and Pip Jakeman for TP camaraderie and daily frivolities. Andrew Demianyk, Paul McDermid, and Aaron Lobb for social allegiance. Eva Kruuse and Kairi Mänd in Estonia for fellow music fanaticism and for welcoming me as their own. Mark Nichols and Marcus Zeilerbauer for Carnaby Street solidarity. Carla Moran for Irish sentimentality. Victoria Cousins for sensitivity and generosity. Lizzie for grammar. Muffie for rock cakes. Joe for mutual WW2 fascination. Josephine for drool. Izzie for growling. Martha for blinking. Louisa Greenwood for exquisiteness and early writing encouragements. Lars Olsen for natural coolness and his work with the kids. Michelle Eva May for artistic brilliance and for inspiring the London return. Sheritta Nesbitt for wit and bunnies. Nicole Wilson for grace and intuition. Jennifer Hayes for arty directness. Michelle Dosson for banter and salad. Phil *PJGPS* Goen for 382 antics. Kristina Lundy for exquisite linguistics. Samantha Hemrich for wisdom and humility. Joe Rehmet for ink and rock star charm. Jess Davis for playfulness and profundity. Homer Tapia for nerve and driving in the middle lane. Yolanda Lopez for vivacity. Eric Munoz, Nicole Kresse, Beth Atchley, Lucy Morquecho, Joseph *Little Bro* Curry, Elouisa Hernandez, Emily Mendez, Holli Odom, Sharon Nichols, Hanna Peterson, Luis Negrete, Erin Coleman, Rick Munoz, Valentin Eduardo Calderon, Chris Buchanan, Geoffrey Glass, Arthur Trujillo, Robert Golembeski, Heather Weaver, Regan Goins, Amanda Shindler, Jean Becraft, Ashley Niels, Dennis Weaver, Josh Rowland, Katy Fendrich, Brunie Drumond, MaryLou Stauffer, Sherry Stephens, Robin D Sirles, Sara Shannon, Terry Colgan, Susan Reda, Soo Lee, Daria Kelly, Aaron Scott, Lisa Wolverton, Carrie Wells,

Elizabeth Kasey Mancera, Sophie Love, Van Gogh and Bordeaux for unyielding devotion to the four-legged. Lauralei Combs, Aly Kerr, Dave Froehlich, Amanda Cunningham, Kaye Reznick, Pitt Garrett, Vickie Garrett, Scott Fischer, Shawn Howard, Mike Mathis Sr, Roy Headrick, Steve Valentine, Robert Salas, Brian Mullin, Doug White, Laura Hicks, Lynn Cowles, and Jim Matthews for Austin music scene comradeship. Willie Nelson for photo op. Sean Alcott and Peter Dolan for Austin running camaraderie. Serena Stewart for southern hospitality and hairdressing wisdom. Diggs Christie for z'n-ology and comradeship in the trim-mark trenches. Archie Haramis for tribal fellowship. Fi Pirola for sharpness and life-saving lunch breaks. CML soldiers Richard Gardiner, Mark Pether, Michael Bartzis, Renate Wolf, Lynette Wallace-Carroll, and Timothy Slater for sharing in the plight of PMS485. Anthony Rooney for solid Irish counsel from St Augustine's to the Chevron. Colin Birney for Elvis impersonation. Johnny Ielo for generosity and soulfulness. Morgan Belbruno for spinning the vinyl dream. Alison Jane Lee for perfection. Suzanne Snooks for curls and cleverness. Marnie Stilo for expatriate understanding. Dale *Oyster* Trickett for four-stringed devilry. Sandra Dureau for maternal interest. Donnie Dureau Sr for George nostalgia. Jenny and Robert McUtchen for big-heartedness. The Spillane brothers for being natural masters of ceremony. Brendan Keogh for writing the song *The Usual Way*. Peter McUtchen for perceptiveness. Chris McUtchen for the unparalleled comedic marriage of Cartman and Céline Dion. Pedro Salinas and Agustina Zembo for instant B.A. brotherhood and sisterhood. Josh Slocum for sincerity and artistic encouragements. Georgina Smith and Kate Murray for charisma and abiding Kerg love. Jade Vidal for appetite. Shiran De Soysa for shoulders. Donna McGlynn for kind-heartedness and directions to the world of Adobe. Darryl Matthews for effortless style. Nicole Petrie for contagious laughter. Matt Petrie for lighting up every room. Andrew Petrie for earnestness. Lisa Smith for sincerity, for early readings, and for sharing the Vipassana battle. James Nicholls for serenity... so much serenity. Tanya Clark for introspection and mutual nomadic tendencies. Richard Macionis and John Foreman for original Crackerology. Marina Berger for intuition and maternality. Pete Saccuzzo for taking us under his musical wing. Gill Maxwell for love of cats and being as equally confused by choice when in a DVD shop. Gary Morris, Duane Voss, Dan Clarke, Anthony Scafidi, and Derek Mulvihill for glistening good times. Wendy Ryan for unreserved artistic passion. Katherine Castles for Dad(s) camaraderie. Dicko Donnellan for his commitment to freedom, and proving that even old people like to dance. Jon Hall the Kiwi artist-blacksmith for Kraków collaboration. Julie Anne Baker for charm and teeth. Dan Rockett in L.A. for writing the song *Still Dreaming*. Olivia Rowley for astuteness and early writing encouragements. Victoria Havard for smarts and for urging me to head east from Fiji. Jojo Moyes, Lisa Hanrahan, Julia Beaven, Roisin Fitzgerald, Sharon Smith, and Erin Vargo for much-welcomed direction through the literary jungle. Kaye Thomas and Deborah Koken for fellow B.T. love. Lynn Fausett in Utah the been-there-done-that author who insisted the pain of writing a book is 'gonna be worth it in the end'. David Felton up in Hemel for early submission advice. Suzan Rubin Felton for photography and vocal appreciation. British Stephen Long for banter and heart-warming correspondence. Jo Davies for love fireworks. Albert Cox and Peter Raeburn for Hamburg highlights. Neil Whiting for patriarchal leanings. Mick Corrigan for certified commentary. Debs Tilley for critique. Bagheera Livingstone for colours and Soho nest takeover. Sophie Kipner for literary understanding. Dr Paul the Scot for humour and for being quick to discourage the studying of medicine. Alexandra Girard the French fashion guru for fierce humour and early writing encouragements. Leigh Marino for curls and cleverness. Tassie Steve for helping me differentiate an apple and an orange. Cam Andrews (the Dalai Lama) for invaluable common sense and for bringing home to the mountain. Matt Brennan for the mountain hut expedition. Dave Huebel in San Fran for innate kindliness. Matt Owen for miles surpassed by none. Taylor Feltner in Florida for mutual admiration of staves. Ben Groundwater for equal dedication to story and road. Gilbert Gabriel for writing the song *Life In A Northern Town*. Ben and Smurf the boys from Budapest for their tour of the old town. Owen Kerr and Alex Topaloski for Kraków slow down. Lior Fain for coolness beyond the freeze. Tom from the Shetland Islands for his inspiring unanimity with nature. Swedish Jack Jensen for wisdom and harmonies. Rocio Rodiel in Madrid for warmth and wittiness. Panos Skala the man about Paleochora. Patroclus the dog for sitting by my feet for much of the writing of the first draft. The nice landlady that left cake and oranges at the flat in Crete. Errol Dixon for being the coolest of all cats. Gregor Erjavec for inspiring us inwards. Lisa Johnston for acceptance and profuse heat. Alethea Jones for wit and early readings. Ian Campbell for helping me watch the watcher. Sharon McNamara for banter and understanding. Mr Myles for anecdotes and Q10 recommendation. Neighbours the Skoski's, the Barrie's, the Dyer's, and the Holub's. Dale McMahon and Jay Hanson for skills, stories, and OZ music scene comradeship. Sandy Greenwood for relating to the pain and passion of an artist endeavour. Caitlin Seawell for our Sunday kitchen chats. Runner the Rabbit for making the daily ritual of trying to put him back in his cage, the only exercise a writer gets. Matt Dills for magnetism. Scott Wilson, Peter Dearsley, Barry McManus, and Jim MacGregor for being the men about Melbourne town. Tezz Bergagna for charisma and original swear coaching. Casa soldiers Mark Kaylar Thompson, Chris Liem, Shannon Creasey, Danielle Maas and Vanessa Elliott for creating a workplace as comically dynamic as creatively brilliant. Daniel McKeag for being a living testament that young people actually *do* like reading. Marianne Haughton for clarity. Joe Manariti for time. Brother Darren Wallace for instinct and interest. Megan Blandford Lewis for exquisiteness inside and out. Jesus Marquez for charm and hunger for knowledge. Adelia Griffin the specialist baker from Hawaii for explaining that the bigger the wedding cake the shorter the marriage. Casper, Sandra Blakemore and the Kiwi connection in London for dossing. Bruno Campara Diniz, Fernando Unanue, Cagri Demirbas, Madalena Arrobas Ferrada, Malion-Debora Milbradt Rosa, Teka Ferreira, Elizabeth Assmann Da Silva, Giovanni Leme Da Silva, and David Topchishvili for _ _ _ _ of a day times at Bethune Road. Manon Klein Hesseling for original 10kms. Rosie Pimenta for being the coolest of cool bosses. Alison Von Hoegan for laugh and Wonder Year bus journeys. St Bernard's soldiers Simon Lynch, Sam Doyle, Danny Rogers, Bernard McMullen, Josh Hudson, Chris Hayes, Brendan Turley, Mick Conway, Ben Hardwick, Jason Sofra, Warwicke Newman, and Danny Roberts for fellow sanitarium survival. Sandra Jane for teaching me to draw what I *see* not what I *think I see*. Peter Crow for being one of the few teachers cool enough to treat his students like equals. Gerry Brown and the *Farck Are We* tribe. St Augustine's soldiers Ben Warner, Shane Manton, Mark Viduka, Joe Musco, Chris Anstey, Luke French, Fabian Sanza, Michael Kelly, Antony Masquapasqua, Peter Kong, Brynley Donoghue, Simon Rashilla, Sacha Kaluri, Cristina Munoz, Vanessa Spalvero, Denise Ferrante, Justine Quayle, Belinda Khalifeh, and Nicole Jamieson for being the original tribe. Marlene Sant for Maltese camaraderie. Maurie Shaw in Brisbane for insight. Peter Carr for fervent story hunting. Sharon O'Rourke for casting a sisterly wing. Alison Dines for catching the mic stand when I knocked it over at piano recital. Dr Liz for listening. Hilton Murphy up in Edmonton. Eric Wong for demonstrating the true powers of antagonism. NMIT soldiers Aaron Mascara, Jenny Petelin, Justin Caddeo, and Joe Puccio for sharing in the graphic's mountain climb. Dan Peterson for early art direction. Stela Brinzeanu for early readings. Susan from biodynamics. Sheng for ch'i. Julie Kenyon for animation. Rory Ferguson for merriment. Stacy Reichert for mountain talk. Jenn Hix for smarts. Dr Varadsti for delivery. Peter Jackson, Fran Walsh and Philippa Boyens for whose glistening trilogy adaptation helped me realise the writer within. Working Dog for reasons best known to themselves choosing the name *Kerrigan* for their movie *The Castle*. Andrew Denton for whose fabulous show I miss to this day. The voice of Morgan Freeman in *The Shawshank Redemption*. And it's with a deep heartfelt sincerity that I thank Kevin Trudeau's *Mega Memory* for helping me to remember things that at this moment in time I can't quite remember. Taylors Lakes Gym for no matter how doggedly I applied its weight-training program making me grow only punier. To my nameless primary schoolteacher for telling us about her and her elderly husband's sexual problems. To my year seven art teacher for spending the entire duration of a 90-minute lesson enlightening us to the midrange wonders of the HB pencil. And refraining, only just, from getting down on one knee, it's with an earnest sense of humility that I thank the bogan galah in 1985 who, devoid of the gentlemanly qualities that come with fighting, wouldn't allow me to remove my Stackhat before smacking me in the mouth at the top milk bar in Keilor. To the Catholic priests of my childhood whose long-winded sermons first introduced me to the feeling known as depression. To the word the for without which I'd have limited means to introduce a noun. To oranges for the simple fact they're the only thing I can think of that are named after their colour. To the three-day Scientology course in Brisbane for helping me realise that doing a three-day Scientology course is a complete waste of three days. And it's near wiping a tear from my eye that I salute, sincerely, the silly old man who, unable to control his Rottweiler when it reared onto its back legs, let go of its leash letting it b-line and bite my Labrador. To Spring Valley for making fruit juice bottles that once drained of their fine product make for even finer bongs. To Billy Hyde's for no matter how many times I ring to inform that I no longer want be on their mailing list continuing to send me their shite nonetheless. To the fucked up opportunistic caterpillars that, mistaking it for herbs, ate that entire bowl of weed we left in the backyard that time…

Made in the USA
Monee, IL
21 March 2022

93261778R00256